FOUNDATIONS OF INFORMATION SECURITY

FOUNDATIONS OF INFORMATION SECURITY

A Straightforward Introduction

by Jason Andress

no starch press

San Francisco

Printed in USA

First printing

23 22 21 20 19   1 2 3 4 5 6 7 8 9

ISBN-10: 1-7185-0004-1
ISBN-13: 978-1-7185-0004-4

Publisher: William Pollock
Production Editor: Meg Sneeringer
Cover Illustration: Rick Reese
Developmental Editor: Frances Saux
Technical Reviewer: Cliff Janzen
Copyeditor: Kim Wimpsett
Compositor: Meg Sneeringer
Proofreader: James Fraleigh
Indexer: Beth Nauman-Montana

For information on distribution, translations, or bulk sales, please contact No Starch Press, Inc. directly:
No Starch Press, Inc.
245 8th Street, San Francisco, CA 94103
phone: 1.415.863.9900; info@nostarch.com
www.nostarch.com

The Library of Congress issued the following Cataloging-in-Publication Data for the first edition:

Names: Andress, Jason, author.
Title: Foundations of information security: a straightforward introduction / Jason Andress.
Description: 1st ed. | San Francisco : No Starch Press, 2019. | Includes
    bibliographical references and index. | Summary: "Begins with an
    introduction to information security, including key topics such as
    confidentiality, integrity, and availability, and then moves on to
    practical applications of these ideas in the areas of operational,
    physical, network, application, and operating system security"--
    Provided by publisher.
Identifiers: LCCN 2019024099 (print) | LCCN 2019024100 (ebook) | ISBN
    9781718500044 (paperback) | ISBN 1718500041 (paperback) | ISBN
    9781718500051 (ebook)
Subjects: LCSH: Computer security. | Computer networks--Security measures.
    | Electronic information resources--Access control.
Classification: LCC QA76.9.A25 A5445 2019 (print) | LCC QA76.9.A25
    (ebook) | DDC 005.8--dc23
LC record available at https://lccn.loc.gov/2019024099
LC ebook record available at https://lccn.loc.gov/2019024100

Le meglio è l'inimico del bene.

—Voltaire

About the Author

Dr. Jason Andress is a seasoned security professional, security researcher, and technophile. He has been writing on security topics for over a decade, covering data security, network security, hardware security, penetration testing, and digital forensics, among others.

About the Technical Reviewer

Since the early days of Commodore PET and VIC-20, technology has been a constant companion (and sometimes an obsession!) to Cliff. He discovered his career passion when he moved into information security in 2008 after a decade of IT operations. Since that time, Cliff is grateful to have had the opportunity to work with and learn from some of the best people in the industry including Jason and the fine people at No Starch. Cliff spends a majority of the work day managing and mentoring a great team, but strives to stay technically relevant by tackling everything from security policy reviews to penetration testing. He feels lucky to have a career that is also his favourite hobby and a wife that supports him.

BRIEF CONTENTS

CONTENTS IN DETAIL

8
HUMAN ELEMENT SECURITY 107

9
PHYSICAL SECURITY 121

10
NETWORK SECURITY 133

11
OPERATING SYSTEM SECURITY
145

12
MOBILE, EMBEDDED, AND INTERNET OF THINGS SECURITY
159

ACKNOWLEDGMENTS

I want to thank my wife for bearing with me through another writing project, especially during my excessive complaining and foot dragging over (*ahem*) certain chapters <3.

I also want to thank the whole crew at No Starch Press for all their time and hard work in making this a better book. Without all the many rounds of editing, reviewing, and feedback, this book would have been a considerably less polished version of itself.

INTRODUCTION

When I was in school, I was faced with a choice between pursuing a concentration in either information security or software engineering. The software engineering courses had terribly boring-sounding titles, so information security it was. Little did I know what a twisted and winding path I'd embarked on.

Information security as a career can take you many different places. Over the years, I've dealt with large-scale malware outbreaks, collected forensic information for court cases, hunted for foreign hackers in computer systems, hacked into systems and applications (with permission!), pored over an astonishing amount of log data, implemented and maintained all manner of security tooling, authored many thousands of lines of code to fit square pegs into round holes, worked on open source projects, spoken at security conferences, taught classes, and written somewhere into the upper regions of hundreds of thousands of words on the topic of security.

This book surveys the information security field as a whole. It's well-suited to anyone wondering what people mean when they use the term *information security*—or anyone interested in the field and wondering where to start. The chapters offer clear, nontechnical explanations of how information security works and how to apply these principles to your own career. It should help you learn about information security without making you consult a massive textbook. I'll first cover the fundamental ideas, such as authentication and authorization, needed to understand the field's key concepts, such as the principle of least privilege and various security models. I'll then dive into a survey of real-world applications of these ideas in the areas of operations, human, physical, network, operating system, mobile, embedded, Internet of Things (IoT), and application security. I'll finish up by looking at how to assess security.

Who Should Read This Book?

This book will be a valuable resource to beginning security professionals, as well as to network and system administrators. You should use the information provided to develop a better understanding of how you protect your information assets and defend against attacks, as well as how to apply these concepts systematically to make your environment more secure.

Those in management positions will find this information useful as well, because it should help you develop better overall security practices for your organizations. The concepts discussed in this book can be used to drive security projects and policies and to mitigate some of the issues discussed.

About This Book

This book is designed to take you through a foundational understanding of information security from the ground up, so it's best read from start to finish. Throughout the book you will see numbered references to the Notes section at the end of the book, where you can find more information on some of these topics. Here's what you'll find in each chapter:

Chapter 1: What Is Information Security?   Introduces some of the most basic concepts of information security, such as the confidentiality, integrity, and availability triad; basic concepts of risk; and controls to mitigate it.

Chapter 2: Identification and Authentication   Covers the security principles of identification and authentication.

Chapter 3: Authorization and Access Controls   Discusses the use of authorization and access controls, which are means of determining who or what can access your resources.

Chapter 4: Auditing and Accountability   Explains the use of auditing and accountability for making sure you're aware of what people are doing in your environment.

Chapter 5: Cryptography   Covers the use of cryptography for protecting the confidentiality of your data.

Chapter 6: Compliance, Laws, and Regulations   Outlines the laws and regulations relevant to information security and what it means to comply with them.

Chapter 7: Operations Security   Covers operations security, which is the process you use to protect your information.

Chapter 8: Human Element Security   Explores issues pertaining to the human element of information security, such as the tools and techniques that attackers use to con us and how to defend against them.

Chapter 9: Physical Security   Discusses the physical aspects of information security.

Chapter 10: Network Security   Examines how you might protect your networks from a variety of different angles, such as network design, security devices, and security tooling.

Chapter 11: Operating System Security   Explores the strategies you can use for securing the operating system, such as hardening and patching, and the steps that you can take to do so.

Chapter 12: Mobile, Embedded, and Internet of Things Security Covers how to ensure security for mobile devices, embedded devices, and IoT devices.

Chapter 13: Application Security   Considers the various methods for securing applications.

Chapter 14: Assessing Security   Discusses tools such as scanning and penetration testing that you can use to suss out security issues in your hosts and applications.

Writing this book was an adventure for me, as always. I hope you enjoy the result and that your understanding of the world of information security expands. The security world can be an interesting and, at times, hair-raising field to work in. Welcome and good luck!

1

WHAT IS INFORMATION SECURITY?

Today, many of us work with computers, play on computers at home, go to school online, buy goods from merchants on the internet, take our laptops to the coffee shop to read emails, use our smartphones to check our bank balances, and track our exercise with sensors on our wrists. In other words, computers are ubiquitous.

Although technology allows us to access a host of information with only a click of the mouse, it also poses major security risks. If the information on the systems used by our employers or our banks becomes exposed to an attacker, the consequences could be dire indeed. We could suddenly find the contents of our bank account transferred to a bank in another country in the middle of the night. Our employer could lose millions of dollars, face legal prosecution, and suffer damage to its reputation because of a system configuration issue that allowed an attacker to gain access to a database containing personally identifiable information (PII) or proprietary information. Such issues appear in the news media with disturbing regularity.

Thirty years ago, such breaches were nearly nonexistent, largely because the technology was at a relatively low level and few people were using it. Although technology changes at an increasingly rapid rate, much of the theory about keeping ourselves secure lags behind. If you can gain a good understanding of the basics of information security, you're on a strong footing to cope with changes as they come.

In this chapter, I'll cover some of the basic concepts of information security, including security models, attacks, threats, vulnerabilities, and risks. I'll also delve into some slightly more complex concepts when discussing risk management, incident response, and defense in depth.

Defining Information Security

Generally speaking, *security* means protecting your assets, whether from attackers invading your networks, natural disasters, vandalism, loss, or misuse. Ultimately, you'll attempt to secure yourself against the most likely forms of attack, to the best extent you reasonably can, given your environment.

You may have a broad range of potential assets you want to secure. These could include physical items with inherent value, such as gold, or those that have value to your business, such as computing hardware. You may also have valuables of a more ethereal nature, such as software, source code, or data.

In today's computing environment, you're likely to find that your logical assets (assets that exist as data or intellectual property) are at least as valuable as your physical assets (those that are tangible objects or materials), if not more valuable. That's where information security comes in.

Information security is defined as "protecting information and information systems from unauthorized access, use, disclosure, disruption, modification, or destruction," according to US law.[1] In other words, you want to protect your data and systems from those who seek to misuse them, intentionally or unintentionally, or those who should not have access to them at all.

When Are You Secure?

Eugene Spafford once said, "The only truly secure system is one that is powered off, cast in a block of concrete and sealed in a lead-lined room with armed guards—and even then, I have my doubts."[2] A system in such a state might be secure, but it's not usable or productive. As you increase the level of security, you usually decrease the level of productivity.

Additionally, when securing an asset, system, or environment, you must consider how the level of security relates to the value of the item being secured. If you're willing to accommodate the decrease in performance, you can apply very high levels of security to every asset for which you're responsible. You could build a billion-dollar facility surrounded by razor-wire fences and patrolled by armed guards and vicious attack dogs, complete with a hermetically sealed vault, to safeguard your mom's chocolate chip cookie recipe, but that would be overkill. The cost of the security you put in place should never outstrip the value of what it's protecting.

In some environments, however, such security measures might not be enough. In any environment where you plan to put heightened levels of security in place, you also need to consider the cost of replacing your assets if you happen to lose them and make sure you establish reasonable levels of protection for their value.

Defining the exact point at which you can be considered secure presents a bit of a challenge. Are you secure if your systems are properly patched? Are you secure if you use strong passwords? Are you secure if you're disconnected from the internet entirely? From my point of view, the answer to all these questions is no. No single activity or action will make you secure in every situation.

That's because even if your systems are properly patched, there will always be new attacks to which you're vulnerable. When you're using strong passwords, an attacker will exploit a different avenue instead. When you're disconnected from the internet, an attacker could still physically access or steal your systems. In short, it's difficult to define when you're truly secure. On the other hand, defining when you're insecure is a much easier task. Here are several examples that would put you in this state:

- Not applying security patches or application updates to your systems
- Using weak passwords such as "password" or "1234"
- Downloading programs from the internet
- Opening email attachments from unknown senders
- Using wireless networks without encryption

I could go on for some time adding to this list. The good thing is that once you can point out the areas in an environment that can make it insecure, you can take steps to mitigate these issues. This problem is similar to cutting something in half over and over. There will always be some small portion left to cut in half again. Although you may never get to a state that you can definitively call "secure," you can take steps in the right direction.

Models for Discussing Security Issues

When discussing security issues, it's often helpful to have a model that you can use as a foundation or a baseline. This provides a consistent set of terminology and concepts that we, as security professionals, can refer to.

The Confidentiality, Integrity, and Availability Triad

Three of the primary concepts in information security are confidentiality, integrity, and availability, commonly known as the *confidentiality, integrity, and availability (CIA) triad*, as shown in Figure 1-1.

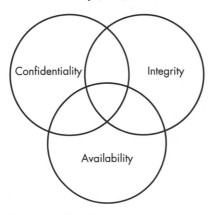

Figure 1-1: The CIA triad

The CIA triad is a model by which you can think about and discuss security concepts. It's also sometimes written as CAI or expressed in its negative form as disclosure, alteration, and denial (DAD).

Confidentiality

Confidentiality refers to our ability to protect our data from those who are not authorized to view it. You could implement confidentiality at many levels of a process.

As an example, imagine a person is withdrawing money from an ATM. The person in question will likely seek to maintain the confidentiality of the personal identification number (PIN) that allows him to draw funds from the ATM if he has his ATM card. Additionally, the owner of the ATM will maintain the confidentiality of the account number, balance, and any other information needed to communicate to the bank from which the funds are being drawn. The bank will also maintain the confidentiality of the transaction with the ATM and the balance change in the account after the funds have been withdrawn.

Confidentiality can be compromised in a number of ways. You could lose a laptop containing data. A person could look over your shoulder while you enter a password. You could send an email attachment to the wrong person, or an attacker could penetrate your systems, to name a few ways.

Integrity

Integrity is the ability to prevent people from changing your data in an unauthorized or undesirable manner. To maintain integrity, not only do you need to have the means to prevent unauthorized changes to your data, but you need the ability to reverse unwanted authorized changes.

A good example of mechanisms that allow you to control integrity are in the file systems of many modern operating systems, such as Windows and Linux. For the purposes of preventing unauthorized changes, such systems often implement permissions that restrict what actions an unauthorized user can perform on a given file. For example, the owner of a file might have permission to read it and write to it, while others might have permission only to read, or no permission to access it at all. Additionally, some such systems and many applications, such as databases, can allow you to undo or roll back changes that are undesirable.

Integrity is particularly important when it concerns data that provides the foundation for other decisions. If an attacker were to alter the data that contained the results of medical tests, a doctor might prescribe the wrong treatment, which could kill the patient.

Availability

The final leg of the CIA triad is availability. *Availability* refers to the ability to access our data when we need it. You could lose availability due to a power loss, operating system or application problems, network attacks, or the compromising of a system, for example. When an outside party, like an attacker, causes such issues, we typically call this a *denial-of-service* (DoS) attack.

How Does the CIA Triad Relate to Security?

Given the elements of the CIA triad, we can begin to discuss security issues with more detail than we otherwise could. For example, let's consider a shipment of backup tapes on which you've stored the only existing, unencrypted copies of some sensitive data.

If you were to lose the shipment in transit, you would have a security issue. This is likely to include a breach of confidentiality since your files were not encrypted. The lack of encryption could also cause integrity issues. If you recover the tapes in the future, it may not be immediately obvious to you if an attacker had altered the unencrypted files, as you would have no good way to discern altered from unaltered data. As for availability, you'll have an issue unless the tapes are recovered since you don't have backup copies of the files.

Although you can describe the situation in this example with relative accuracy using the CIA triad, you might find that the model is too restrictive to describe the entire situation. A more extensive model, the Parkerian hexad, exists for these cases.

The Parkerian Hexad

The Parkerian hexad, a less well-known model named after Donn Parker and introduced in his book *Fighting Computer Crime*, provides a somewhat more complex variation of the classic CIA triad. Where the CIA triad consists only of confidentiality, integrity, and availability, the *Parkerian hexad* consists of these three principles as well as possession or control, authenticity, and utility,[3] for a total of six principles, as shown in Figure 1-2.

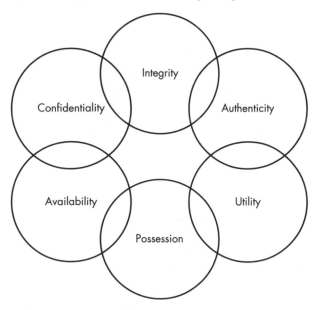

Figure 1-2: The Parkerian hexad

Confidentiality, Integrity, and Availability

As I mentioned, the Parkerian hexad includes the three principles of the CIA triad, with the same definitions just discussed. Parker describes integrity slightly differently; he doesn't account for authorized, but incorrect, modification of data. For him, the data must be whole and completely unchanged from its previous state.

Possession or Control

In the Parkerian hexad, *possession* or *control* refers to the physical disposition of the media on which the data is stored. This enables you to discuss your loss of the data in its physical medium without involving other factors such as availability. Returning to the example of your lost shipment of backup tapes, let's say that some of them were encrypted and some of them were not. The principle of possession would enable you to more accurately describe the scope of the incident; the encrypted tapes in the lot cause a possession problem but not a confidentiality problem, while the unencrypted tapes cause a problem on both counts.

Authenticity

The principle of *authenticity* allows you to say whether you've attributed the data in question to the proper owner or creator. For example, if you send an email message that is altered so that it appears to have come from a different email address than the one from which it was actually sent, you would be violating the authenticity of the email. Authenticity can be enforced using digital signatures, which I'll discuss further in Chapter 5.

A similar, but reversed, concept to this is *nonrepudiation*, which prevents people from taking an action, such as sending an email and then later denying that they have done so. I'll discuss nonrepudiation at greater length in Chapter 4 as well.

Utility

Finally, *utility* refers to how useful the data is to you. Utility is also the only principle of the Parkerian hexad that is not necessarily binary in nature; you can have a variety of degrees of utility, depending on the data and its format. This is a somewhat abstract concept, but it does prove useful in discussing certain situations in the security world.

For instance, in the shipment of backup tapes example, imagine that some of the tapes were encrypted and some were not. For an attacker or other unauthorized person, the encrypted tapes would likely be of very little utility, as the data would not be readable. The unencrypted tapes would be of much greater utility, as the attacker or unauthorized person would be able to access the data.

The concepts discussed in both the CIA triad and the Parkerian hexad provide a practical basis to discuss all the ways in which something can go wrong in the world of information security. These models enable you to better discuss the attacks that you might face and the types of controls that you need to put in place to combat them.

Attacks

You may face attacks from a wide variety of approaches and angles. You can break these down according to the *type* of attack, the *risk* the attack represents, and the *controls* you might use to mitigate it.

Types of Attacks

You can generally place attacks into one of four categories: interception, interruption, modification, and fabrication. Each of the categories can affect one or more of the principles of the CIA triad, as shown in Figure 1-3.

C	Interception
I	Interruption Modification Fabrication
A	Interruption Modification Fabrication

Figure 1-3: The CIA triad and categories of attacks

The line between the categories of attack and the effects they can have are somewhat blurry. Depending on the attack in question, you might include it in more than one category or have more than one type of effect.

Interception

Interception attacks allow unauthorized users to access your data, applications, or environments, and they are primarily attacks against confidentiality. Interception might take the form of unauthorized file viewing or copying, eavesdropping on phone conversations, or reading someone else's email, and you can conduct it against data at rest or in motion (concepts explained in the "Data at Rest and in Motion" box). When they're properly executed, interception attacks can be difficult to detect.

DATA AT REST AND IN MOTION

You will find, repeatedly throughout this book, that I refer to data being either "at rest" or "in motion," so let's talk about what this means. *Data at rest* is stored data that is not in the process of being moved from one place to another. It may be on a hard drive or flash drive, or it may be stored in a database, for example. This type of data is generally protected with some sort of encryption, often at the level of the file or entire storage device.

Data in motion is data that is moving from one place to another. When you are using your online banking session, the sensitive data flowing between your web browser and your bank is data in motion. Data in motion is also protected by encryption, but in this case the encryption protects the network protocol or path used to move the data from one place to another.

Some may also posit a third category, *data in use*. Data in use would be data that an application or individual was actively accessing or modifying. Protections on data in use would include permissions and authentication of users. Often you will find the concept of data in use conflated with data in motion. Sound arguments can be made on both sides about whether we should treat this type of data as its own category.

Interruption

Interruption attacks make your assets unusable or unavailable to you on a temporary or permanent basis. These attacks often affect availability but can affect integrity, as well. You would classify a DoS attack on a mail server as an availability attack.

On the other hand, if an attacker manipulated the processes on which a database runs to prevent access to the data it contains, you might consider this an integrity attack because of the possible loss or corruption of data, or you might consider it a combination of the two. You might also consider such a database attack to be a modification attack rather than an interruption attack, as you'll see next.

Modification

Modification attacks involve tampering with an asset. Such attacks might primarily be considered attacks on integrity but could also represent attacks on availability. If you access a file in an unauthorized manner and alter the data it contains, you've affected the integrity of the file's data. However, if the file in question is a configuration file that manages how a service behaves—perhaps one that is acting as a web server—changing the contents of the file might affect the availability of that service. If the configuration you altered in the file for your web server changes how the server deals with encrypted connections, you could even call this a confidentiality attack.

Fabrication

Fabrication attacks involve generating data, processes, communications, or other similar material with a system. Like the last two attack types, fabrication attacks primarily affect integrity but could affect availability, as well. Generating fake information in a database would be a kind of fabrication attack. You could also generate email, a common method for propagating malware. If you generated enough additional processes, network traffic, email, web traffic, or nearly anything else that consumes resources, you might be conducting an availability attack by rendering the service that handles such traffic unavailable to legitimate users.

Threats, Vulnerabilities, and Risk

To speak more specifically about attacks, I need to introduce a few new terms. When you look at how an attack might affect you, you can speak of it in terms of threats, vulnerabilities, and the associated risk.

Threats

When I spoke of the types of attacks you might encounter earlier in this chapter, I discussed several types of attacks that could harm your assets— for instance, the unauthorized modification of data. Ultimately, a threat is something that has the potential to cause harm. Threats tend to be specific to certain environments, particularly in the world of information security. For example, although a virus might be problematic on a Windows operating system, the same virus will be unlikely to have any effect on a Linux operating system.

Vulnerabilities

Vulnerabilities are weaknesses, or holes, that threats can exploit to cause you harm. A vulnerability might involve a specific operating system or application that you're running, the physical location of your office building, a data center that is overpopulated with servers and producing more heat than its air-conditioning system can handle, a lack of backup generators, or other factors.

Risk

Risk is the likelihood that something bad will happen. For you to have a risk in an environment, you need to have both a threat and a vulnerability that the threat could exploit. For example, if you have a structure that is made from wood and you light a fire nearby, you have both a threat (the fire) and a matching vulnerability (the wood structure). In this case, you most definitely have a risk.

Likewise, if you have the same threat of fire but your structure is made of concrete, you no longer have a credible risk because your threat doesn't have a vulnerability to exploit. You could argue that a sufficiently hot flame could damage the concrete, but this is a much less likely event.

We often talk about potential, but unlikely, attacks in computing environments. The best strategy is to spend your time mitigating the most likely attacks. If you sink your resources into trying to plan for every possible attack, however unlikely, you'll spread yourself thin and lack protection where you need it the most.

Impact

Some organizations, such as the US National Security Agency (NSA), add a factor to the threat/vulnerability/risk equation called *impact*. Impact takes into account the value of the asset being threatened and uses it to calculate risk. In the backup tape example, if you consider that the unencrypted tapes contain only your collection of chocolate chip cookie recipes, you may not actually have a risk because the data exposed contains nothing sensitive and you can make additional backups from the source data. In this case, you might safely say that you have no risk.

Risk Management

Risk management processes compensate for risks in your environment. Figure 1-4 shows a typical risk management process at a high level.

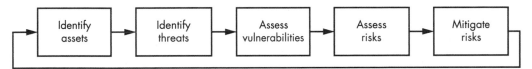

Figure 1-4: A risk management process

As you can see, you need to identify your important assets, figure out the potential threats against them, assess your vulnerabilities, and then take steps to mitigate these risks.

Identify Assets

One of the first and, arguably, most important parts of the risk management process is identifying the assets you're protecting. If you can't enumerate your assets and evaluate the importance of each, protecting them can become a difficult task indeed.

Although this may sound like an exceedingly simple task, it can be a more complex problem than it might seem on the surface, particularly in larger enterprises. In many cases, an organization might have various generations of hardware, assets from acquisitions of other companies lurking in unknown areas, and scores of unrecorded virtual hosts in use, any of which may be critical to the continued functionality of the business.

Once you've identified the assets in use, deciding which of them are critical business assets is another question entirely. Making an accurate determination of which assets are truly critical to conducting business will generally require the input of functions that make use of the asset, those that support the asset itself, and potentially other involved parties as well.

Identify Threats

After enumerating your critical assets, you can then begin to identify the threats that might affect them. It's often useful to have a framework for discussing the nature of a given threat, and the CIA triad or Parkerian hexad discussed earlier in this chapter serves nicely for this purpose.

For instance, let's apply the Parkerian hexad to examine the threats you might face against an application that processes credit card payments.

Confidentiality   If you expose data inappropriately, you could potentially have a breach.

Integrity   If data becomes corrupt, you may incorrectly process payments.

Availability   If the system or application goes down, you won't be able to process payments.

Possession   If you lose backup media, you could potentially have a breach.

Authenticity   If you don't have authentic customer information, you may process a fraudulent transaction.

Utility   If you collect invalid or incorrect data, that data will have limited utility.

While this is clearly a high-level pass at assessing threats for this system, it does point out a few problem areas immediately. You need to be concerned with losing control of data, maintaining accurate data, and keeping the system up and running. Given this information, you can begin to look at areas of vulnerability and potential risk.

Assess Vulnerabilities

When assessing vulnerabilities, you need to do so in the context of potential threats. Any given asset may have thousands or millions of threats that could impact it, but only a small fraction of these will be relevant. In the previous section, you learned about potential threats against a system that processes credit card transactions.

Let's look at the issues that were identified and attempt to determine whether vulnerabilities exist in any of them.

Confidentiality   If you expose data inappropriately, you could have a breach.

Your sensitive data is encrypted at rest and in motion. Your systems are regularly tested by an external penetration testing company. *This is not a risk.*

Integrity   If data becomes corrupt, you may incorrectly process payments.

You carefully validate that payment data is correct as part of the processing workflow. Invalid data results in a rejected transaction. *This is not a risk.*

Availability   If the system or application goes down, you can't process payments.

You do not have redundancy for the database on the back end of the payment processing system. If the database goes down, you can't process payments. *This is a risk.*

Possession   If you lose backup media, you could have a breach.

Your backup media is encrypted and hand-carried by a courier. *This is not a risk.*

Authenticity   If you don't have authentic customer information, you may process a fraudulent transaction.

Ensuring that valid payment and customer information belongs to the individual conducting the transaction is difficult. You do not have a good way of doing this. *This is a risk.*

Utility   If you collect invalid or incorrect data, that data will have limited utility.

To protect the utility of your data, you checksum credit card numbers, make sure that the billing address and email address are valid, and perform other measures to ensure that your data is correct. *This is not a risk.*

These examples are a high-level view of the process you'd need to undertake, but they serve to illustrate the task. From here, you can again see a few areas of concern, namely, in the areas of authenticity and availability, and you can begin to evaluate the areas in which you may have risks.

Assess Risks

Once you've identified the threats and vulnerabilities for a given asset, you can assess the overall risk. As discussed earlier in this chapter, risk is the conjunction of a threat and a vulnerability. A vulnerability with no matching threat or a threat with no matching vulnerability does not constitute a risk.

For example, the following item was both a potential threat and an area of vulnerability:

Availability   If the system or application goes down, you can't process payments.

You don't have redundancy for the database on the back end of your payment processing system, so if the database goes down, you won't be able to process payments.

In this case, you have both a threat and a corresponding vulnerability, meaning you risk losing ability to process credit card payments because of a single point of failure on your database back end. Once you've worked through your threats and vulnerabilities in this manner, you can mitigate these risks.

Mitigate Risks

To mitigate risks, you can put measures in place to account for each threat. These measures are called *controls*. Controls are divided into three categories: physical, logical, and administrative.

Physical controls protect the physical environment in which your systems sit, or where your data is stored. Such controls also control access in and out of such environments. Physical controls include fences, gates, locks, bollards, guards, and cameras, but also systems that maintain the physical environment, such as heating and air-conditioning systems, fire suppression systems, and backup power generators.

Although at first glance physical controls may not seem like they'd be integral to information security, they're one of the most critical controls; if you're not able to physically protect your systems and data, any other controls that you put in place become irrelevant. If attackers can physically access your systems, they can steal or destroy them, rendering them unavailable for your use—in the best case. In the worst case, attackers will be able to access your applications and data directly and steal your information and resources or subvert them for their own use.

Logical controls, sometimes called *technical controls*, protect the systems, networks, and environments that process, transmit, and store your data. Logical controls can include items such as passwords, encryption, access controls, firewalls, and intrusion detection systems.

Logical controls enable you to prevent unauthorized activities; if your logical controls are implemented properly and are successful, an attacker or unauthorized user can't access your applications and data without subverting the controls.

Administrative controls are based on rules, laws, policies, procedures, guidelines, and other items that are "paper" in nature. Administrative controls dictate how the users of your environment should behave. Depending on the environment and control in question, administrative controls can represent differing levels of authority. You may have a simple rule such as "turn the coffee pot off at the end of the day," aimed at avoiding a physical security problem (burning your building down at night). You may also have a more stringent administrative control, such as one that requires you to change your password every 90 days.

One important part of administrative controls is the ability to enforce them. If you don't have the authority or the ability to ensure that people comply with your controls, they are worse than useless because they create a false sense of security. For example, if you create a policy that says employees can't use business resources for personal use, you'll need to be able to enforce this. Outside of a highly secure environment, this can be a difficult task. You'd need to monitor telephone and mobile phone usage, web access, email use, instant message conversations, installed software, and other potential areas for abuse. Unless you were willing to devote a great deal of resources to monitoring these and handling violations of policy, you'd quickly have a policy that you wouldn't be able to enforce. The next time you're audited and asked to produce evidence of policy enforcement, you'll face issues.

Incident Response

If your risk management efforts are not as thorough as you hoped or you're blindsided by something entirely unexpected, you can react with incident response. You should direct your incident response at the items that you feel are most likely to cause your organization pain. You should have already identified these as part of your risk management efforts.

As much as possible, you should base your reaction to such incidents on documented incident response plans, which should be regularly reviewed, tested, and practiced by those who will be expected to enact them in the case of an actual incident. You don't want to wait until an actual emergency to find out documentation that has been languishing on a shelf is outdated and refers to processes or systems that have changed heavily or no longer exist.

The incident response process, at a high level, consists of the following:

- Preparation
- Detection and analysis
- Containment
- Eradication
- Recovery
- Post-incident activity

I'll go over these phases in more detail next.

Preparation

The preparation phase of incident response consists of all the activities you can perform ahead of time to better handle an incident. This typically involves creating policies and procedures that govern incident response and handling, conducting training and education for both incident handlers and those who are expected to report incidents, and developing and maintaining documentation.

You shouldn't underestimate the importance of this phase of incident response. Without adequate preparation, it is extremely unlikely that the response to an incident will go well or according to your unpracticed plans. The time to determine what needs to be done, who needs to do it, and how to do it is not when you're faced with an emergency.

Detection and Analysis

The detection and analysis phase is where the action begins. In this phase, you detect an issue, decide whether it's actually an incident, and respond to it appropriately.

Most often, you'll detect the issue with a security tool or service, like an intrusion detection system (IDS), antivirus (AV) software, firewall logs, proxy logs, or alerts from a security information and event monitoring (SIEM) tool or managed security service provider (MSSP).

The analysis portion of this phase is often a combination of automation from a tool or service, usually a SIEM tool, and human judgment. While you can often use some sort of thresholding to say that a certain number of events in a given amount of time is normal or that a certain combination of events is not normal (two failed logins, followed by a success, a password change, and the creation of a new account, for instance), you'll often want human intervention at a some point. Human intervention might include a review of logs output by various security, network, and infrastructure devices; contact with the party who reported the incident; and general evaluation of the situation. (Unfortunately for the incident handler, these situations often occur at 4 PM on a Friday or 2 AM on a Sunday.)

When the incident handler evaluates the situation, that person will decide whether the issue constitutes an incident, evaluate the criticality of the incident, and contact any additional resources needed to proceed to the next phase.

Containment, Eradication, and Recovery

The containment, eradication, and recovery phase is where most of the work to solve the incident takes place, at least in the short term.

Containment involves taking steps to ensure that the situation doesn't cause any more damage than it already has—or at least lessen any ongoing harm. If the problem involves a malware-infected server actively being controlled by a remote attacker, this might mean disconnecting the server from the network, putting firewall rules in place to block the attacker, and updating signatures or rules on an intrusion prevention system (IPS) to halt the traffic from the malware.

During *eradication*, you'll attempt to remove the effects of the issue from your environment. In the case of your malware-infected server, you've already isolated the system and cut it off from its command-and-control network. Now you'll need to clean the malware from the server and ensure that it doesn't exist elsewhere in your environment. This might involve additional scanning of other hosts in the environment to ensure that the malware is not present and perhaps examining logs on the server and network to determine what other systems the infected server has communicated with. With malware, particularly very new malware or variants, this can be a tricky task. Whenever you're in doubt about whether you've truly evicted malware or attackers from your environment, you should err on the side of caution.

Lastly, you need to recover the state you were in prior to the incident. *Recovery* might involve restoring devices or data from backup media, rebuilding systems, or reloading applications. Again, this can be a more painful task than it initially seems because your knowledge of the situation might be incomplete or unclear. You may find that you are unable to verify that backup media is clean and free or infection or that the backup media is entirely bad. Application install bits may be missing, configuration files may not be available, or many other issues could occur.

Post-Incident Activity

Like preparation, post-incident activity is easy to overlook, but you should ensure that you don't neglect it. In the post-incident activity phase, often referred to as a *post-mortem* (Latin for "after death"), you attempt to determine specifically what happened, why it happened, and what you can do to keep it from happening again. The purpose of this phase is not to point fingers or place blame (although this does sometimes happen) but to ultimately prevent or lessen the impact of future such incidents.

Defense in Depth

Now that you've learned about the potential effects of a security breach, the kinds of attacks you might face, and the strategies for dealing with these attacks, I'll introduce you to a method of working toward preventing these attacks. *Defense in depth* is a strategy common to both military maneuvers and information security. The basic concept is to formulate a multilayered defense that will allow you to still mount a successful resistance should one or more of your defensive measures fail.

In Figure 1-5, you can see an example of layers you might want to put in place to defend your assets.

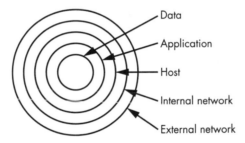

Figure 1-5: Defense in depth

At the least, you would want defenses at the external network, internal network, host, application, and data levels. Well-implemented defenses at each layer make it difficult to successfully penetrate your network and attack your assets directly.

That said, defense in depth is not a magic bullet. No matter how many layers you put in place or how many defensive measures you place at each layer, you won't be able to keep every attacker out for an indefinite period. Nor is this the goal of defense in depth in an information security setting. The goal is to place enough defensive measures between your truly important assets and the attacker so that you'll notice that an attack is in progress and have enough time to prevent it.

An example of such a delaying tactic is requiring employees to change their passwords every 60 or 90 days. This makes it harder for an attacker to crack a password in time to still use it.

Using stringent password construction rules is another delaying tactic. Consider the password "mypassword," which is ten characters long and uses only one character set. Using a relatively slow off-the-shelf system, an attacker might take a week or two to crack this password. With a purpose-built password cracking system or a botnet, an attacker might take only an hour or two.

If you use more secure password construction rules and go with a password along the lines of MyP@ssword1, which is also ten characters long but uses four character sets, cracking the password would take thousands of years on purpose-built hardware and upward of several years for a large botnet.

If you require employees to both change their passwords frequently and create complex passwords, an attacker won't be able to crack one in time to use it.

ENTROPY IN PASSWORDS

The complex password example discussed previously uses a classic strong password construction scheme, consisting of eight or more characters and comprising multiple character sets (upper alpha, lower alpha, numbers, and punctuation). Some would argue it contains insufficient entropy (unpredictability) to be truly secure and that you'd be better served with a longer, more entropic, and more easily remembered password like correcthorsebatterystaple.[4]

Ultimately, your primary concern should be in constructing reasonably secure passwords and changing them at regular intervals.

The layers you include in your defense-in-depth strategy will vary given the situation and environment you're defending. As discussed, from a strictly logical (nonphysical) information security perspective, you'd want to look at the external network, network perimeter, internal network, host, application, and data layers as areas to place your defenses.

You could add complexity to your defensive model by including other vital layers, such as physical defenses, policies, or user awareness and training, but I'll stick with a simpler example for the time being.

Table 1-1 lists some of the defenses you might use for each of the layers discussed.

Table 1-1: Defense by Layer

Layer	Defensive measures
External network	DMZ VPN Logging Auditing Penetration testing Vulnerability analysis
Network perimeter	Firewalls Proxy Logging Stateful packet inspection Auditing Penetration testing Vulnerability analysis
Internal network	IDS IPS Logging Auditing Penetration testing Vulnerability analysis
Host	Authentication Antivirus Firewalls IDS IPS Passwords Hashing Logging Auditing Penetration testing Vulnerability analysis
Application	SSO Content filtering Data validation Auditing Penetration testing Vulnerability analysis
Data	Encryption Access controls Backups Penetration testing Vulnerability analysis

In some cases, a defensive measure appears in multiple layers because it applies to more than one area. A good example of this is *penetration testing*, a method of finding gaps in your security by using some of the same strategies an attacker would use to break in, which appears in every layer. I'll discuss this in greater depth in Chapter 14. You might want to use penetration testing at every layer of your defense. You can also see where specific controls may be tied to particular layers, such as firewalls and proxies at the network perimeter. As with everything else in the security field, you could argue that some or all of these controls could exist at layers other than what is shown here, but this is a good general guideline. As you move through the book, I'll discuss each of these areas shown in Table 1-1 in greater detail, as well as the specific defenses you might want to use for each.

Summary

When discussing issues pertaining to information security, such as attacks and controls, it's helpful to have a model by which to do so. This chapter discussed two potential models: the CIA triad, composed of confidentiality, integrity, and availability; and the Parkerian hexad, composed of confidentiality, integrity, availability, possession or control, authenticity, and utility.

As you look toward preventing attacks, it is also helpful to understand the general categories of damage that you might see occur in the event of an attack. Attacks may impact environments through interception, interruption, modification, or fabrication. Each of these effects would impact particular areas of the CIA triad.

When discussing specific threats you might face, it's important to understand the concept of risk. You only face risk from an attack when a threat is present and you have a vulnerability that threat can exploit. To mitigate risk, you use three main types of controls: physical, logical, and administrative.

Finally, this chapter covered defense in depth, a particularly important concept in the world of information security. To build defensive measures using this concept, you put in place multiple layers of defense to delay an attacker long enough to alert you to the attack and to allow you to mount a more active defense.

The concepts discussed in this chapter are foundational to information security. They're used on a regular basis during normal information security tasks in many organizations; you might hear someone talking about breaches of confidentiality, for example, or the authenticity of a given email message.

Information security is a daily concern for organizations of any size, particularly those that handle any type of personal information, financial data, healthcare data, educational data, or other types of information regulated by the laws of the country in which the organization operates. When an organization doesn't invest in information security, the repercussions can be severe. They might face fines, lawsuits, or even the inability to continue conducting business if they lose control of critical or sensitive data. In short, information security is a key component of the modern business world.

Exercises

Here are some questions to help you review the key concepts of this chapter:

1. Explain the difference between a vulnerability and a threat.
2. What are six items that might be considered logical controls?
3. What term might you use to describe the usefulness of data?
4. Which category of attack is an attack against confidentiality?
5. How do you know at what point you can consider your environment to be secure?
6. Using the concept of defense in depth, what layers might you use to secure yourself against someone removing confidential data from your environment on a USB flash drive?
7. Based on the Parkerian hexad, what principles are affected if you lose a shipment of encrypted backup tapes that contain personal and payment information for your customers?
8. If the web servers in your environment are based on Microsoft's Internet Information Services (IIS) and a new worm is discovered that attacks Apache web servers, what do you not have?
9. If you develop a new policy for your environment that requires you to use complex and automatically generated passwords that are unique to each system and are a minimum of 30 characters in length, such as "!Qa4(j0nO$&xn1%2AL34ca#!Ps321$," what will be adversely impacted?
10. Considering the CIA triad and the Parkerian hexad, what are the advantages and disadvantages of each model?

2

IDENTIFICATION AND AUTHENTICATION

When you're developing security measures, whether they're specific mechanisms or entire infrastructures, identification and authentication are key concepts. In short, *identification* makes a claim about what someone or something is, and *authentication* establishes whether this claim is true. You can see such processes taking place daily in a wide variety of ways.

One common example of an identification and authentication transaction is the use of payment cards that require a personal identification number (PIN). When you swipe the magnetic strip on the card, you're asserting that you're the person indicated on the card. At this point, you've given your identification, but nothing more. When you're prompted to enter the PIN associated with the card, you're completing the authentication portion of the transaction, proving you're the legitimate cardholder.

Some of the identification and authentication methods that we use daily are particularly fragile, meaning they depend largely on the honesty and diligence of those involved in the transaction. If you show your ID card to buy alcohol, for example, you're asking people to trust that your ID is genuine and accurate; they can't authenticate it unless they have access to the system that maintains the ID in question. We also depend on the competence of the person or system performing the authentication; they must be capable not only of performing the act of authentication but also of detecting false or fraudulent activity.

You can use several methods for identification and authentication, from requiring simple usernames and passwords to implementing purpose-built hardware tokens that serve to establish your identity in multiple ways. In this chapter, I'll discuss several of these methods and explore their uses.

Identification

Identification, as you just learned, is simply an assertion of who we are. This may include who we claim to be as people, who a system claims to be over the network, or who the originating party of an email claims to be. You'll see some methods for determining identity and examine how trustworthy those methods are.

Who We Claim to Be

Who we claim to be is a tenuous concept at best. We can identify ourselves by our full names, shortened versions of our names, nicknames, account numbers, usernames, ID cards, fingerprints, or DNA samples. Unfortunately, with a few exceptions, such methods of identification are not unique, and even some of the supposedly unique methods of identification, such as fingerprints, can be duplicated.

Who we claim to be can, in many cases, be subject to change. For instance, women often change their last names upon getting married. In addition, we can generally change logical forms of identification—such as account numbers or usernames—easily. Even physical identifiers, such as height, weight, skin color, and eye color, can change. One of the most crucial factors to realize is that a claim of identity alone is not enough.

Identity Verification

Identity verification is a step beyond identification, but it's still a step short of authentication, which I'll discuss in the next section. When you're asked to show a driver's license, Social Security card, birth certificate, or other similar form of identification, this is generally for identity verification, not authentication. It's the rough equivalent of someone claiming the identity John Smith; you asking if the person is indeed John Smith and being satisfied with an answer of "Sure, I am" from the person (plus a little paperwork).

We can take the example a bit further and validate the form of identification (say, a passport) against a database holding an additional copy of the information that it contains, matching the photograph and physical specifications with the person standing in front of us. This may get us a bit closer to ensuring we've correctly identified the person, but it still doesn't qualify as authentication; we may have validated the status of the ID itself, and we know that the person meets the general specifications of the person it was originally issued to, but we've taken no steps to prove that the person is really the right one. The more than we trend toward verification and away from authentication, the weaker our controls are.

Computer systems use identity verification, too. When you send an email, the identity you provide is taken to be true; the system rarely takes any additional steps to authenticate you. Such gaps in security contribute to the enormous amount of spam traffic, which Cisco's Talos Intelligence Group estimated to have accounted for approximately 85 percent of all emails sent from mid-2017 to mid-2018.[1]

Falsifying Identification

As I've discussed, methods of identification are subject to change. As such, they are also subject to falsification. Minors often use fake IDs to get into bars or nightclubs, while criminals and terrorists might use them for a variety of more nefarious tasks. You could use some methods of identification, such as birth certificates, to gain additional forms of identification, such as Social Security cards or driver's licenses, thus strengthening a false identity.

Identity theft based on falsified information is a major concern today; identity thieves stole an estimated $16.8 billion from US consumers in 2017.[2] This type of attack is unfortunately common and easy to execute. Given a minimal amount of information—usually a name, address, and Social Security number are sufficient—it's possible to impersonate someone just enough to be able to conduct a variety of transactions in their name, such as opening a line of credit. Such crimes occur because many activities lack authentication requirements. Although most people think identity verification is sufficient, verification is easy to circumvent by using falsified forms of identification.

Many of the same difficulties exist in computer systems and environments. For example, it's entirely possible to send an email from a falsified email address. Spammers use this tactic on a regular basis. I'll address such issues at greater length in Chapter 9.

Authentication

In information security, authentication is the set of methods used to establish whether a claim of identity is true. Note that authentication does not decide what the party being authenticated is permitted to do; this is a separate task, known as *authorization*. I'll discuss authorization in Chapter 3.

Factors

There are several approaches to authentication: something you know, something you are, something you have, something you do, and where you are. These approaches are known as *factors*. When you're attempting to authenticate a claim of identity, you'll want to use as many factors as possible. The more factors you use, the more positive your results will be.

Something you know, a common authentication factor, includes passwords or PINs. However, this factor is somewhat weak, because if the information the factor depends on is exposed, your authentication method may no longer be unique.

Something you are is a factor based on the relatively unique physical attributes of an individual, often referred to as *biometrics.* Although biometrics can include simple attributes such as height, weight, hair color, or eye color, these aren't usually distinctive enough to make very secure identifiers. Complex identifiers such as fingerprints, iris or retina patterns, or facial characteristics are more common. These are a bit stronger than, say, a password, because forging or stealing a copy of a physical identifier is somewhat more difficult, although not impossible. There is some question as to whether biometrics truly count as an authentication factor or whether they only constitute verification. I'll discuss this again later in this chapter, when I cover biometrics in greater depth.

Something you have is a factor generally based on a physical possession, although it can extend into some logical concepts. Common examples are automatic teller machine (ATM) cards, state or federally issued identity cards, or software-based security tokens, as shown in Figure 2-1.[3] Some institutions, such as banks, have begun to use access to logical devices, such as cell phones or email accounts, as methods of authentication, as well.

This factor can vary in strength depending on the implementation. If you wanted to use a security token sent to a device that doesn't belong to you, you'd need to steal the device to falsify the authentication method. On the other hand, if the security token was sent to an email address, it would be much easier to intercept, and you'd have a measure of considerably less strength.

Figure 2-1: Sending a security token to a mobile phone is a common authentication method.

Something you do, sometimes considered a variation of something you are, is a factor based on the actions or behaviors of an individual. This may include an analysis of the individual's gait or handwriting or of the time delay between keystrokes as he or she types a passphrase. These factors present a strong method of authentication and are difficult to falsify. They do, however, have the potential to incorrectly reject legitimate users at a higher rate than some of the other factors.

Where you are is a geographically based authentication factor. This factor operates differently than the other factors, as it requires a person to be present in a specific location. For example, when changing an ATM PIN, most banks will require you to go into a branch, at which point you will also be required to present your identification and account number. If the bank allowed the PIN to be reset online, an attacker could change your PIN remotely and proceed to clean out your account. Although potentially less useful than some of the other factors, this factor is difficult to counter without entirely subverting the system performing the authentication.

Multifactor Authentication

Multifactor authentication uses one or more of the factors discussed in the preceding section. When you're using only two factors, this practice is also sometimes called *two-factor authentication*.

Let's return to the ATM example because it illustrates multifactor authentication well. In this case, you use something you know (your PIN) and something you have (your ATM card). Your ATM card serves as both a factor for authentication and a form of identification. Another example of multifactor authentication is writing checks. In this case, you're using something you have (the checks themselves) and something you do (signing them). Here, the two factors involved in writing a check are rather weak, so you sometimes see a third factor—a fingerprint—used with them.

Depending on the factors selected, you can assemble stronger or weaker multifactor authentication schemes particular to each situation. In some cases, although certain methods may be more difficult to defeat, they're not practical to implement. For example, DNA makes for a strong method of authentication but isn't practical in most situations. In Chapter 1, I said that your security should be proportional to what you're protecting. You certainly could install iris scanners on every credit card terminal, but this would be expensive, impractical, and potentially upsetting to customers.

Mutual Authentication

Mutual authentication is an authentication mechanism in which both parties in a transaction authenticate each other. These parties are typically software-based. In the standard, one-way authentication process, the client authenticates to the server. In mutual authentication, not only does the client authenticate to the server, but the server authenticates to the client. Mutual authentication often relies on digital certificates, which I'll discuss in Chapter 5. Briefly, both the client and the server would have a certificate to authenticate the other.

In cases where you don't perform mutual authentication, you leave yourself open to impersonation attacks, often referred to as *man-in-the-middle attacks*. In a man-in-the-middle attack, the attacker inserts himself between the client and the server. The attacker then impersonates the server to the client and the client to the server, as shown in Figure 2-2, by circumventing the normal pattern of traffic and then intercepting and forwarding the traffic that would normally flow directly between the client and the server.

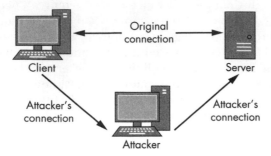

Figure 2-2: A man-in-the-middle attack

This is typically possible because the attacker needs to subvert or falsify authentication only from the client to the server. If you implement mutual authentication, this becomes a considerably more difficult attack because the attacker would have to falsify two different authentications.

You can also combine mutual authentication with multifactor authentication, although the latter generally takes place only on the client side. Multifactor authentication from the server back to the client would be not only technically challenging but also impractical in most environments because it would involve some technical heavy-lifting on the client side, potentially on the part of the user. You'd likely lose a significant amount of productivity.

Common Identification and Authentication Methods

I'll conclude this discussion by exploring three common identification and authentication methods in detail: passwords, biometrics, and hardware tokens.

Passwords

Passwords are familiar to most us who use computers regularly. When combined with a username, a password will generally allow you access to a computer system, an application, a phone, or a similar device. Although they're only a single factor of authentication, passwords can represent a relatively high level of security when constructed and implemented properly.

People often describe certain passwords as being *strong*, but a better descriptive term might be *complex*. If you construct a password that uses lowercase letters only and is eight characters long, you can use a password-cracking utility to crack it quickly, as discussed in Chapter 1. Adding character sets to the password makes it increasingly harder to figure out. If you use uppercase letters, lowercase letters, numbers, and symbols, you'll end up with a password that is potentially more difficult to remember, such as *$sU&qw!3*, but much harder to crack.

In addition to constructing strong passwords, you also need to practice good password hygiene. Don't write your password down and post it under your keyboard or on your monitor; doing so completely defeats the purpose of having a password in the first place. Applications called *password managers* exist to help us manage all the logins and passwords we have for different accounts, some as locally installed software and others as web or mobile device applications. There are many arguments for and against such tools; some people think keeping all of your passwords in one place is a bad idea, but when used carefully, they can help you maintain good password hygiene.

Another common problem is the manual synchronization of passwords—in short, using the same password everywhere. If you use the same password for your email, for your login at work, and for your online knitting discussion forum, you're putting the security of all the accounts in the hands of those system owners. If any one of them is compromised, all of your accounts become vulnerable; all an attacker needs to do to access the others is look up your account name on the internet to find your other accounts and log in using your default password. By the time the attacker gets into your email account, the game is over because an attacker can generally use it reset account credentials for any other accounts you have.

Biometrics

Although some biometric identifiers may be more difficult to falsify than others, this is only because of the limitations of today's technology. At some point in the future, we'll need to develop more robust biometric characteristics to measure or else stop using biometrics as an authentication mechanism.

Using Biometrics

Biometrics-equipped devices are becoming increasingly common and inexpensive. You can find a wide selection of them for less than $20. It pays to research such devices carefully before you depend on them for security, as some of the cheaper versions are easy to bypass.

You can use biometric systems in two ways. You can use them to verify the identity claim someone has put forth, as discussed earlier, or you can reverse the process and use biometrics as a method of identification. This process is commonly used by law enforcement agencies to identify the owner of fingerprints left on various objects. It can be a time-consuming effort, considering the sheer size of the fingerprint libraries held by such organizations. To use a biometric system in either manner, you need to put the user through some sort of enrollment process. Enrollment involves recording the user's chosen biometric characteristic—for instance, making a copy of a fingerprint—and saving it in a system. Processing the characteristic may also include noting elements that appear at certain parts of the image, known as *minutiae* (Figure 2-3).

Figure 2-3: Biometric minutiae

You can use the minutiae later to match the characteristic to the user.

Characteristics of Biometric Factors

Biometric factors are defined by seven characteristics: universality, uniqueness, permanence, collectability, performance, acceptability, and circumvention.[4]

Universality means you should be able to find your chosen biometric characteristic in the majority of people you expect to enroll in the system. For instance, although you might be able to use a scar as an identifier, you can't guarantee that everyone will have a scar. Even if you choose a common characteristic, such as a fingerprint, you should take into account the fact that some people may not have an index finger on their right hand and be prepared to compensate for this.

Uniqueness is a measure of how unique a characteristic is among individuals. For example, if you choose to use height or weight as a biometric identifier, you'd stand a good chance of finding several people in any given group who have the same height or weight. You should try to select characteristics with a high degree of uniqueness, such as DNA or iris patterns, but even these could be duplicated, whether intentionally or otherwise. For example, identical twins have the same DNA, and an attacker could replicate a fingerprint.

Permanence tests how well a characteristic resists change over time and with advancing age. If you choose a factor that can easily vary, such as height, weight, or hand geometry, you'll eventually find yourself unable to authenticate a legitimate user. It's better to use factors such as fingerprints, which are unlikely to change without deliberate action.

Collectability measures how easy it is to acquire a characteristic. Most commonly used biometrics, such as fingerprints, are relatively easy to acquire, which is one reason they are common. On the other hand, a DNA sample is more difficult to acquire because the user must provide a genetic sample to enroll and to authenticate again later.

Performance measures how well a given system functions based on factors such as speed, accuracy, and error rate. I'll discuss the performance of biometric systems at greater length later in this section.

Acceptability is a measure of how acceptable the characteristic is to the users of the system. In general, systems that are slow, difficult to use, or awkward to use are less likely to be acceptable to the user.[5] Systems that require users to remove their clothes, touch devices that have been repeatedly used by others, or provide tissue or bodily fluids are unlikely to have a high degree of acceptability.

Circumvention describes how easy it is to trick a system by using a falsified biometric identifier. The classic example of a circumvention attack against the fingerprint as a biometric identifier is the "gummy finger." In this type of attack, a fingerprint is lifted from a surface and used to create a mold with which the attacker can cast a positive image of the fingerprint in gelatin. Some biometric systems have secondary features specifically designed to defeat such attacks by measuring skin temperature, pulse, or pupillary response.

Measuring Performance

There are many ways to measure the performance of a biometric system, but a few primary metrics are particularly important. The *false acceptance rate (FAR)* and *false rejection rate (FRR)* are two of these.[6] FAR measures how often you accept a user who should be rejected. This is also called a *false positive.* FRR measures how often we reject a legitimate user and is sometimes called a *false negative.*

You want to avoid both of these situations in excess. You should aim for a balance between the two error types, referred to as an *equal error rate (EER).* If you plot both the FAR and the FRR on a graph, as I've done in Figure 2-4, the EER marks the point where the two lines intersect. We sometimes use EER as a measure of the accuracy of biometric systems.

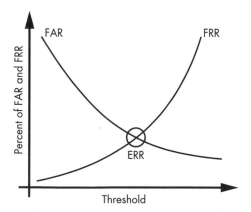

Figure 2-4: The equal error rate is the intersection of the false acceptance rate and false rejection rate.

Flaws in Biometric Systems

Biometric systems are prone to several common issues. As I mentioned when discussing circumvention, it's easy to forge some biometric identifiers. Moreover, once they're forged, it's hard to re-enroll a user in the system. For example, if you enroll a user with both index fingers and those fingerprints get compromised, you could remove these from the system and enroll two of their other fingers. However, if you've already enrolled all of their fingers in the system, you'd have no means of re-enrolling them using fingers at all. Depending on the system in question, you may be able to select a different set of minutiae for the same identifier, but this avoids the point of the discussion, which is that biometric identifiers are finite. This issue became tangible in 2015, when an attacker hacked the US Office of Personnel Management and stole the fingerprint records of 5.6 million federal employees holding security clearances.[7]

You also face possible privacy issues in the use of biometrics. When you're enrolled in a biometric system, you're essentially giving away a copy of the identifier, whether it's a fingerprint, iris pattern, or DNA sample. Once such an item has been entered into a computer system, you have little, if any, control over what happens to it. We can hope that once you're no longer associated with the institution in question, the institution would destroy such materials, but you have no way to guarantee this. Particularly in the case of DNA sampling, the repercussions of surrendering genetic material could affect you for the rest of your life.

Hardware Tokens

A standard hardware token (Figure 2-5) is a small device, typically in the general form factor (size and shape) of a credit card or keychain fob.[8] The simplest hardware tokens look identical to universal serial bus (USB) flash drives and contain a certificate or unique identifier. They're often called *dongles*. More complex hardware tokens incorporate liquid-crystal displays (LCDs), keypads for entering passwords, biometric readers, wireless devices, and additional features to enhance security.

Figure 2-5: A hardware token

Many hardware tokens contain an internal clock that generates a code based on the device's unique identifier, an input PIN or password, and other potential factors. Usually, the code is output to a display on the token and changes on a regular basis, often every 30 seconds. The infrastructure used to keep track of these tokens can predict what the proper output will be at any given time in order to authenticate the user.

The simplest kind of hardware token represents only the something you have factor and is thus susceptible to theft and potential use by a knowledgeable criminal. Although these devices represent an increased level of security for the user's accounts and aren't generally useful without the associated account credentials, you do need to remember to safeguard them.

More sophisticated hardware tokens could represent the something you know or something you are factors, as well. They might require a PIN or fingerprint, which enhances the security of the device considerably; in addition to getting the hardware token, an attacker would need to either subvert the infrastructure that uses the device or extract the something you know or something you are factor from the legitimate owner of the device.

Summary

Identification is an assertion of the identity of some party, whether it be a person, process, system, or other entity. Identification is only a claim of identity; it doesn't say anything about any privileges that might be associated with the identity.

Authentication is the process used to validate whether the claim of identity is correct. It's different than verification, which is a much weaker way of testing someone's identity.

When you perform authentication, you can use several factors. The main factors are something you know, something you are, something you have, something you do, and where you are. An authentication mechanism that includes more than one factor is known as multifactor authentication. Using multiple factors gives you a much stronger authentication mechanism than you might otherwise have.

The common set of tools used for authentication includes passwords, tokens, and biometric identifiers. Each of these has its own set of unique challenges that you will need to deal with when you are implementing them as part of your set of security controls.

In the next chapter, I'll discuss the steps that take place after identification and authentication: authorization and access control.

Exercises

1. What is the difference between verification and authentication of an identity?
2. How do you measure the rate at which you fail to authenticate legitimate users in a biometric system?

3. What do you call the process in which the client authenticates to the server and the server authenticates to the client?

4. A key would be described as which type of authentication factor?

5. What biometric factor describes how well a characteristic resists change over time?

6. If you're using an identity card as the basis for your authentication scheme, what steps might you add to the process to allow you to move to multifactor authentication?

7. If you're using an eight-character password that contains only lowercase characters, would increasing the length to ten characters represent any significant increase in strength? Why or why not?

8. Name three reasons why an identity card alone might not make an ideal method of authentication.

9. What factors might you use when implementing a multifactor authentication scheme for users who are logging onto workstations that are in a secure environment and are used by more than one person?

10. If you're developing a multifactor authentication system for an environment where you might find larger-than-average numbers of disabled or injured users, such as a hospital, which authentication factors might you want to use or avoid? Why?

3

AUTHORIZATION AND ACCESS CONTROLS

After you've received a party's claim of identity and established whether that claim is valid, as discussed in Chapter 2, you have to decide whether to allow the party access to your resources. You can achieve this with two main concepts: authorization and access control. *Authorization* is the process of determining exactly what an authenticated party can do. You typically implement authorization using *access controls*, which are the tools and systems you use to deny or allow access.

You can base access controls on physical attributes, sets of rules, lists of individuals or systems, or other, more complex factors. When it comes to logical resources, you'll probably find simple access controls implemented in everyday applications and operating systems and elaborate, multilevel configurations in military or government environments. In this chapter, you'll learn about access controls in more detail and look at some ways of implementing them.

What Are Access Controls?

Although the term *access controls* may sound technical, like it belongs only in high-security computing facilities, we all deal with access controls daily.

- When you lock or unlock the doors of your house, you're using a form of physical access control, based on your keys. (Your keys are something you have, as discussed in Chapter 2; in this case, they function as methods of both authentication and authorization.)

- When you start your car, you're also likely to use a key. For some newer cars, your key may even include an extra layer of security with radio-frequency identification (RFID) tags, which are certificate-like identifiers stored on the key.

- Upon reaching your place of employment, you might use a badge (again, something you have) to enter the building.

- When you sit down in front of your computer at work and enter your password (something you know), you're authenticating yourself and using a logical access control system to access the resources for which you've been given permission.

Most of us regularly encounter multiple implementations like these while working, going to school, and performing the other activities that make up our day.

You'll probably want to use access controls to carry out four basic tasks: allowing access, denying access, limiting access, and revoking access. We can describe most access control issues or situations using these four actions.

Allowing access is giving a party access to a given resource. For example, you might want to give a user access to a file, or you may want to give an entire group of people access to all the files in a given directory. You might also allow someone physical access to a resource by giving your employees a key or badge to your facility.

Denying access is the opposite of granting access. When you deny access, you are preventing a given party from accessing the resource in question. You might deny access to a person attempting to log onto a machine based on the time of day, or you might block unauthorized individuals from entering the lobby of your building beyond business hours. Many access control systems are set to deny by default.

Limiting access is allowing only some degree of access to your resources. In a physical security scheme, you might have a master key that can open any door in the building, an intermediate key that can open only a few doors, and a low-level key that can open only one door. You might also implement limited access when you're using applications that may be exposed to attack-prone environments, like web browsers used on the internet.

One way to limit access is by running sensitive applications in *sandboxes*, which are isolated environments containing a set of resources for a given purpose (Figure 3-1).

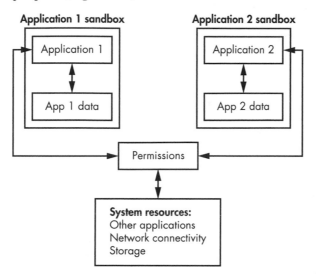

Figure 3-1: A sandbox is an isolated environment that protects a set of resources.

We use sandboxes to prevent their contents from accessing files, memory, and other system resources with which they shouldn't be interacting. Sandboxes can be useful for containing things that you can't trust, such as code from public websites. One example of a sandbox is the Java Virtual Machine (JVM) used to run programs written in the Java programming language. The JVM is specifically constructed to protect users against potentially malicious downloaded software.

Revoking access is taking access away from a party after you've granted it. Being able to revoke access is vital to the security of your system. If you were, for instance, to fire an employee, you'd want to revoke any accesses they might have, including access to their email account, your virtual private network (VPN), and your facility. When you're working with computer resources, it may be particularly important to be able to revoke access to a given resource quickly.

Implementing Access Controls

The two main methods of implementing access controls are with access control lists and capabilities. Both of these methods have strengths and weaknesses, as well as different ways of carrying out the four basic tasks we covered earlier.

Access Control Lists

Access control lists (ACLs), often pronounced "ackles," are lists containing information about what kind of access certain parties are allowed to have to a given system. We often see ACLs implemented as part of application software or operating systems and in the firmware of some hardware appliances, such as network infrastructure devices. We may even see ACL concepts extend into the physical world, through software systems that control physical resources, such as badge readers for door control systems. According to the ACL in Figure 3-2, Alice is allowed access to the resource, while Bob is specifically denied access.

Alice	Allow	✓
Bob	Deny	✗

Figure 3-2: A simple access control list

This may seem like a simple concept, but in larger implementations, ACLs can become quite complex. Organizations commonly use ACLs to control access in the file systems on which their operating systems run and to control the flow of traffic in the networks to which their systems are attached. You'll learn about these two types of ACLs in this chapter.

File System ACLs

The ACLs in most file systems will have three types of permissions (the authorizations that allow access to specific resources in a specific manner): *read*, which allows a user to access the contents of a file or directory; *write*, which allows a user to write to a file or directory; and *execute*, which allows a user to execute the contents of the file if that file contains either a program or a script capable of running on the system in question.

A file or directory may also have multiple ACLs attached to it. In UNIX-like operating systems, for instance, a given file might have separate access lists for specific users or groups. The system might give a certain individual user (like a specific developer) specific read, write, and execute permissions; a certain group of users (like the entire developer group) different read, write, and execute permissions; and any other authenticated users a third set of read, write, and execute permissions. On Linux-based operating systems, you can view these three sets of permissions by issuing the following command:

```
ls -la
```

Figure 3-3 shows these permissions displayed in the system.

```
                          root@ubuntu: /etc                           _  □  ×

 File  Edit  View  Search  Terminal  Help
-rw-r--r--   1 root root   1260 Mar 16  2016 ucf.conf
drwxr-xr-x   4 root root   4096 Aug 13 15:15 udev
drwxr-xr-x   2 root root   4096 Jan  4  2018 udisks2
drwxr-xr-x   3 root root   4096 Jan  4  2018 ufw
-rw-r--r--   1 root root    403 Apr 27  2017 updatedb.conf
drwxr-xr-x   3 root root   4096 Jul 19 14:09 update-manager
drwxr-xr-x   2 root root   4096 Aug 13 15:46 update-motd.d
drwxr-xr-x   2 root root   4096 Mar 14  2017 update-notifier
drwxr-xr-x   2 root root   4096 Jan  4  2018 UPower
-rw-r--r--   1 root root   1523 Aug 26  2017 usb_modeswitch.conf
drwxr-xr-x   2 root root   4096 Jan 22  2017 usb_modeswitch.d
-rw-r--r--   1 root root     51 Feb 19  2016 vdpau_wrapper.cfg
drwxr-xr-x   2 root root   4096 Jan  4  2018 vim
lrwxrwxrwx   1 root root     23 Dec  4  2017 vtrgb -> /etc/alternatives/vtrgb
-rw-r--r--   1 root root   4942 Jul 15  2016 wgetrc
-rw-r--r--   1 root root     30 Jan  4  2018 whoopsie
drwxr-xr-x   2 root root   4096 Dec  4  2017 wildmidi
drwxr-xr-x   2 root root   4096 Jan  4  2018 wpa_supplicant
drwxr-xr-x  11 root root   4096 Jan  4  2018 X11
drwxr-xr-x   5 root root   4096 Jan  4  2018 xdg
drwxr-xr-x   2 root root   4096 Aug 13 15:07 xml
drwxr-xr-x   2 root root   4096 Jan  4  2018 zm
-rw-r--r--   1 root root    477 Jul 19  2015 zsh_command_not_found
root@ubuntu:/etc#
```

Figure 3-3: File permissions on a UNIX-like operating system

Each line in Figure 3-3 represents the permissions for an individual file. The permissions for the first file, *ucf.conf*, are displayed as follows:

```
- r w - r - - r - -
```

This may seem a bit cryptic. To interpret the permissions, it'll help to divide them into the following sections:

```
- | r w - | r - - | r - -
```

The first character generally represents the file type: - represents a regular file, and d represents a directory. The second segment represents the *user* who owns the file's permissions and is set to r w -, meaning that the user can read and write to the file but not execute it.

The third segment, the *group* permissions, is set to r - -, meaning that members of the group that was given ownership of the file can read it but not write or execute it. The last segment, *other*, is also set to r - -, meaning that anyone who is not the user who owns the file or in the group that owns the file can also read it but not write or execute it. In Linux, the user permissions apply to a single user only, and the group permissions apply to a single group.

By using sets of file permissions, you can control access to the operating systems and applications that use your file system. Most file systems use systems that are similar to the one described for assigning permissions.

Network ACLs

If you look at the variety of activities that take place on networks, both private and public, you'll notice ACLs regulating the activity. In network ACLs, you typically filter access based on identifiers used for network transactions, such as Internet Protocol (IP) addresses, Media Access Control addresses, and ports. You can see such ACLs at work in network infrastructure such as routers, switches, and firewall devices, as well as in software firewalls, websites like Facebook and Google, email, and other forms of software.

Permissions in network ACLs tend to be binary in nature; rather than read, write, and execute, they generally either allow or deny some activity. Instead of users, network ACLs typically grant permissions to traffic. For example, when you set up the ACL, you use your chosen identifier or identifiers to dictate which traffic you're referring to and whether the traffic is allowed. It's best to rely on multiple identifiers to filter traffic, for reasons that will become clear shortly.

Media Access Control address filtering is one of the simplest forms of network-oriented ACLs. Media Access Control addresses are unique identifiers hard-coded into each network interface in a given system.

Unfortunately, the software settings in most operating systems can override a network interface's Media Access Control address. Changing this address is easy, so it's not a good choice for a unique identifier of a device on the network.

You could use *IP addresses* instead. Theoretically, an IP address is a unique address assigned to each device on any network that uses the Internet Protocol for communication. You can filter based on individual addresses or an entire range of IP addresses. For instance, you could allow the IP addresses 10.0.0.2 through 10.0.0.10 to pass traffic but deny any traffic from 10.0.0.11 and higher. Unfortunately, like Media Access Control addresses, you can falsify IP addresses, and they're not unique to a network interface. Additionally, IP addresses issued by internet service providers are subject to frequent change, so making IP addresses the sole basis for filtering is a shaky prospect at best.

BLACK HOLES

Some organizations, such as those that operate web servers, mail servers, and other services exposed to the internet, apply large-scale filtering to block out known attacks, spammers, and other undesirable traffic. Such filtering might include dropping traffic from individual IP addresses, ranges of IP addresses, or the entire IP spaces of large organizations, internet service providers, or even entire countries. This practice is commonly called *blackholing*, because from the user's perspective, any traffic sent to filtered destinations appears to have vanished into a black hole.

A third way of filtering traffic is by the *port* used to communicate over the network. The network port is a numerical designation for one side of a connection between two devices, and we use them to identify the application to which traffic should be routed. Many common services and applications use specific ports. For instance, FTP uses ports 20 and 21 to transfer files, Internet Message Access Protocol (IMAP) uses port 143 for managing email, and Secure Shell (SSH) uses port 22 to manage remote connections to systems. There are many more examples, since there are 65,535 ports in all.

You can control the use of many applications over the network by allowing or denying traffic originating from or sent to any ports that you care to manage. However, like Media Access Control and IP addresses, the specific ports used for applications are conventions, not absolute rules. You can, with relative ease, change the ports that applications use to entirely different ones.

As you just saw, if you use any single attribute to construct a network ACL, you'll likely encounter a variety of issues. If you're using IP addresses, your attribute might not necessarily be unique. If you're using Media Access Control addresses, your attribute will be easy to alter, and if you use ports, you're banking on conventions rather than rules.

When you combine several attributes, you begin to arrive at a more secure technique. For example, it's common to use both an IP address and a port, a combination typically called a *socket*. Using sockets, you can allow or deny network traffic from one or more IP addresses with one or more applications on your network in a workable fashion.

You can also construct ACLs to filter based on a wide variety of other criteria. In some cases, you want to allow or deny traffic based on more specific information, such as the content of an individual packet or a related series of packets. Using such techniques, you could, for example, filter out traffic related to networks used to illegally share copyrighted material.

Weaknesses of ACL Systems

Systems that use ACLs to manage permissions are vulnerable to a type of attack called the *confused deputy problem*. This problem occurs when the software with access to a resource (the deputy) has a greater level of permission to access the resource than the user who is controlling the software. If you can trick the software into misusing its greater level of authority, you can potentially carry out an attack.[1]

Several attacks take practical advantage of the confused deputy problem. These often involve tricking the user into taking some action when they really think they are doing something else entirely. Many of these attacks are *client-side* attacks, which take advantage of weaknesses in applications running on the user's computer. These attacks might be code sent through the web browser and executed on the local machine, malformed PDF files, or images and videos with attack code embedded. In the past several years, software vendors have become increasingly aware of such attacks and have begun building defensive measures into their software, but new attacks appear on a regular basis. Two of the more common attacks that exploit the confused deputy problem are cross-site request forgery (CSRF) and clickjacking.

CSRF is an attack that misuses the authority of the browser on the user's computer. If the attacker knows of, or can guess, a website that has already authenticated the user—perhaps a common site such as Amazon.com—the attacker can embed a link in a web page or HTML-based email, generally to an image hosted from a site controlled by the attacker. When the target's browser attempts to retrieve the image in the link, it also executes the additional commands the attacker has embedded in it, often in a fashion completely invisible to the target.

In the example in Figure 3-4, the attacker has embedded a request to transfer funds from an account at BankCo to the attacker's offshore account. As the BankCo server sees the request as coming from an authenticated and authorized user, it proceeds with the transfer. In this case, the confused deputy is the bank server.

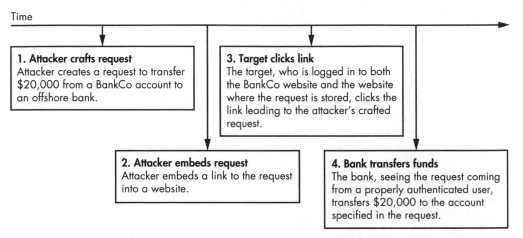

Figure 3-4: An example of a CSRF attack

Clickjacking, also known as *user interface redressing*, is a particularly sneaky and effective client-side attack that takes advantage of some of the page rendering features that are available in newer web browsers. To carry out a clickjacking attack, the attacker must legitimately control or have taken control of some portion of a website. The attacker constructs or modifies the site by placing an invisible layer over something the client would normally click. This causes the client to execute a command that's different than the one they think they're performing. You can use clickjacking to trick the client into making purchases, changing permissions in their applications or operating systems, or performing other unwanted activities.

Capabilities

Whereas ACLs define permissions based on a given resource, an identity, and a set of permissions, all generally held in a file of some sort, you can also define permissions based on a user's *token*, or key, otherwise known as a *capability*. Although the token isn't a physical object in most cases, you can think of it as the badge you might use to open the door of a building. The building has one door, and many people have a token that will open it, but each person has a different level of access. One person might be able to access the building only during business hours on weekdays, while another person may have permission to enter the building at any time of day on any day of the week.

In capability-based systems, the right to access a resource is based entirely on possession of the token, rather than *who* possesses it. If you were to give your badge to someone else, he would be able to use it to access the building with whatever set of permissions you have. When it comes to logical assets, applications can share their token with other applications.

If you were to use capabilities instead of ACLs to manage permissions, you could protect against confused deputy attack. Neither of the attacks you learned about earlier, CSRF and clickjacking, would be possible, because the attacker wouldn't be able to misuse the authority of the user unless they had access to the user's token.

Access Control Models

An *access control model* is a way of determining who should be allowed access to what resources. There are quite a few different access control models out there. The most common ones, covered here, include discretionary access control, mandatory access control, rule-based access control, role-based access control, attribute-based access control, and multilevel access control.

Discretionary Access Control

In the *discretionary access control* (DAC) model, the owner of the resource determines who gets access to it and exactly what level of access they can have. You can see DAC implemented in most operating systems; if you decide to create a network share in a Microsoft operating system, for instance, you're in charge of people's access to it.

Mandatory Access Control

In the *mandatory access control* (MAC) model, the owner of the resource doesn't get to decide who gets to access it. Instead, a separate group or individual has the authority to set access to resources. You can often find MAC implemented in government organizations, where access to a given resource is largely dictated by the sensitivity label applied to it (secret or top secret, for example), by the level of sensitive information the individual is allowed to access (perhaps only secret), and by whether the individual actually has a need to access the resource (a concept called the *principle of least privilege*, discussed in the box).

THE PRINCIPLE OF LEAST PRIVILEGE

The principle of least privilege dictates that you should give a party only the bare minimum level of access it needs to perform its functionality. For example, someone working in an organization's sales department should not need access to data in the organization's internal human resources system to do their job. Violation of the principle of least privilege is at the heart of many of the security problems we face today.

One of the more common ways the principle of least privilege gets improperly implemented is in the permissions given to operating system user accounts. In Microsoft operating systems in particular, you'll often find that casual users, who are performing tasks such as creating documents in word processors and exchanging emails, are configured with administrative access, allowing them to carry out any task that the operating system allows.

Because of this, whenever the over-privileged user opens an email attachment containing malware or encounters a website that pushes attack code to the client computer, these attacks have free rein on the system. The attacker can simply turn off anti-malware tools, install any additional attack tools they care to, and proceed with completely compromising the system.

Rule-Based Access Control

Rule-based access control allows access according to a set of rules defined by the system administrator. If the rule is matched, access to the resource will be granted or denied accordingly.

A good example of rule-based access control is an ACL used by a router. You might see a rule specifying that traffic coming from source A to destination B on port C is allowed. Any other traffic between the two devices would be denied.

Role-Based Access Control

The *role-based access control* (RBAC) model allows access based on the role of the individual being granted access. For example, if you have an employee whose only role is to enter data into an application, RBAC would mandate that you allow the employee access to only that application.

If you have an employee with a more complex role—customer service for an online retailer, perhaps—the employee's role might require him to have access to information about customers' payment status and information, shipping status, previous orders, and returns. In this case, RBAC would grant him considerably more access. You can see RBAC implemented in many large-scale applications that are oriented around sales or customer service.

Attribute-Based Access Control

Attribute-based access control (ABAC) is based on the specific attributes of a person, resource, or environment. You can often find it implemented on infrastructure systems, such as those in network or telecommunications environments.

Subject attributes belong to an individual. We could choose any number of attributes, such as height in the classic "you must be this tall to ride" access control in amusement park rides. Another common example of subject attributes are *CAPTCHAs*, or "completely automated public Turing tests to tell humans and computers apart" (Figure 3-5).[2] CAPTCHAs control access based on whether the party on the other end can pass a test that is (in theory) too difficult for a machine to complete.

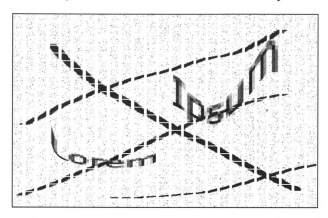

Figure 3-5: A CAPTCHA, designed to prove that the user is human

Resource attributes belong to a resource, such as an operating system or application. You'll often see access controlled by resource attributes, although usually this is for technical reasons rather than security reasons; some software runs only on a particular operating system, and some websites work only with certain browsers. You might apply this type of access control as a security measure by requiring someone to use specific software or protocols for communication.

You can use *environmental attributes* to enable access controls based on environmental conditions. People commonly use time to control access to physical and logical resources. Access controls on buildings often allow access only during business hours. Many VPN connections have time limits that force the user to reconnect every 24 hours to prevent users from keeping a connection running after their authorization for using it has been removed.

Multilevel Access Control

Multilevel access control models combine several of the access control models discussed in this section. They're used when the simpler access control models aren't considered robust enough to protect the information to which you're controlling access. Military and government organizations, which handle data of a sensitive nature, often use multilevel access control models to control access to a variety of data, from nuclear secrets to protected health information. You'll learn about a few of these models now.

The Bell–LaPadula Model

The *Bell–LaPadula* model implements a combination of discretionary and mandatory access controls (DAC and MAC) and is primarily concerned with the confidentiality of the resource in question—in other words, making sure unauthorized people can't read it. Generally, in cases where you see these two models implemented together, MAC takes precedence over DAC, and DAC works within the accesses allowed by the MAC permissions.

For example, you might have a resource that is classified as secret and a user who has a secret level of clearance; under a mandatory access model, the user would have access to the resource. However, you might also have an additional layer of DAC under the MAC access so that if the resource owner has not given the user access, they would not be able to access it, despite the MAC permissions. In Bell–LaPadula, two security properties define how information can flow to and from the resource.[3]

The Simple Security Property   The level of access granted to an individual must be at least as high as the classification of the resource in order for the individual to access it. In other words, an individual cannot read a resource classified at a higher level, but they can read resources at a lower level.

The * Property (or Star Property)   Anyone accessing a resource can only write (or copy) its contents to another resource classified at the same level or higher.

You can summarize these properties as "no read up" and "no write down," respectively, as shown in Figure 3-6.

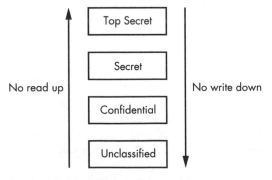

Figure 3-6: The Bell–LaPadula model

In short, this means that when you're handling classified information, you can't read any higher than your clearance level, and you can't write classified data down to any lower level.

The Biba Model

The *Biba* model of access control is primarily concerned with protecting the integrity of data, even at the expense of confidentiality. That means it's more important to keep people from altering the data than from viewing it. Biba has two security rules that are the exact opposite of those discussed in the Bell–LaPadula model.[4]

The Simple Integrity Axiom   The level of access granted to an individual must be no lower than the classification of the resource. In other words, access to one level does not grant access to lower levels.

The * Integrity Axiom (or Star Integrity Axiom)   Anyone accessing a resource can only write its contents to a resource classified at the same level or lower.

We can summarize these rules as "no read down" and "no write up," respectively, as shown in Figure 3-7. This means that assets that are of high integrity (meaning they shouldn't be altered) and assets that are of low integrity are kept strictly apart.

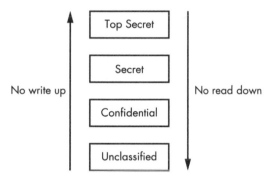

Figure 3-7: The Biba model

This may seem completely counterintuitive when it comes to protecting information. However, these principles protect integrity by ensuring that your resource can be written to only by those with a high level of access and that those with a high level of access do not access a resource with a lower classification. Consider an organization that performs both a low-integrity process that collects (potentially malicious) PDF uploads from users and a high-integrity process that scans document inputs from highly classified systems. In the Biba model, the upload process wouldn't be able to send data to the scanning process, so it wouldn't be able to corrupt the classified input; on top of this, the scanning process would be unable to access the low-level data, even if it was directed to.

The Brewer and Nash Model

The *Brewer and Nash* model, also known as the *Chinese Wall* model, is an access control model designed to prevent conflicts of interest. Brewer and Nash is commonly used in industries that handle sensitive data, such as the financial, medical, or legal industries. This model considers three main resource classes.[5]

- *Objects*: Resources, such as files or information, pertaining to a single organization
- *Company groups*: All objects pertaining to an organization
- *Conflict classes*: All groups of objects concerning competing parties

A commercial law firm that represents companies in a certain industry might have files that pertain to various competing individuals and companies. Since an individual lawyer at the firm accesses files for different clients, the lawyer could potentially access confidential data that would generate a conflict of interest. In the Brewer and Nash model, the level of access to resources and case materials that the lawyer is allowed would dynamically change based on the materials previously accessed (Figure 3-8).

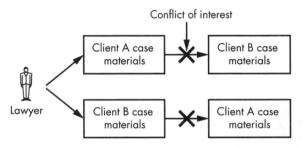

Figure 3-8: Brewer and Nash model

In this example, after the lawyer views Client A's case materials, the lawyer would no longer be able to access information pertaining to Client B or any other parties competing with the current client, resolving any conflicts of interest.

Physical Access Controls

So far you've seen logical examples to illustrate the access control concepts discussed in this chapter, but many of these methods apply to physical security, as well. Let's go over some examples of those now.

Physical access controls are often concerned with controlling the movement of individuals and vehicles. Access controls for individuals typically regulate their movement in and out of buildings or facilities, often using badges that open a facility's doors (something you have, from Chapter 2). Door control systems that make use of badges frequently use ACLs in the software that runs them to permit or deny access for certain doors and times of day.

One of the more common security issues with regulating people's access into buildings is *tailgating*, which occurs when you authenticate your physical access control measure, such as a badge, and another person follows directly behind you without also being authenticated. Tailgating can cause a variety of issues, including creating an inaccurate representation of who is in the building in the case of emergencies.

We can attempt to solve tailgating in a variety of ways, including implementing a policy that forbids it, posting a guard in the area, or simply (but expensively) installing a physical access control solution that allows only one person to pass through at a time, such as a turnstile. All of these are reasonable solutions, but, depending on the environment in question, they may or may not be effective. You'll often find that a combination of several solutions works better than any single one.

A much more complex example of a physical access control is the security system in use at many airports. After the terrorist attacks of September 11, 2001, in the United States, the level of security at airports increased. Once you've entered the airport security system, you are required to present a boarding pass and identification (something you have, times two). You typically pass through several steps to ensure that you're not carrying any dangerous devices—a form of attribute-based access control. You then proceed to your gate and, once again, present your boarding pass before stepping on the airplane. Such processes may differ slightly depending on the country, but they're generally the same from an access control perspective.

Physical access control for vehicles often revolves around keeping said vehicles from moving through unauthorized areas, typically using various simple barriers, including Jersey barriers (Figure 3-9), bollards, one-way spike strips, and fences. You may also see more complex installations that include staffed or unstaffed rising barriers, automated gates or doors, and other similar controls.

Figure 3-9: A Jersey barrier

There are, of course, a huge number of other physical access controls and methods. Additionally, when referring to physical access control devices, or access controls in general, the line between an authentication device and an access control device often becomes rather blurry, or overlaps entirely. For example, a key for a physical lock could be considered identification, authentication, and authorization, all the while being a component of a physical access control. Often these terms are used inaccurately or inappropriately, even within the security field, which does not help matters.

Summary

Authorization is a key step in the process of allowing parties to access resources—in other words, the identification, authentication, and authorization process. You implement authorization by using access controls. Typically, you use one of two access control methods: access control lists or capabilities. Although capabilities can provide safeguards against confused deputy attacks, they're not implemented as often as they should be.

When putting together an access control system, you use an access control model that outlines who should be given access to what resources. In our daily lives, we often encounter simpler access control models, such as discretionary access control, mandatory access control, role-based access control, and attribute-based access control. Environments that handle more sensitive data, such as those involved in the government, military, medical, or legal industry, typically use multilevel access control models, including Bell–LaPadula, Biba, and Brewer and Nash.

The next chapter will discuss auditing and accountability, which is how you keep track of the activities that have taken place after you've gone through the process of identification, authentication, and authorization.

Exercises

1. Discuss the difference between authorization and access control.
2. What does the Brewer and Nash model protect against?
3. Why does access control based on the Media Access Control address of the systems on our network not represent strong security?
4. Which should take place first, authorization or authentication?
5. What are the differences between the MAC and DAC models of access control?
6. The Bell–LaPadula and Biba multilevel access control models both have a primary security focus. Can these two models be used together?
7. If you have a file containing sensitive data on a Linux operating system, would setting the permissions to rw-rw-rw- cause a potential security issue? If so, which portions of the CIA triad might be affected?
8. Which access control model could you use to prevent users from logging into their accounts after business hours?
9. Explain how the confused deputy problem could allow users to carry out activities for which they are not authorized.
10. What are some of the differences between access control lists and capabilities?

4

AUDITING AND ACCOUNTABILITY

When you've successfully gone through the identification, authentication, and authorization processes (or even while you're still completing them), you need to keep track of the activities taking place in your organization. Even after you've allowed a party access to your resources, you still need to ensure that they behave in accordance with your rules, particularly those relating to security, business conduct, and ethics. Essentially, you need to make sure you can hold users of your systems accountable (Figure 4-1).

Figure 4-1: You should always hold users accountable.

Holding someone *accountable* means making sure that person is responsible for their actions. This is particularly important now that most organizations house a great deal of information in digital form. If you don't keep track of how people are accessing sensitive data stored digitally, you can suffer business losses, intellectual property theft, identity theft, and fraud. In addition, a data breach could have legal consequences for your organization. Some types of data—medical and financial, for example—are protected by law in several countries; in the United States, two such well-known laws are the Health Insurance Portability and Accountability Act of 1996, which protects medical information, and the Sarbanes–Oxley Act of 2002, which protects against corporate fraud.

Many of the measures you put in place to ensure accountability are examples of *auditing*, which is the process of reviewing an organization's records or information. You perform audits to ensure that people comply with laws, policies, and other bodies of administrative control. Auditing can also prevent attacks, such as credit card companies recording and auditing the purchases you make through your account. If you decide to buy half a dozen laptops in one day, your unusual behavior might trigger an alert in the company's monitoring system, and the company might temporarily freeze any purchases made with your card. In this chapter, you'll learn about accountability in more detail and see how to use auditing to enforce it.

Accountability

To hold people accountable for their actions, you have to trace all activities in your environment back to their sources. That means you have to use identification, authentication, and authorization processes so you can know who a given event is associated with and what permissions allowed them to carry it out.

It's easy to criticize accountability and its associated auditing tools. You could argue that implementing surveillance techniques is like having Big Brother watching over your shoulder. In some senses, this is true; if you monitor people excessively, you can create an unhealthy environment.

But you can also go too far in the other direction. If you don't have sufficient controls in place to deter or prevent people from breaking your rules and abusing your resources, you'll end up with security disasters. The "Equifax Breach" box covers an example of this.

THE EQUIFAX BREACH

In 2017, Equifax's shareholders, board of directors, and auditors, as well as the US government, failed to hold Equifax accountable for protecting consumers' personal and financial information. As a result, attackers stole data relating to 147 million Americans, and Equifax suffered very little in the way of consequences, aside from a brief dip in stock price. Although Equifax was brought to testify in front of Congress and lawmakers said they would enact new regulations because of the incident, Equifax has faced no consequences, and Congress has not passed any new laws on the matter.

The breach occurred when attackers exploited a vulnerability (designated as CVE-2017-5638) in Apache Struts2, a framework for developing Java applications for web use. This vulnerability allowed attackers to perform remote code execution (RCE) on the web servers in question, giving them a foothold in the Equifax environment. At the time of the attack, Equifax had a solution to the vulnerability but hadn't implemented it yet.

Although Equifax has not publicly disclosed the exact details of the breach beyond the initial entry as of the fall of 2018, we can infer that, since attackers were able to breach an internet-facing server and access personally identifiable information belonging to Equifax customers, the system included significant lapses in security; Equifax might not have separated servers containing sensitive data, for example, or it might have used poor access controls, among other issues. (The US Government Accountability office released a report confirming these types of issues.[1])

Although outside agencies might often prompt accountability, the impetus to comply with these requirements must come from within your organization. For example, when a company experiences a breach in the United States, laws often require it to notify those whose information has been exposed. As of March 2018, all 50 US states now have breach disclosure laws.[2]

In many cases, however, few people outside the company know of the breaches until the company notifies those who are directly involved. You can certainly see why an organization might be tempted, in such a case, to not say anything about the incident. If you don't comply with legal requirements, however, you'll likely be discovered eventually. When that happens, you'll face greater personal, business, and legal repercussions than if you had handled the situation properly in the first place.

Security Benefits of Accountability

When you hold people accountable, you can keep your environment secure in several ways: by enabling a principle called nonrepudiation, by deterring those who would otherwise misuse your resources, and by detecting and preventing intrusions. The processes you use to ensure accountability can also assist you in preparing materials for legal proceedings.

Nonrepudiation

The term *nonrepudiation* refers to a situation in which an individual is unable to successfully deny that they have made a statement or taken an action, generally because we have sufficient evidence that they did it. In information security settings, you can achieve nonrepudiation in a variety of ways. You may be able to produce proof of the activity directly from system or network logs or recover such proof through the use of digital forensic examination of the system or devices involved.

You may also be able to establish nonrepudiation using encryption technologies, like hash functions, to digitally sign a communication or a file. You'll learn more about such methods in Chapter 5, which covers encryption. Another example is when a system digitally signs every email that is sent from it, making it impossible for someone to deny the fact that the email came from that system.

Deterrence

Accountability can also prove to be a great *deterrent* against misbehavior in your environments. If people are aware that you're monitoring them and if you've communicated to them that there will be penalties for acting against the rules, individuals may think twice before straying outside the lines.

The key to deterrence lies in letting people know they will be held accountable for their actions. You typically achieve deterrence with the auditing and monitoring processes, both of which are discussed in the "Auditing" section of this chapter. If you don't make your intentions clear, your deterrent will lose most of its strength.

For example, if, as part of your monitoring activities, you keep track of the badge access times that tell you when your employees pass in and out of your facility, you can validate this activity against the times they have submitted on their time card for each week to prevent your employees from falsifying their time card and defrauding the company for additional and undeserved pay. Since the employees are aware that this cross-checking takes place, they're deterred from lying on their time cards. While this might seem intrusive, real companies often use such methods when they have large numbers of employees working specific shifts, like at technical support help desks.

Intrusion Detection and Prevention

When you audit information in your environment, you can detect and prevent intrusions in both the logical and physical sense. If you implement alerts based on unusual activities and regularly check the information you have recorded, you stand a much better chance of detecting attacks in progress and the precursors of future attacks.

Particularly in the logical realm, where attacks can take place in fractions of a second, you would also be wise to implement automated tools to monitor the system and alert you to any strange activity. You can divide such tools into two major categories: intrusion detection systems (IDSs) and intrusion prevention systems (IPSs).

An IDS is strictly a monitoring and alerting tool; it notifies you when an attack or other undesirable activity is taking place. An IPS, which often works from information sent by the IDS, can take action based on events happening in the environment. In response to an attack over the network, an IPS might refuse traffic from the source of the attack. Chapters 10 and 11 will discuss IDSs and IPSs at greater length.

Admissibility of Records

When you seek to introduce records into legal settings, you're more likely to have them accepted when they're produced by a regulated and consistent tracking system. For instance, if you plan to submit digital forensic evidence for use in a court case, you'll likely have to provide a solid and documented *chain of custody* for the evidence in order for the court to accept it. That means you need to be able to track information such as the location of the evidence over time, how exactly it passed from one person to another, and how it was protected while it was stored.

Your accountability methods for evidence collection should create an unbroken chain of custody. If it doesn't, your evidence will likely only be taken as hearsay, at best, considerably weakening your case.

Auditing

Auditing is a methodical examination and review of an organization's records.[3] In nearly any environment, from the lowest level of technology to the highest, you usually ensure that people remain accountable for their actions by using some kind of auditing.

One of the primary ways you can ensure accountability through technical means is by keeping accurate records of who did what and when they did it—and then checking those records. If you don't have the ability to assess your activities over a period, you won't be able to facilitate accountability on a large scale. Particularly in larger organizations, your capacity to audit directly equates to your ability to hold anyone accountable for anything.

You may also be bound by contractual or regulatory requirements that subject you to audits on some sort of recurring basis. In many cases, such audits are carried out by unrelated and independent third parties certified and authorized to perform such a task. Good examples of such audits are those mandated by the Sarbanes–Oxley Act, mentioned earlier, which ensures that companies report their financial results honestly.

What Do You Audit?

In the information security world, organizations commonly audit the factors that determine access to their various systems. For example, you might audit passwords, allowing you to enforce the policies dictating how to construct and use them. As discussed in Chapter 2, if you don't construct passwords in a secure manner, an attacker can easily crack them. You should also verify how often users change their passwords. In many cases, systems can check password strength and manage password changes automatically, using functions within an operating system or other utilities. You'll also have to audit those tools to ensure that they're working properly.

Organizations often audit software licenses as well. The software you use should have a license that proves you obtained it legally. If an outside agency were to audit you and found that you were running large quantities of unlicensed software, the financial penalties could be severe. It is often best if you can find and correct such matters yourself before receiving a notification from an external company.

The Business Software Alliance (BSA) is one such company that works on behalf of software firms (Adobe or Microsoft, for instance). It regularly audits other organizations to ensure that they're complying with software licensing. Legal settlements with the BSA can reach $250,000 *per occurrence* of unlicensed software,[4] plus additional charges of up to $7,500 to pay BSA legal fees. The BSA also sweetens the pot for whistle-blowers by offering rewards of up to $1 million for reporting violations.[5]

Finally, organizations commonly audit internet usage, including websites its employees visit, instant messaging, email, and file transfers. In many cases, organizations have configured proxy servers to funnel all such traffic through just a few gateways, which allows them to log, scan, and potentially filter such traffic. Such tools can give you the ability to examine exactly how employees are using those resources, allowing you to act if you encounter misuse.

Logging

Before you can audit something, you have to create the records to review. *Logging* gives you a history of the activities that have taken place in an environment. You typically generate logs automatically in operating systems to keep track of the activities that take place on most computing, networking, and telecommunications equipment, as well as on the devices that incorporate or connect to a computer. Logging is a *reactive* tool; it allows you to view the record of an event after it has taken place. To immediately react to something taking place, you would need to use a tool like an IDS or IPS, which will be covered in detail in Chapter 10.

You typically configure logging mechanisms to record critical events only, but you could also log every action carried out by the system or software. You'd probably want to do this for troubleshooting purposes. A log might include records of events such as software errors, hardware failures, user logins or logouts, resource accesses, and tasks requiring increased privileges, depending on the logging settings and the system in question.

Generally, only system administrators can review logs. Usually, users of the system can't modify them, except maybe to write to them. For instance, an application running under the context of a particular user will generally have permissions to write messages to system or application logs. Keep in mind that collecting logs without reviewing them is pointless. If you never review the content of the logs, you might as well have failed to collect them in the first place. It is important that you schedule a regular review of your logs to catch anything unusual in their contents.

You may also be asked, in the course of normal security duties, to analyze the contents of logs in relation to an incident or situation. In the case of investigations, incidents, and compliance checks, these types of activities often fall to security personnel. Reviewing logs can be a difficult task if the period in question is greater than a few days. Even searching the contents of a relatively simple log, such as that generated by a web proxy server, can mean sifting through enormous amounts of data. In such cases, custom scripts or even a tool such as grep (a UNIX and Linux tool for searching text) can help accomplish the task in a reasonable amount of time.

Monitoring

A subset of auditing, *monitoring* is observing information about an environment to discover undesirable conditions such as failures, resource shortages, and security issues, as well as trends that might signal the arrival of such conditions. Like logging, monitoring is largely a reactive activity; it takes action based on gathered data, typically from logs generated by various devices. Even when you're trying to predict future events, you're still relying on past data to do so.

When monitoring a system, you're typically watching for specific kinds or patterns of data, such as increased resource usage on computers, unusual network latency (the time it takes a packet to get from one point to another on a network), certain types of attacks occurring repeatedly against servers with network interfaces that are exposed to the internet, traffic passing through your physical access controls at unusual times of day, and so on.

When you detect unusual levels of such activity, called the *clipping level*, your monitoring system might send an alert to a system administrator or physical security personnel, or it might trigger a more direct action, such as dropping traffic from a particular IP address, switching to a backup system for a critical server, or summoning law enforcement officials.

Auditing with Assessments

As mentioned, logging and monitoring are reactive measures. To assess the state of your systems more actively, you might use a kind of audit called *assessments*, which are tests that find and fix vulnerabilities before any attackers do. If you can conduct assessments successfully and on a recurring basis, you will considerably increase your security posture and stand a much better chance of resisting attacks. You can take two approaches to this: vulnerability assessments and penetration testing. While people often use these terms interchangeably, they are two distinct sets of activities.

Vulnerability assessments generally involve using vulnerability scanning tools, such as Qualys,[6] shown in Figure 4-2, to locate weaknesses in an environment. Such tools generally work by scanning the target systems to discover open ports and then interrogating each open port to find out exactly which service is listening on it. Additionally, you may choose to provide credentials, if you have them, to allow a vulnerability scanner to authenticate to the device in question and collect considerably more detailed information, such as the specific software installed, the users on the system, and the information contained in or regarding files.

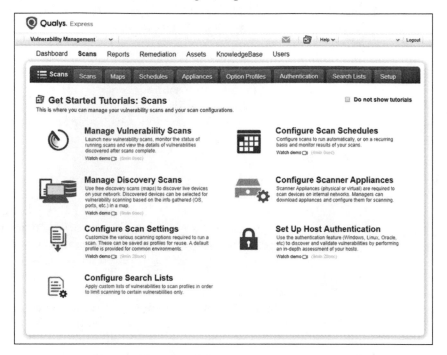

Figure 4-2: Qualys, a tool for vulnerability scanning

Given this information, the vulnerability assessment tool can then consult its database of vulnerability information to determine whether the system might contain any weaknesses. Although these databases tend to be thorough, new or uncommon attacks will often escape their notice.

Penetration testing takes the assessment process several steps further. When you conduct a penetration test, you mimic the techniques an actual attacker would use to breach a system. You may attempt to gather additional information on the target environment from users or other systems in the vicinity, exploit security flaws in web-based applications or web-connected databases, or conduct attacks through unpatched vulnerabilities in applications or operating systems.

You'll learn more about assessing security at greater length in Chapter 14. As with any security measure that you can put in place, security assessments should be only a single component of your overall defensive strategy.

Summary

For nearly any action you might care to take, some system somewhere creates an associated audit record. Organizations regularly query and update your medical history, grades in school, purchases, and credit history, and they use this data to make decisions that can impact your life for better or worse.

When you allow others to access your business's resources or personal information of a sensitive nature, you need to hold them accountable for what they do with the resources or information.

You go through the auditing process to hold people accountable and ensure that your environment is compliant with the laws, regulations, and policies that bind it. You may carry out a variety of auditing tasks, including logging, monitoring, and conducting assessments. Through these processes, you can both react to threats and actively prevent them.

In the next chapter, you'll get an overview of the main cryptographic algorithms that serve as the backbone of today's security systems.

Exercises

1. What is the benefit of logging?
2. Discuss the difference between authorization and accountability.
3. Describe nonrepudiation.
4. Name five items you might want to audit.
5. Why is accountability important when dealing with sensitive data?
6. Why might auditing your installed software be a good idea?
7. When dealing with legal or regulatory issues, why do you need accountability?
8. What is the difference between vulnerability assessment and penetration testing?
9. What impact can accountability have on the admissibility of evidence in court cases?
10. Given an environment containing servers that handle sensitive customer data, some of which are exposed to the internet, would you want to conduct a vulnerability assessment, a penetration test, or both? Why?

5

CRYPTOGRAPHY

Cryptography, the science of protecting the confidentiality and integrity of data, is a key part of the vast set of transactions that take place over your devices daily. You use cryptography when you have conversations on your cell phones, check your email, buy things from online retailers, and file your taxes, among other activities. Without the ability to protect the information you send over such channels, your Internet-based activities would be much riskier.

In cryptography, *encryption* is the process of transforming readable data, called *plaintext* or *cleartext*, into an unreadable form, called *ciphertext*. *Decryption* is the process of recovering the plaintext message from the ciphertext. You encrypt the plaintext or decrypt the ciphertext using a specific computational procedure called a *cryptographic algorithm*. You'll explore several examples of these in this chapter. Cryptographic algorithms generally use a *key*, or multiple keys, to encrypt or decrypt the message. You can think of a key as a password that you can apply to the algorithm to retrieve the message.

In this chapter, you'll look at some of the earliest examples of cryptography and then dive into modern cryptographic practices.

The History of Cryptography

Some of the oldest examples of cryptography date back to ancient Greece and Rome. To hide information, Greeks and Romans used codes, as well as unorthodox methods such as tattooing information on the shaved heads of messengers and allowing hair to grow over it. Enough historical information about cryptography exists to fill an entire volume, and indeed many books have been written on the subject, so I'll go over just a few highlights.

The Caesar Cipher

The Caesar cipher, a classic example of ancient cryptography, is said to have been used by Julius Caesar. The Caesar cipher involves shifting each letter of the plaintext message by a certain number of spaces in the alphabet, historically three, as shown in Figure 5-1. After the shift, you would write the letter *A* as *D*, the letter *B* as *E*, and so on. To decrypt the ciphertext, you would apply the same number of shifts in the opposite direction.

S	E	C	R	E	T	M	E	S	S	A	G	E
V	H	F	U	H	W	P	H	V	V	D	J	H

Figure 5-1: Encrypting the phrase "secret message" with the Caesar cipher

We call this type of encryption a *substitution cipher*, because it substitutes each letter in the alphabet with a different one. A more recent variation of the Caesar cipher is the ROT13 cipher, which uses the same mechanism as the Caesar cipher but moves each letter 13 places forward in the alphabet. Moving each letter by 13 places makes the message convenient to decrypt, because all you have to do to retrieve the original is apply another round of encryption with ROT13; two rotations will return each letter to its original starting place in the alphabet. Utilities for performing ROT13 are part of the basic set of tools that ship with many Linux and UNIX operating systems.

Cryptographic Machines

Before the advent of the modern computer, people used machines to simplify encryption and make more complex encryption schemes feasible. Initially, such devices were basic mechanical machines, but as technology progressed, they began to include electronics and considerably more complex systems.

The Jefferson Disk, invented by Thomas Jefferson in 1795, is a purely mechanical cryptographic machine. It is composed of 36 disks, each marked with the letters *A* through *Z* in a circle around its rim, as shown in Figure 5-2.[1]

Each disk represents one character in a message. The letters on each disk are arranged in a different order, and each disk is marked with a unique identifier so you can tell them apart.

To encrypt a message, you line up the characters in a row across the set of disks so they spell out the message in plaintext, like in row A of Figure 5-3. Then you choose a different row of characters to use as the ciphertext, as shown in row B.

Figure 5-2: The Jefferson Disk, one of the earliest crypto-graphic machines

A	F	T	K	D	A	R	X	Z	X	Z	X
B	K	O	E	E	Q	U	T	Y	U	I	A
P	I	P	Q	U	W	Z	W	V	Y	U	C
I	L	Y	G	L	B	C	V	D	Z	P	R
U	Q	G	B	M	K	W	B	T	W	F	U
L	A	L	D	A	R	N	U	E	P	E	P
H	V	C	O	Z	P	M	N	W	S	K	Q
A M	E	E	T	I	N	G	I	S	A	G	O
X	C	H	W	V	U	O	S	M	O	Y	J
O	U	Z	N	Y	H	B	E	X	T	D	B
E	Z	A	P	N	F	Q	M	U	B	A	G
V	J	U	X	F	J	I	C	P	E	N	F
Y	G	R	L	Q	E	A	L	L	K	S	W
C	Y	M	V	T	O	P	G	K	C	O	D
G	M	K	A	B	G	S	A	I	C	H	V
X	W	N	M	W	I	F	D	F	N	R	L
K	D	F	U	J	D	T	R	B	D	L	M
F	O	W	H	R	M	J	Q	H	G	X	E
S	X	N	I	S	T	E	K	O	R	M	Y
D	B	D	Y	G	V	Y	F	Q	V	T	H
R	H	Q	Z	K	S	L	J	A	I	J	S
B T	N	J	R	O	C	H	O	N	L	Q	I
Q	P	I	F	C	X	K	P	G	F	V	N
J	R	B	S	X	Z	D	Z	C	M	W	K
W	S	V	J	H	L	V	H	J	J	B	Z
N	T	G	C	P	Y	X	Y	R	Q	C	T

Figure 5-3: Encrypting the message "Meeting is a go" using the Jefferson Disk

The key to this cipher is in the order of the disks. If the encrypting and decrypting devices arrange their disks in the same order, all you need to do to decrypt the message is rewrite the ciphertext using the disks and then look at all the rows until you find the plaintext message. This is, of course, merely a more complex version of a substitution cipher, made possible using a mechanical aid, in which the substitution changes with each letter.

A more intricate example of a cryptographic machine is the German-made Enigma machine (Figure 5-4).[2] Created by Arthur Scherbius in 1923, the Enigma secured German communications during World War II.

Figure 5-4: An Enigma machine

Conceptually, the Enigma resembles the Jefferson Disk. It's based on a series of wheels, or rotors, each with 26 letters and 26 electrical contacts. It also has a keyboard for entering the plaintext message and a set of 26 characters above the keyboard, which light up to indicate the encrypted equivalent. When you press a key on the Enigma keyboard, one or more of the rotors physically rotates, changing the orientation of the electrical contacts between them. Current flows through the entire series of disks and then back through them again to the original disk, lighting up the scrambled version of each letter on the series of characters above the keyboard.

For two Enigma machines to communicate during the war, they needed to have the same configuration. This took a lot of work since both the rotors and the rings marked with the alphabet on each rotor needed to be identical and in the same position, and any cables plugged in needed to be set up in the same fashion. Once the message was encrypted, it would be sent via Morse code to the receiving end. When the receiver got the encrypted Morse code message, they would enter the equivalent characters on the keyboard, and presuming everything was set up properly, the decrypted character would light up.

There were several models of Enigma machine and a variety of accessories and add-ons you could attach to them. To add further possible variations, some models had a patch panel, allowing you to swap some or all the letters by plugging cables into different positions. On each rotor, the ring containing the letters of the alphabet could also be rotated independently of the electrical contacts to change the relationship between the character selected and the character output.

Between the inherent strengths of the device and the knowledge of the required configuration needed for decryption, the Enigma posed quite a difficult task for those attempting to break the messages generated by it. But a large portion of the device's strength was in the secrecy surrounding the equipment and the configurations used for specific messages; this is a strategy we call *security through obscurity* in the security field. Once these secrets became exposed, the encrypted messages were no longer as secure.

In 1939, when cryptographers at Bletchley Park, a British code-breaking base during World War II, were given an Enigma to study, they were able to construct a computer called the Bombe that decoded a large portion of the Germans' messages, even though they didn't have access to the Enigma settings rotated on a daily basis.

MORE ON THE ENIGMA MACHINE

Anyone interested in getting hands-on experience with a classic item of cryptographic history can interact with the Enigma in several ways. The DIY inclined can purchase a kit that re-creates the functionality of the Enigma using modern electronics components.[3] Additionally, a variety of software-based Enigma simulators exist.[4] These are particularly useful for representing the relationship between the rotors and the paths running through them, which change with each character entered. A great many books have also been written on this topic, but a particularly good one is *The German Enigma Cipher Machine: Beginnings, Success, and Ultimate Failure* by Brian J. Winkel, Cipher Deavours, David Kahn, and Louis Kruh. *Seizing the Enigma: The Race to Break the German U-Boat Codes, 1933–1945* by David Kahn is another excellent source for further detail on some of this work.

Kerckhoffs's Principles

In 1883, the *Journal des Sciences Militaires* published an article by Auguste Kerckhoffs, a Dutch linguist and cryptographer, titled "La cryptographie militaire." In the article, Kerckhoffs outlined six principles he thought should serve as a basis for all cryptographic systems.[5]

1. The system must be substantially, if not mathematically, undecipherable.
2. The system must not require secrecy; even if stolen by the enemy, the system should remain secure.
3. The keys must be easy to communicate and remember without written notes, and they must be easy to change or modify to use with different participants.
4. The system ought to be compatible with communication via telegraph.
5. The system must be portable, and its use must not require more than one person.
6. Finally, the system must be easy to use, requiring neither complex thinking nor the knowledge of a long series of rules.

Although several of these principles, such as requiring the system to support telegraph use or be physically portable, became outmoded once people started using computers for cryptography, the second principle remains a key tenet of modern cryptographic algorithms. Claude Shannon, an American mathematician and cryptographer, later restated the idea as "the enemy knows the system";[6] in other words, cryptographic algorithms should be robust enough that even if people know every bit of the encryption process except for the key itself, they should still not be able to break the encryption. This idea represents the opposite approach to security through obscurity.

Modern Cryptographic Tools

Although efficient electromechanical cryptographic systems like Enigma enabled highly secure means of communication for a period, the increasing complexity of computers quickly rendered these systems obsolete. One reason was that the systems were not completely compliant with Kerckhoffs's second principle and still largely depended on security through obscurity to protect the data they processed.

Modern cryptographic algorithms used by computers are truly open, meaning you can understand the encryption process and still not be able to break the cipher. These algorithms depend on difficult mathematical problems, sometimes referred to as *one-way problems*. One-way problems are easy to perform in one direction but difficult to perform in the other direction. Factorization of large numbers is an example of a one-way problem; it's easy to create an algorithm that returns a product of multiple integers, but it's much more difficult to create one that does the inverse of that operation— finding the factors of a given integer—especially if that number is very large. Such problems form the basis of many modern cryptographic systems.

Keyword Ciphers and One-Time Pads

Two technologies, keyword ciphers and one-time pads, helped bridge the gap between older cryptographic methods and modern ones. Although simpler than the algorithms used today, these techniques increasingly met the standard set by Kerckhoffs's second principle.

Keyword Ciphers

Keyword ciphers are substitution ciphers, like the Caesar cipher discussed earlier in the chapter. But, unlike the Caesar cipher, they use a key to determine what to substitute for each letter of the message. Rather than shifting all letters by the same number of spaces in the alphabet, you'd shift each letter to match the corresponding letter in the keyword. For example, if you use the keyword MYSECRET, you'd have the substitution shown in Figure 5-5.

Plaintext

A	B	C	D	E	F	G	H	I	J	K	L	M	N	O	P	Q	R	S	T	U	V	W	X	Y	Z
M	Y	S	E	C	R	T	A	B	D	F	G	H	I	J	K	L	N	O	P	Q	U	V	W	X	Z

Substitution

Figure 5-5: Encryption using a keyword cipher

The letter *A* turns into the letter *M*, which is the first letter in the key; the letter *B* turns into the letter *Y*, which is the second letter in the key. You continue like this, removing any repeating letters in the key—notice the second *E* in SECRET is missing—and once the keyword ends, you assign the rest of the characters are in alphabetical order, minus any letter used in the key. If you started with the plaintext THE QUICK BROWN FOX, you'd get the ciphertext PAC LQBSF YNJVI RJW.

Ciphers such as this one have weaknesses. Like all the other historical ciphers we've discussed, they're vulnerable to *frequency analysis*, which means you can make guesses about what the message contents might be based on the frequency of characters used, where those characters appear in words, and when they're repeated. For example, the letter *E* is the most commonly used letter in the English alphabet, so you could assume that the most frequent letter in the substitution might be an *E*, as well, and work from there to decrypt the message.

To fix this flaw, cryptographers invented the one-time pad.

One-Time Pads

The *one-time pad*, also known as the Vernam cipher, is an unbreakable cipher when used properly. To use it, you create two copies of the same pad of paper containing a completely random set of numbers, known as *shifts*, and give one copy to each party. These pads are the key. To encrypt the message, you use the shifts to move each letter of the message forward. Like with the keyword cipher, if the first number on the pad were 4, you'd shift the first letter of your message by 4 spots, and if the second number were 6, you'd shift the second letter of the message by 6 spots. Figure 5-6 shows an example of this.

One-time pad

4	5	13	1	13
2	14	19	6	23
8	2	26	5	2
16	24	1	25	3
6	14	6	10	20

Plaintext	A	T	T	A	C	K	A	T	D	A	W	N
Shift	4	5	13	1	13	2	14	19	6	23	8	2
Substitution	E	Y	G	B	P	M	O	M	J	X	E	P

Figure 5-6: Encryption using a one-time pad

In this example, you'd send the message ATTACKATDAWN as EYGBPMOMJXEP. The receiving party would consult their one-time pad and then perform the relative shifts backward to decrypt the message.

The encrypted text could generate an infinite number of possible plaintext messages. In the case of the Caesar cipher, where you shift the entire message by the same number of characters, there are only 26 possible combinations. *Brute forcing*, or testing every possible key to retrieve the original message, takes little time, and you'll likely have no trouble recognizing the correct message when you've succeeded. But since the one-time pad uses a different shift for each letter, the message could contain any combination of letters or words that fits the message length. From the previous example, you could just as easily decrypt the incorrect messages ATTACKATNOON or NODONTATTACK.

The one-time pad is a primitive version of a stream cipher, which we'll come back to shortly. You can use it with more complex pads and mathematical operations, and modern methods of encryption and key exchange use some of these same concepts.

Symmetric and Asymmetric Cryptography

Today, we can separate most cryptographic algorithms into two types: symmetric and asymmetric. In this section, I will discuss each type, as well as a few specific examples of each.

Symmetric Cryptography

Also known as private key cryptography, *symmetric key cryptography* uses a single key to both encrypt the plaintext and decrypt the ciphertext. Technically, the ciphers we've explored so far in this chapter use symmetric keys; to decode the Caesar cipher, for example, you would apply the same key to the message as the one used to encrypt it. That means you must share the key between the sender and the receiver. This process, known as *key exchange*, constitutes an entire subtopic of cryptography. I'll discuss key exchange at greater length later in this chapter.

The fact that you must share a single key among all users of the system is one of the chief weaknesses of symmetric key cryptography. If attackers gain access to the key, they could decrypt the message—or, worse yet, decrypt it, alter it, and then encrypt it once more and pass it on to the receiver in place of the original message (a tactic called a *man-in-the-middle attack*).

Block vs. Stream Ciphers

Symmetric key cryptography in the digital age makes use of two types of ciphers: block ciphers and stream ciphers. A *block cipher* takes a predetermined number of bits (or binary digits, which are either a 1 or a 0), known as a *block*, and encrypts that block. Blocks typically have 64 bits, but they can be larger or smaller depending on the algorithm used and the various modes the algorithm can operate in. A *stream cipher* encrypts each bit in the plaintext message one bit at a time. You can make a block cipher act as a stream cipher by setting the block size to one bit.

The majority of the encryption algorithms currently in use are block ciphers. Although block ciphers are often slower than stream ciphers, they tend to be more versatile. Since block ciphers operate on larger blocks of the message at a time, they're usually more resource intensive and more complex to implement. They're also more susceptible to errors in the encryption process. For example, an error in block cipher encryption would render a large segment of data unusable, whereas in a stream cipher, an error would corrupt only a single bit. You can generally use specific block modes to detect and compensate for such errors. A *block mode* defines the specific processes and operations that the cipher uses. You'll learn more about these modes in the next section when I discuss the algorithms that use them.

Typically, block ciphers work better with messages whose sizes are fixed or known in advance, such as files, or messages whose sizes are reported in protocol headers. It's generally better to use stream ciphers when encrypting data of an unknown size or data in a continuous stream, such as information moving over a network, where the kind of data being sent and received is variable.

Symmetric Key Algorithms

Some of the most well-known cryptographic algorithms are symmetric key algorithms. The US government has used several of these, such as DES, 3DES, and AES, as standard algorithms for protecting highly sensitive data. I'll discuss these three examples in this section.

DES is a block cipher that uses a 56-bit key (meaning the key used by its cryptographic algorithm is 56 bits long). As you saw when discussing keyword ciphers, the length of the key determines the strength of the algorithm, because the longer the key is, the more possible keys there are. For example, an 8-bit key has a keyspace (range of possible keys) of 2^8. DES has a keyspace of 2^{56}—that's 72057594037927936 possible keys attackers must test.

DES first came into use in 1976 in the United States and has since spread globally. People considered it very secure until 1999, when a distributed computing project attempted to break a DES key by testing every possible key in the entire keyspace. They succeeded in a little more than 22 hours. It turned out the keyspace was too short; to compensate for this, cryptographers began using *3DES* (pronounced "triple DES"), which is simply DES used to encrypt each block three times, with three different keys.

Eventually, the US government replaced DES with *AES*, a set of symmetric block ciphers. AES uses three different ciphers: one with a 128-bit key, one with a 192-bit key, and one with a 256-bit key, all of which encrypt blocks of 128 bits. Briefly, there are a few key differences between AES and 3DES.

1. 3DES is three rounds of DES, while AES uses a newer and completely different algorithm developed in 2000.
2. AES uses longer and stronger keys than 3DES, as well as a longer block length, making AES harder to attack.
3. 3DES is slower than AES.

Hackers have attempted a variety of attacks against AES, most of them against the encryption using the 128-bit key. Most of these have either failed or had only partial success. At the time of this writing, the US government still considers AES to be secure.

Other well-known symmetric block ciphers include Twofish, Serpent, Blowfish, CAST5, RC6, and IDEA. Popular stream ciphers include RC4, ORYX, and SEAL.

Asymmetric Cryptography

Martin Hellman and Whitfield Diffie first described asymmetric cryptography in their 1976 paper, "New Directions in Cryptography."[7] While symmetric key cryptography makes use of only one key, *asymmetric key cryptography*, also known as public key cryptography, uses two keys: a public key and a private key. You use the public key to encrypt data, and anyone can access the public key. You can see them included in email signatures or posted on servers that exist specifically to host public keys. Private keys, used to decrypt messages, are carefully guarded by the receiver. Cryptographers use complex mathematical operations to create the private and public keys. These operations—which typically involve factorizing very large prime numbers, as I discussed earlier in the chapter—are difficult enough that, currently, no method exists to discover the private key by using the public key.

The main advantage of asymmetric key cryptography over symmetric key cryptography is that you no longer need to distribute the key. In symmetric key cryptography, as discussed, the message sender needs to find a way of sharing the key with whomever they want to communicate with. They might do this by exchanging keys in person, sending a key in an email, or repeating it verbally over the phone, but the method must be secure enough to ensure the key isn't intercepted. But with asymmetric key cryptography, you don't have to share a secret key. You simply make your public key available, and anyone who needs to send you an encrypted message can use it without compromising the security of the system.

Asymmetric Key Algorithms

The *RSA* algorithm, named after the initials of its creators, Ron Rivest, Adi Shamir, and Leonard Adleman, is an asymmetric algorithm used across the world, including in the Secure Sockets Layer (SSL) protocol. (*Protocols* are the rules that define communication between devices. SSL secures many common transactions, such as web and email traffic.) Created in 1977, RSA is still one of the most widely used algorithms in the world to this day.

Elliptic curve cryptography (ECC) is a class of cryptographic algorithms, although people sometimes refer to it as though it were a single algorithm. Named for the type of mathematical problem on which its cryptographic functions are based, elliptic curve cryptography has several advantages over other types of algorithms.

ECC can use short keys while maintaining a higher cryptographic strength than many other types of algorithms. It's also a fast and efficient type of algorithm that allows us to easily implement it on hardware that has less processing power and memory, such as a cell phone or portable device. A variety of cryptographic algorithms, including the Secure Hash Algorithm 2 (SHA-2) and Elliptic Curve Digital Signature Algorithm (ECDSA), use ECC.

Other asymmetric algorithms include ElGamal, Diffie–Hellman, and Digital Signature Standard (DSS). Many protocols and applications are based on asymmetric cryptography, including Pretty Good Privacy (PGP) for securing messages and files, SSL and Transport Layer Security (TLS) for common internet traffic, and some voice over IP (VoIP) protocols for voice conversations.

PGP

PGP, created by Phil Zimmerman, was one of the first strong encryption tools to reach the eye of the public and the media. Created in the early 1990s, the original release of PGP was based on a symmetric algorithm, and you could use it to secure data such as communications and files. The original version of PGP was given away as free software, including the source code. At the time of its release, PGP was regulated as munitions under the US International Traffic in Arms Regulations (ITAR) law. Zimmerman spent several years under investigation for criminal activities when he was suspected of exporting PGP out of the country, which was illegal at the time and considered to be arms trafficking.

Hash Functions

Hash functions represent a third type of modern cryptography, which we call keyless cryptography. Instead of using a key, hash functions, or message digests, convert the plaintext into a largely unique and fixed-length value, commonly referred to as a *hash*. You can think of these hash values as finger-prints because they're unique identifiers of a message. Moreover, hashes of similar messages look completely different. Figure 5-7 shows some hashes.

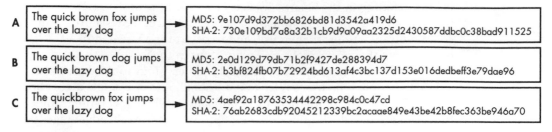

Figure 5-7: A hash function generates a unique value for every message, no matter how similar the messages are.

Notice that the message we're hashing in B differs from message A by only a single word, but it produces a completely different hash. The same is true for message C, which removes only a single space from the original message but still generates a unique hash. You can't use hashes to discover the contents of the original message, or any of its other characteristics, but you can use it to determine whether the message has changed. This means that if you're distributing files or sending communications, you can send the hash with the message so that the receiver can verify its integrity. To do this, the receiver simply hashes the message again using the same algorithm and then compares the two hashes. If the hashes match, the message has not changed. If they don't match, the message has been altered.

Although it's theoretically possible to engineer a matching hash for two different sets of data, called a *collision*, this is difficult and generally happens only if you're using a broken hashing algorithm. Some algorithms, such as Message-Digest algorithm 5 (MD5) and Secure Hash Algorithm 1 (SHA-1), have been attacked in this fashion, although it's uncommon (Figure 5-8).

Figure 5-8: In a hash collision, two distinct messages produce the same hash.

When collisions occur, you generally stop using the compromised algo-rithm. Those who require stringent hash security have mostly stopped using MD5 and replaced it with SHA-2 and SHA-3.

Other hash algorithms include MD2, MD4, and RACE.

Digital Signatures

Another way to use asymmetric algorithms and their associated public and private keys is to create digital signatures. A *digital signature* allows you to sign a message so that others can detect any changes to the message after you've sent it, ensure that the message was legitimately sent by the expected party, and prevent the sender from denying that they sent the message (a principle known as *nonrepudiation*, covered in Chapter 4).

To digitally sign a message, the sender generates a hash of the message and then uses their private key to encrypt the hash. The sender then sends this digital signature along with the message, usually by appending it to the message itself.

When the message arrives at the receiving end, the receiver uses the public key corresponding to the sender's private key to decrypt the digital signature, thus restoring the original hash of the message. The receiver can then verify the message's integrity by hashing the message again and comparing the two hashes. This may sound like a considerable amount of work just to verify the integrity of the message, but software applications usually do it for you, so the process is typically invisible to the user.

Certificates

In addition to hashes and digital signatures, you can use digital certificates to sign your messages. *Digital certificates*, as shown in Figure 5-9, link a public key to an individual by validating that the key belongs to the proper owner, and they're often used as a form of electronic identification for that person.

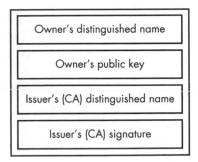

Owner's distinguished name

Owner's public key

Issuer's (CA) distinguished name

Issuer's (CA) signature

Figure 5-9: A digital certificate

You typically create a certificate by taking the public key and identifying information, such as a name and address, and having them signed by a trusted entity that handles digital certificates, called a *certificate authority*. A certificate authority is the entity that issues certificates. It acts as a trusted third party to both sides of transactions that involve certificates by signing the certificate to begin with and later verifying that it is still valid. One well-known certificate authority is VeriSign. Some large organizations, such as the US Department of Defense, may choose to implement their own certificate authority to keep costs down.

A certificate allows you to verify that a public key is truly associated with an individual. In the case of the digital signature discussed in the preceding section, someone might have falsified the keys used to sign the message;

maybe those keys did not actually belong to the original sender. If the sender had a digital certificate, you could easily check with the certificate authority to ensure that the public key for the sender is legitimate.

A certificate authority is only a small part of the infrastructure that you can put in place to handle certificates on a large scale. This infrastructure is known as a *public key infrastructure (PKI)*. A PKI usually has two main components: the certificate authorities that issue and verify certificates, and the registration authorities that verify the identity of the individual associated with the certificate, although some organizations may separate some functions out into more than just these.

A PKI might also revoke certificates if they reach their expiration date, are compromised, or shouldn't be used for some other reason. In this case, the certificate will likely be added to a certificate revocation list, which is generally a public list that holds all an organization's revoked certificates for a time.

Protecting Data at Rest, in Motion, and in Use

You can divide the practical uses of cryptography into three major categories: protecting data at rest, protecting data in motion, and protecting data in use. Data at rest includes the large amount of stored data on devices such as backup tapes, flash drives, and hard drives in portable devices such as laptops. Data in motion is the enormous amount of information sent over the internet, including financial transactions, medical information, tax filings, and other similarly sensitive exchanges. Data in use is data actively being accessed.

Protecting Data at Rest

People often neglect to protect *data at rest*, which is data on a storage device of some kind that isn't moving over a network, through a protocol, or across some other communication platform.

Somewhat illogically, data at rest can also, technically, be in motion. For example, you might ship a load of backup tapes containing sensitive data, carry a flash drive containing a copy of your tax forms in your pocket, or leave a laptop containing the contents of a customer database in the back seat of your car.

Attackers exploit this fact on a regular basis. For example, in 2017, someone found a USB flash drive in the street outside Heathrow Airport in London and discovered it contained information about the routes and security measures used to protect Queen Elizabeth II, as well as other high-ranking officials and dignitaries, when they move through the airport.[8]

Had necessary steps been taken to protect the flash drive's data at rest by encrypting it, the security incident would not have occurred (and authorities would not have had to publicly disclose that the incident had occurred, saving them from quite a bit of embarrassment).

Data Security

We primarily use encryption to protect data at rest, particularly when we know that the device containing the data could be physically stolen.

An enormous number of commercial products provide encryption for portable devices. These often target hard drives and portable storage devices, including products from large companies such as Intel and Symantec, to name a few. These commercial products often encrypt entire hard disks (a process known as *full disk encryption*) and a variety of removable media, and they report back to centralized management servers or other security and administrative features. There are also several free or open source encryption products on the market, such as VeraCrypt,[9] BitLocker[10] (which ships with some versions of Windows), and dm-crypt[11] (which is specific to Linux).

Physical Security

Physical security, which I'll discuss at length in Chapter 9, is an important part of protecting data at rest. If you make it more difficult for attackers to physically access or steal the storage media that contains sensitive data, you have solved a large portion of your problem.

In many cases, large businesses have databases, file servers, and workstations that contain customer information, sales forecasts, business strategy documents, network diagrams, and other kinds of data they want to keep from becoming public or falling into the hands of their competitors. If the physical security at the building that houses the data is weak, an attacker might be able to simply enter the building, steal a device, and walk right out with the data.

You also need to be aware of the areas you cannot physically protect and limit the data that leaves your protected spaces. In an office building, you could apply extra layers of physical security to the data center containing your servers, for example. Once sensitive data leaves such areas, your ability to protect it becomes more limited. In the case of the Heathrow flash drive that I discussed earlier, officials might have kept this sensitive data from being copied to an external drive to prevent it from walking out the door and being lost in the street.

Protecting Data in Motion

Often, data travels over networks, whether it be a closed wide area network (WAN) or local area network (LAN), a wireless network, or the internet. To protect data exposed on a network, you will usually choose to either encrypt the data itself or encrypt the entire connection.

Protecting the Data Itself

You can take a variety of approaches to encrypting the data you are sending over the network, depending on the kind of data you are sending and the protocols over which you are sending it.

You will often use SSL and TLS to encrypt a connection between two systems communicating over a network. SSL is TLS's predecessor, although the terms are often used interchangeably, and they are nearly identical. SSL and TLS operate in conjunction with other protocols, such as Internet Message Access Protocol (IMAP) and Post Office Protocol (POP) for email, Hypertext Transfer Protocol (HTTP) for web traffic, and VoIP for voice conversations and instant messaging.

However, SSL and TLS protections generally apply to only a single application or protocol, so although you might be using them to encrypt your communications with the server that holds your email, this doesn't necessarily mean the connections made through your web browser have the same level of security. Many common applications are capable of supporting SSL and TLS, but you generally need to configure them to do so independently.

Protecting the Connection

Another approach to protecting data in motion is encrypting all your network traffic with a virtual private network (VPN) connection. VPN connections use a variety of protocols to create a secure connection between two systems. You might use a VPN when you're accessing data from a potentially insecure network, such as the wireless connection in a hotel.

The two most common protocols currently used to secure VPNs are Internet Protocol Security (IPsec) and SSL. You can configure these two types of VPN connections to have a nearly identical set of features and functionality, from the perspective of the user, but they require a slightly different set of hardware and software to set up.

Typically, an IPsec VPN requires a more complex hardware configuration on the back end, as well as a software client you have to install, whereas an SSL VPN often operates from a lightweight plug-in downloaded from a web page and a less complex hardware configuration on the back end. From a security standpoint, the two methods have relatively similar levels of encryption. One weakness of the SSL VPN client, however, is that you could download it to a public computer or other random insecure device and provide an avenue for data leakage or an attack.

Protecting Data in Use

The last category of data to protect is the data currently being used. Although we can use encryption to protect data while it's stored or moving across a network, we are somewhat limited in our ability to protect data while legitimate entities have access to it. Authorized users can print files, move them to other machines or storage devices, email them, share them on peer-to-peer file-sharing networks, and generally make a mockery of our meticulous security measures.

In June 2013, the public discovered that a government contractor named Edward Snowden had deliberately leaked classified information containing details about the US National Security Agency PRISM program, which was ostensibly designed to collect and review terrorism-related communications.[12] Although this incident occurred more than five years ago at the time of this writing, the US intelligence community is still cleaning up after it and working to prevent another such incident.

Summary

Cryptography has existed in one form or another for most of recorded history. Early cryptographic practices varied in complexity, from the simple substitution ciphers of the Roman era to the complex electromechanical machines used before the invention of modern computing systems. Although such primitive cryptographic methods would not protect against modern cryptographic attacks, they form the basis for our modern algorithms.

Today, you conduct cryptography by using computers to create complex algorithms that encrypt your data. There are three main kinds of cryptographic algorithms: symmetric key cryptography, asymmetric key cryptography, and hash functions. In symmetric key cryptography, you encrypt and decrypt data with the same key, to which all parties operating on the plaintext or ciphertext have access. In asymmetric cryptography, you use both a public and a private key. The sender encrypts the message with the receiver's public key, and the receiver decrypts the message with their private key. This resolves the problem of having to find a secure way to share a single private key between the receiver and the sender. Hash functions don't use a key at all; they create a (theoretically) unique fingerprint of the message so that we can tell if the message has been altered from its original form.

Digital signatures are an extension of hash functions that allow you to not only create a hash to ensure that the message has not been altered but also encrypt the hash with the public key of an asymmetric algorithm to ensure that the message was sent by the expected party and to ensure nonrepudiation.

Certificates allow you to link a public key to an identity so that you can ensure that an encrypted message really represents a communication from a particular individual. The receiver can check with the issuer of the certificate—the certificate authority—to determine whether the certificate presented is, in fact, legitimate. Behind the certificate, you may find a PKI, which issues, verifies, and revokes certificates.

In general, cryptography provides a mechanism to protect data at rest, data in motion, and, to a certain extent, data in use. It provides the core of many of the basic security mechanisms that enable you to communicate and carry out transactions when the data involved is of a sensitive nature.

Exercises

1. What type of cipher is a Caesar cipher?
2. What is the difference between a block and a stream cipher?
3. ECC is classified as which type of cryptographic algorithm?

4. What is the key point of Kerckhoffs's second principle?

5. What is a substitution cipher?

6. What are the main differences between symmetric and asymmetric key cryptography?

7. Explain how 3DES differs from DES.

8. How does public key cryptography work?

9. Try to decrypt this message using the information in this chapter: V qb abg srne pbzchgref. V srne gur ynpx bs gurz. —Vfnnp Nfvzbi.

10. How is physical security important when discussing the cryptographic security of data?

6

COMPLIANCE, LAWS, AND REGULATIONS

In information security, external rules and regulations often govern your ability to collect information, pursue investigations, and monitor networks, among other activities. To comply with these rules, you can set requirements for protecting your organization, designing new systems and applications, deciding on how long to retain data, or encrypting or tokenizing sensitive data.

In this chapter, I'll outline some rules that might affect your organization and discuss how to ensure compliance to them.

What Is Compliance?

Simply put, *compliance* is your adherence to the rules and regulations that govern the information you handle and the industry within which you operate.

A decade ago, most information security efforts followed only a few policies and a general mandate to keep attackers out. Regulations aimed at protecting data and consumers had loose definitions, and governing parties enforced them less strictly.

Today, laws and regulations are more stringent, in part because large breaches, such as the British Airways breach of 380,000 payment cards in August 2018,[1] put compliance issues under increased scrutiny. Modern regulations update and evolve constantly, creating a moving target for companies that need to comply with the rules.

In general, you measure compliance against the standard to which you're adhering. In several industries, you may even have to comply with more than one set of rules. While you'll rarely encounter contradictory sets of standards, you may find that they disagree on the specifics. For example, one set of compliance rules might specify a one-year retention period for server backups, while another might specify six months. When faced with these situations, you'll likely find yourself adopting the strictest set of items across all compliance efforts, for the sake of simplicity.

Keep in mind that compliance isn't the same thing as security. Even if you've put hundreds or thousands of hours toward complying with a specific set of rules and even if you've passed an audit, you may not be secure against attacks. You carry out compliance to meet the needs of specific third parties—namely, your customers or business partners, auditors, and the compliance bodies responsible for ensuring your compliance. Compliance fulfills a business need rather than any technical security need. Furthermore, you are "compliant" whenever these third parties are satisfied with your efforts—regardless of how well you've actually met the requirements. An organization will usually put their "best foot forward" when the inspector comes.

Types of Compliance

There are two main types of compliance: regulatory compliance and industry compliance.

Regulatory compliance is your adherence to the laws specific to the industry in which you're operating. In almost every case, regulatory compliance involves cyclical audits and assessments to ensure that you're carrying everything out according to specification. Preparing for these audits can be a valuable part of a compliance program, as they can both educate participants and provide opportunities to find and fix issues.

Industry compliance is adherence to regulations that aren't mandated by law but that can nonetheless have severe impacts upon your ability to conduct business. For example, organizations that accept credit cards must typically comply with the Payment Card Industry Data Security Standard (PCI DSS), a set of rules created by a group of credit card issuers (including Visa, American Express, and Mastercard) for processing credit card transactions. The standard defines requirements for a security program, specific criteria for protecting data, and necessary security controls. Credit card issuers update the standard every few years to keep pace with current conditions and threats.

Although these credit card issuers can't legally enforce compliance with their standards, their mandate certainly has teeth. Merchants processing credit card transactions based on cards from PCI members must submit to yearly assessments of their security practices. Organizations with low numbers of transactions can simply complete a self-assessment consisting of a short questionnaire. As the number of transactions grows, however, the requirements become progressively stringent, culminating in visits by specially certified external assessors, mandated penetration tests, requirements for internal and external vulnerability scanning, and a great deal of other measures.

Consequences of Noncompliance

Noncompliance can trigger a variety of consequences, depending on the set of regulations in question.

In the case of industry compliance, you may lose the privileges associated with being compliant. For instance, if you fail to comply with the PCI DSS regulations that govern processing credit card transactions and protecting associated data, you may face hefty fines or lose your merchant status and be unable to process further transactions. For a business that depends heavily on credit card transactions, such as a retail store, losing the ability to process credit cards could put them out of business.

In the case of regulatory compliance, you may face even stiffer penalties, including incarceration for violating the laws in question.

Achieving Compliance with Controls

To comply with standards and regulatory requirements, you will typically implement physical, administrative, and technical controls.

Types of Controls

Physical controls mitigate risks to physical security. Examples include fences, guards, cameras, locked doors, and so on. These controls typically physically prevent or deter unauthorized access to or through specific areas.

Administrative controls mitigate risks by implementing certain processes and procedures. Whenever you accept, avoid, or transfer risk, you're likely using administrative controls because you're putting processes, procedures, and standards in place to prevent your organization from hurting itself by taking on too much risk. You'll also have to document your administrative controls by keeping records of policies, procedures, and standards you've put in place and providing evidence that your organization has followed them.

For example, almost every standard or regulation requires you to have an *information security policy*, which is a document that defines information security for an organization. To comply with this requirement, you must both put a policy in place and be able to prove that you've followed it with regular documentation. The day of the audit is not a good time to discover that you lack the documentation to show your policy in use. Proper documentation could include emails, tickets from your ticketing system, and files from investigations.

Technical controls manage risk using technical measures. You might mitigate risks by putting firewalls, intrusion detection systems, access control lists, and other technical measures in place to prevent attackers from getting into your systems.

None of these controls is sufficient by itself, but each contributes to the layered defense necessary to provide good security and meet requirements. Often, the regulations themselves stipulate certain controls. For instance, the PCI DSS requirements include a variety of specific controls that organizations must implement to comply with the standard. Also, keep in mind that your controls are only as good as your implementation of them. If you implement a control improperly, then you might be worse off than if you hadn't implemented it at all, because you've created a false sense of security.

Key vs. Compensating Controls

In addition to distinguishing types of controls, you can divide your controls into two levels of importance. *Key controls* are the primary controls used to manage risk in your environment and have the following characteristics:

1. They provide a reasonable degree of assurance that the risk will be mitigated.
2. If the control fails, it is unlikely that another control could take over for it.
3. The failure of this control will affect an entire process.

What you consider a key control will vary based on your environment and the present risks, and you should always test key controls as part of compliance or audit efforts. An example of a key control might be the use of antivirus software on all systems processing payment card information in an environment.

Compensating controls are controls that replace impractical or unfeasible key controls. When you put a compensating control in place, you'll likely have to explain to auditors how it will fulfill the intent and purpose of the control you're replacing.

For example, although regulations may require you to run antivirus tools on all systems, certain systems might not have sufficient resources to run these utilities without adverse impacts. In this case, as a compensating control, you might use Linux operating systems, which are less susceptible to malware.

Maintaining Compliance

To maintain your compliance over time, you can cycle through the following set of activities, as shown in Figure 6-1: monitoring, reviewing, documenting, and reporting.

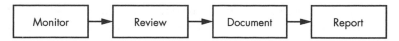

Figure 6-1: Maintaining compliance

Following each step in this process helps you maintain the health of your controls.

Monitoring

You must monitor your controls (and the data produced by or related to them) on an ongoing basis to determine whether they effectively mitigate or reduce risk. In the information security world, no news often just means no good news. Since your environment and technology might change, it's important to check that your controls—especially your key controls—continue to play their intended role. Without such monitoring, your controls quickly stop being useful, possibly without your knowledge.

Reviewing

Controls need to undergo a periodic review to determine whether they're still effective and meet the objectives for managing risk in your particular environment. As old risks evolve and new risks arise, you'll need to make sure your controls still cover these risks appropriately, determine whether you need any new controls, or decide whether you should retire old controls.

Documenting

You should document the results of your reviews and carefully track any changes to a control's environment. Documentation helps you evaluate trends and maybe even predict future control changes, which can allow you to forecast the resources you'll need later.

Reporting

After monitoring, reviewing, and documenting the state of your controls, you must report the results to your leadership. This not only keeps them aware of the state of your controls and enables them to make informed decisions for the organization but also provides you with a means of requesting the staff and resources you need for these efforts.

Laws and Information Security

When it comes to information security, enforcing laws and regulations is often trickier than in cases of physical incidents. Matters such as attributing attacks to a particular party or assessing the damage resulting from an attack—which can be simple when they concern, say, the vandalism of a building—are made considerably more difficult in the world of information security.

Many laws and regulations developed in recent years seek to address these types of situations. Some of them leave gaps, while others overlap significantly. You'll be measured against these laws when preparing for or being assessed for compliance. Let's look at a few of them.

Government-Related Regulatory Compliance

In the United States, standards frequently form the basis for the laws and regulations that govern the behavior of the government and those who work closely with it. In the world of information security and compliance, these standards are often from the series of Special Publications (SPs) created by the US National Institute of Standards and Technology (NIST). While NIST is not itself a regulatory agency, the standards it produces have compliance requirements, generally through other government compliance standards based on NIST's SPs (yes, this is somewhat convoluted). Security professionals often play a major role in making sure that an organization complies with these government-related standards.

WHAT IS NIST?

What is now called NIST was originally created in the early 1900s to develop standards for weights and measures and serve as a national laboratory. Over time, its mission has evolved to include promoting technology and innovation in the United States. NIST's Special Publications have a significant impact on information security.

Two of the most common government compliance standards are the Federal Information Security Management Act (FISMA) and the Federal Risk and Authorization Management Program (FedRAMP), which are both based on NIST SP 800-53, "Security and Privacy Controls for Information Systems and Organizations."

Federal Information Security Management Act

The Federal Information Security Management Act of 2002 applies to all US federal government agencies, all state agencies that administer federal programs (such as Medicare), and all private companies that support, sell to, or receive grant money from the federal government.

FISMA requires that an organization implement information security controls that use a *risk-based* approach—one that handles security by enumerating and compensating for specific risks.

After an organization passes an audit, the federal agency they're working with grants it an *authority to operate (ATO)*. Since the ATO is specific to each agency, a company working with ten different agencies must obtain ten different ATOs.

Federal Risk and Authorization Management Program

The Federal Risk and Authorization Management Program, established in 2011, defines rules for government agencies contracting with cloud providers.[2] This applies to both cloud platform providers, such as AWS and Azure, and companies providing software as a service (SaaS) tools that are based in the cloud. I'll discuss this distinction later in this chapter.

Unlike FISMA, FedRAMP certification consists of a single ATO that allows an organization to do business with any number of federal agencies. Since the FedRAMP ATO is considerably broader, the requirements to obtain it are more stringent than FISMA's. As of this writing, FedRAMP marketplace lists only 91 companies that possess an ATO.[3]

Industry-Specific Regulatory Compliance

Many regulatory compliance requirements pertain to a specific area of operation, such as the healthcare industry, public companies, and financial institutions. Let's look at a few of these requirements.

Health Insurance Portability and Accountability Act

The Health Insurance Portability and Accountability Act (HIPAA) of 1996 protects the rights and data of patients in the US healthcare system. Security professionals should pay specific attention to Title II of HIPAA, which lays out requirements for safeguarding protected health information (PHI) and electronic protected health information (e-PHI). (You can generally interpret these as consisting of any portion of a patient's medical records or medical transactions.) While HIPAA primarily applies to organizations involved in healthcare or health insurance, it may also apply in other odd cases, such as employers that self-insure.

HIPAA requires that you ensure the confidentiality, integrity, and availability of any information that you handle or store; protect this information from threats and unauthorized disclosures; and ensure that your workforce is compliant with all of its rules. This can be a tall order, especially in institutions that handle large amounts of PHI.

Sarbanes–Oxley Act

The Sarbanes–Oxley Act (SOX) of 2002 regulates financial data, operations, and assets for publicly held companies. The government-enacted SOX as a response to incidents of financial fraud among several large companies, most notably the Enron scandal of 2001, in which the public learned that the company had falsified years' worth of financial reporting.[4]

Among other provisions, SOX places specific requirements on an organization's electronic recordkeeping, including the integrity of records, retention periods for certain kinds of information, and methods of storing electronic communications. Security professionals often help design and implement systems impacted by SOX, so it pays for you to understand these regulations and your requirements under them.

Gramm–Leach–Bliley Act

The Gramm–Leach–Bliley Act (GLBA) of 1999 aims to protect information (such as personally identifiable information (PII), which is any data that can identify a specific person) and financial data belonging to customers of financial institutions. Interestingly, GLBA defines *financial institution* broadly to include "banks, savings and loans, credit unions, insurance companies and securities firms . . . some retailers and automobile dealers that collect and share personal information about consumers to whom they extend or arrange credit," as well as businesses that use financial data to collect debts from customers.[5]

To comply with GLBA, you must secure every pertinent record against unauthorized access, track people's access to these records, and notify customers when you share their information. Organizations must also have a documented information security plan in place and specifically have an overarching information security program to handle security for the organization.

Children's Internet Protection Act

The Children's Internet Protection Act (CIPA) of 2000 requires schools and libraries to prevent children from accessing obscene or harmful content over the Internet. CIPA requires these institutions to have policies and technical protection measures in place to block or filter such content. Additionally, these institutions must monitor the activities of minors and provide education regarding appropriate online behavior.

CIPA encourages institutions to adopt these standards not by imposing penalties for noncompliance but by providing cheap internet access for eligible institutions that choose to comply with them.

Children's Online Privacy Protection Act

The Children's Online Privacy Protection Act (COPPA) of 1988 protects the privacy of minors younger than 13 by restricting organizations from collecting their PII, requiring the organizations to post a privacy policy online, make reasonable efforts to obtain parental consent, and notify parents that information is being collected. Many companies choose to charge a small fee for accounts belonging to a minor as a way of verifying parental consent, while others refuse service to minors entirely.

COPPA is a bit of a hot potato in the information security world, as it requires organizations to judge the age of its users and provides for an even more restrictive class of PII for children if such data is to be collected, even by accident, both of which are difficult to execute with a high level of surety. In 2016, the mobile advertising company InMobi was fined $950,000 under COPPA for unknowingly tracking the location of minors younger than 13 with its advertising software.[6] As you can see, compliance here can be difficult, even when organizations are honestly attempting to do so.

Family Educational Rights and Privacy Act

The Family Educational Rights and Privacy Act (FERPA) of 1974 protects students' records. FERPA applies to student at all levels, and when students turn 18, the rights to these records shift from the parents to the students.

FERPA defines how institutions must handle student records to protect them and how people can view or share them. As schools now largely hold educational records in digital form, it's not uncommon for a security professional to participate in incidents and design discussions, and to address general security issues when working at an institution that handles educational records.

Laws Outside of the United States

Foreign laws governing computing and data can differ greatly from US laws. If your organization operates internationally, you need to research the relevant laws in every country in which you plan to conduct business. You should also check for any treaties that regulate security practices and the exchange of information between those countries.

It pays to know ahead of time where you might encounter regulatory issues. For example, in one country, you might be able to gather log data containing a list of machines and associated usernames, cross-referenced with the owner's employee number and email address. But in another country, collecting this data might be more difficult, or perhaps even illegal.

One example of an international regulation relevant to information security is the General Data Protection Regulation (GDPR), which the European Union enacted in 2018. GDPR covers data protection and privacy for all individuals in the European Union. The regulation applies to anyone collecting data about EU citizens, regardless of the country in which you're working.

GDPR requires that organizations get consent before collecting people's data, report data breaches, give individuals the right to access and remove collected data, and set specific guidelines for privacy and privacy programs. Given the broad applicability of GDPR, security and privacy programs all over the world had to adapt when this law came into effect, prompting a great many customer communications, new privacy-oriented banners on websites, and updates to many organizations' policies.[7]

Adopting Frameworks for Compliance

In addition to the frameworks provided by specific regulations, it's helpful to choose a framework for your overall compliance efforts. For example, if your organization is bound to comply with separate, unrelated regulations— HIPAA and PCI DSS, for example—you might want to choose a more over-arching framework to guide the entire compliance effort and security program and then adjust it as needed for specific areas of compliance.

In this section, you'll learn about some frameworks you can use. Choosing a well-known framework can also ease the path of an audit, as you're able to give the auditor an idea of what to expect of your program and the specific controls that you've implemented.

International Organization for Standardization

The International Organization for Standardization (ISO) is a body first created in 1926 to set standards between nations. It has created more than 21,000 standards "covering almost every industry, from technology, to food safety, to agriculture and healthcare."[8]

The ISO 27000 series that covers information security includes standards such as the following:

- ISO/IEC 27000, "Information security management systems – Overview and vocabulary"
- ISO/IEC 27001, "Information technology – Security Techniques – Information security management systems – Requirements"
- ISO/IEC 27002, "Code of practice for information security controls"

This series of ISO standards, also referred to in the industry as ISO 27k, discusses information security management systems and is intended to help manage the security of the assets within your organization. These documents lay out best practices for managing risk, controls, privacy, technical issues, and a wide array of other specifics.

National Institute of Standards and Technology

A National Institute of Standards and Technology Special Publication provides guidelines for many topics in computing and technology, including risk management. Two of the commonly referenced publications in this area are SP 800-37, "Guide for Applying the Risk Management Framework to Federal Information Systems," and SP 800-53, "Security and Privacy Controls for Federal Information Systems and Organizations."

SP 800-37 lays out the risk management framework in the following six steps, which form the basis of many security programs:

Categorize   Categorize the system based on the information it handles and the impact of exposing or losing such data.

Select   Select controls based on the system's categorization and any extenuating circumstances.

Implement   Implement the controls and document the implementation.

Assess   Assess the controls to ensure that they're properly implemented and performing as expected.

Authorize   Authorize or ban the use of the system based on the risk it faces and the controls implemented to mitigate that risk.

Monitor   Monitor the controls to ensure that they continue to appropriately mitigate risk.

If you intend to select controls based on SP 800-37, you can find specific guidelines for that purpose in SP 800-53.

Custom Frameworks

You could always develop your own framework or modify an existing one, but you should think carefully before doing so. As you've just seen, plenty of frameworks for risk management already exist, all of which have undergone considerable review and testing. You probably shouldn't try to reinvent the wheel here.

Compliance amid Technological Changes

Keeping up with technological change can provide challenges for both the bodies that enforce compliance and those who are attempting to achieve it. An excellent example of this is cloud computing, discussed in this section.

Before hosting data and applications in the cloud became a common technology trend, organizations generally owned their own servers and infrastructure and hosted them either internally or in a co-located data center. This presented a relatively black-and-white set of areas for who owned and was responsible for the security of these devices.

Now that entire companies exist almost entirely in the cloud, compliance efforts have shifted in an attempt to specifically cope with these situations; new policies might govern how to track and evaluate third-party security and compliance efforts, new regulations determine how to manage cloud data, and auditors ask entirely new questions, requiring evidence specific to these types of environments.

While most of the technology change is relatively gradual, allowing the security and compliance industries to slowly shift to keep pace with it, this is not always the case. Two relatively new and potentially disruptive technologies have the potential to cause further shift in compliance requirements for some industries: blockchain and cryptocurrencies.

Compliance in the Cloud

For organizations operating partially or entirely in the cloud, compliance can present an additional set of challenges. That's because cloud offerings come in different models, each of which gives you a differing level of control over the environment. These models are *infrastructure as a service (IaaS)*, *platform as a service (PaaS)*, and *software as a service (SaaS)*, as shown in Figure 6-2.

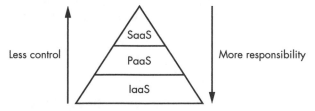

Figure 6-2: Cloud models

At a high level, IaaS provides you with access to virtual servers and storage. Examples include Google Cloud and Amazon Web Services. PaaS provides you with prebuilt servers, such as database or web servers, like Azure, and SaaS provides you with access to a specific application or application suite, as in the case of Google Apps.

PaaS gives you some level of control, and SaaS gives you little or none. Conversely, IaaS requires you to adopt a greater level of responsibility, PaaS requires you to adopt some level of responsibility, and SaaS requires you to adopt very little of it. To quote from *Spider-Man*, "With great power comes great responsibility." (The attribution of this quote is a bit tricky, but I can credit Stan Lee in "Amazing Fantasy #15" with relative safety.)

The choice of which of these types of services to use is a matter of balancing your need for flexibility and configurability with how easy the service should be to use. If you want to send a simple email and be done, it would be logical for you to use a tool like Gmail (SaaS) to do so. It would not make very much sense, in this case, for you to build and configure a virtual server, install and configure mail server software on it (IaaS), and then send your email.

Who Owns the Risk?

In each cloud model, the cloud provider must take responsibility for the portions of the environment that the users can't control. That means that, in some cases, you'll be responsible for securing your data directly; in other cases, you'll be responsible for ensuring that the services you're using secure it appropriately.

In IaaS environments, the cloud provider owns the risks related to the networks and servers on which the virtual infrastructure exists. In other words, it's responsible for securing and maintaining the hosts (the servers that run the virtual machines), the storage arrays on which the customer's storage volumes reside, and the networks used by the hosts, among other components. Because IaaS gives you a large amount of control over the environment and how it is configured, it requires you to adopt a greater level of responsibility.

In PaaS environments, the cloud customers access the servers directly, but they can't access the infrastructure that runs those servers. In this case, the cloud provider assumes responsibility for the security of that infrastructure, including tasks such as patching the operating system, configuring the servers, backing up the servers, and maintaining storage volumes.

In SaaS environments, customers probably won't be able to make changes to the infrastructure or servers at all, which means the cloud provider is responsible for them entirely. Customers might still be responsible for the data they input into the environment, but not for the security of the environment itself.

Audit and Assessment Rights

Your contract with the cloud provider generally stipulates your right to audit and assess the security of the cloud environment. In many cases, the service allows customers to audit and assess the environment within certain specific bounds. For instance, it might stipulate how and when you can ask the provider for an audit by your internal audit team or a third-party audit company. These limits are reasonable, since responding to each audit request takes a lot of work. The provider might also respond to audit requests by providing the result of an annual external audit conducted expressly for the purposes of responding to requests such as these.

If you hope to directly assess the security of a cloud provider, perhaps with a penetration test (which I'll discuss in depth in Chapter 14), you might meet resistance. Many providers deny such requests outright or allow penetration tests only under very specific and tightly restricted conditions. This is also understandable for many of the same reasons that they might limit audits. Additionally, active security testing often impacts the infrastructure, platform, or application being tested, and the provider might experience service issues as a result.

Technology Challenges

Cloud services pose technological challenges related to compliance because they're shared resources. If you're using cloud resources on the same host server as another company, that company's lack of security could easily impact the security of your systems, as well.

Risks increase in cloud services that the provider manages more closely, such as SaaS, because you share a larger portion of the environment with other customers. You may have data intermingled with that of other customers in the same database, with only the application logic keeping your data apart from theirs.

In an IaaS service, on the other hand, although you're sharing some of the same server resources to host virtual machines and some of the same storage space, a sharp divide exists between your resources and the resources of others.

Compliance with Blockchain

Blockchain is a distributed and uneditable digital ledger. Transactions are recorded to the ledger as a block, and each block is attached to the previous block in the chain by a one-way mathematical handshake (similar to a hash, as discussed in Chapter 5). Each participant has a copy of the blockchain, and the consensus of 51 percent of participants defines the accepted chain (generally the longest chain).

In security terms, blockchain promises a strong form of integrity. When you record something to blockchain, you can, with a high degree of certainty, say that it wasn't altered when you look at it later. For example, Walmart uses this technology to track the path of its food products from the supplier with which they originate to the stores that will sell them to customers.[9]

When it comes to compliance, it's important to create controls that demonstrate an understanding of how blockchain works. For example, people often cite the use of blockchain as an indelible record that you can write to something and never be concerned with that data being altered.

Unfortunately, this is true only under certain conditions. You can force consensus on blockchain by controlling 51 percent of the participants, at which point you can write whatever you like to it. Some companies have even gone as far as to promote "private" blockchains, which really amounts to just using encryption to ensure the integrity of the data. Someone trying to regulate blockchain should understand what drawbacks there may be in using it; if you rush from one hot new technology to the next, you may be putting in place controls that are, in actuality, only security theater.

Compliance with Cryptocurrencies

A *cryptocurrency* is a form of digital currency often based on the use of blockchain. Cryptocurrencies are unquestionably a disruptive technology. The first cryptocurrency, Bitcoin, appeared in 2009 and has enjoyed a wild variance in value between now and then.

Bitcoin generates currency through the same means it uses to keep the underlying blockchain functioning. To attach each block in the Bitcoin to the chain, as discussed, it needs to be verified with a mathematical handshake. This function requires some level of computing power from all of those participating in the blockchain, and as an incentive, those who participate are rewarded with a Bitcoin. This process of generating new Bitcoins is known as *Bitcoin mining*.

In February 2019, Gerald Cotton, the founder of Quadriga (which at the time was the largest cryptocurrency exchange in Canada), reportedly perished suddenly. Cotton, a security-minded fellow, maintained the entire exchange from offline accounts stored on his highly encrypted laptop. Upon his death, the entirety of the approximately $190 million in cryptocurrency held by the exchange across 115,000 clients vanished into thin air as his laptop became inaccessible. As of this writing, the exact circumstances surrounding this incident are still under investigation, although there are rumors that the incident involved some sort of chicanery.

As an organization, you are likely bound by a number of laws and regulations that govern financial transactions, as well as those that define the rules for investors and reporting to them. The use of cryptocurrency in business at all is still a gray area, although many businesses do so. It is all but certain, however, that you would, as an organization, be unable to shrug off a multimillion-dollar loss due to a cryptocurrency technology failure without serious repercussions from a legal and regulatory perspective.

Summary

In this chapter, I discussed the laws and regulations relevant to information security and what it means to comply with them. A great number of these are pertinent to computing, and they can vary heavily from one country to the next. Businesses might face both regulatory compliance and industry compliance, which they typically maintain by implementing controls.

I also talked about compliance in newer technologies, such as cloud computing and blockchain, which present additional challenges for those attempting to regulate them.

Exercises

1. Select one of the US laws applicable to computing covered in this chapter and summarize its main stipulations.
2. Why might a compliance audit be a positive occurrence?
3. What type of data is COPPA concerned with?
4. How do compliance and security relate to each other?
5. What issues might make conducting an international information security program difficult?
6. Which NIST Special Publication forms the basis for FISMA and FedRAMP?
7. Why are industry regulations, such as PCI DSS, important?
8. What are the potential impacts of being out of compliance?
9. What set of ISO standards might be useful for an information security program?
10. What two items are an indicator of which sets of compliance standards your company might fall under?

7

OPERATIONS SECURITY

Known in military and government circles as OPSEC, operations security is a process you use to protect your information. Although we've discussed certain elements of operations security previously, such as using encryption to protect data, the entire operations security process encompasses much more.

Operations security involves not only putting security measures in place but also identifying what exactly you need to protect and what to protect it against. If you jump directly to implementing protections, you might fail to direct your efforts toward the most critical information. Moreover, when putting security measures in place, you should implement measures that are relative to the value of what you are protecting. If you apply the same level of security to everything, you may be overprotecting some resources that are not of high value and underprotecting resources of much greater value.

In this chapter, I'll discuss the US government's guidelines for conducting operations security. I'll then outline the origins of some of these concepts and talk about everyday uses for them as tools for protecting yourself and your organizations.

The Operations Security Process

The operations security process laid out by the US government has five parts, as shown in Figure 7-1.

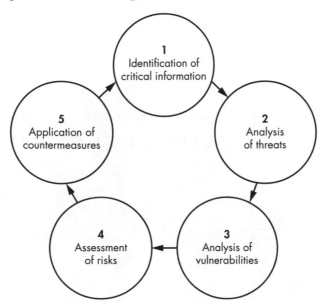

Figure 7-1: The operations security process

First, you identify the information that needs protection. You then analyze the threats and vulnerabilities that might impact it and develop methods of mitigating those threats and vulnerabilities. Although the process is relatively simple, it's effective. Let's go through these steps one by one.

Identification of Critical Information

The first and most important step in the operations security process is to identify your most critical information assets. Any given business, individual, military operation, process, or project is bound to have at least a few critical items of information on which everything else depends. For a soft drink company, it might be their secret recipe. For an application vendor, it might be their source code, while for a military operation, it might be an attack timetable. You should be identifying the assets that would cause you the most harm if exposed.

Analysis of Threats

The next step is to analyze any threats related to the critical information you identified. Remember from Chapter 1 that a threat is something that has the potential to cause you harm. Using your list of critical information, you might evaluate the harm caused if critical information were exposed, as well as who might exploit that exposure. This is the same process many military and government organizations use to classify information and determine who can see it.

For example, if you own a software company, you might identify the proprietary source code of your product as critical information. Exposing this critical information could make the company vulnerable to attackers and competition. Attackers might be able to determine the scheme used to generate license keys and then develop a utility that allows them to pirate your software, costing revenue. Competitors might use exposed source code to copy your software's proprietary features in their own applications, or they might copy large portions of your application and sell it themselves.

Repeat this step for each item of critical information, for each party that might take advantage of it if it were exposed, and for each use they might make of the information. As you can see, the more information assets you identify as critical, the more involved this step becomes. In some circumstances, you may find that only a limited number of parties can make use of the information and then only in a limited number of ways; in other cases, you may find the exact opposite. For example, a secret chocolate-chip cookie recipe, intended for mass production on an industrial food processing line, would be of use only to another organization operating in this type of industry. The same recipe composed and scaled for home use would be usable by anyone.

Analysis of Vulnerabilities

Vulnerabilities are weaknesses that others can exploit to harm you. The third step in operations security is analyzing the vulnerabilities in the protections you've put in place to secure your information assets. You'll do this by looking at how you interact with these assets and what areas an attacker might target to compromise them.

When analyzing the vulnerabilities affecting your source code, you might find that the security controls on the source code aren't very rigorous and that it's possible for anyone with access to the operating system or network shares to access, copy, delete, or alter it. This might make it possible for an attacker who has compromised the system to copy, tamper with, or entirely delete the source code. Or the vulnerability might render the files vulnerable to accidental alteration while the system is undergoing maintenance.

You might also find there are no policies in place that regulate where the source code should be stored, whether copies of it should exist on other systems or on backup media, or how it should be protected in general. These issues might create multiple vulnerabilities and could lead to serious security breaches.

Assessment of Risks

Next, you decide what issues you need to address in the rest of the operations security process. As discussed in Chapter 1, risk occurs when you have a matching threat and vulnerability. In the software source code example, one of the threats was the potential exposure of the application source code. The vulnerabilities were poor controls on access to the source code and a lack of a policy dictating how exactly to control access. These two vulnerabilities could lead to the exposure of your critical information to your competitors or attackers.

Again, you need a matching threat and vulnerability to constitute a risk. If the confidentiality of your source code wasn't a goal—for instance, if you were creating an open source project and the source code were freely available to the public—you wouldn't have a risk. Likewise, if your source code were subject to stringent security requirements that made it nearly impossible to release in an unauthorized manner, you wouldn't have a risk, either, as the vulnerability would not be present.

Application of Countermeasures

Once you've discovered risks to your critical information, you can put measures in place to mitigate them. In operations security, these are called *countermeasures*. As discussed, to constitute a risk, you need a matching set of threats and vulnerabilities. When you construct a countermeasure for a risk, you need to mitigate either the threat or the vulnerability at the bare minimum.

In the source code example, the threat was that your source code might be exposed to your competitors or attackers, and the vulnerability was the poor set of security controls you had in place to protect it. In this instance, there is not much that you can do to protect yourself from the threat itself without changing the nature of your application entirely, so you can't mitigate the threat. You can, however, put measures in place to mitigate the vulnerability.

For example, to mitigate this vulnerability, you can institute stronger measures to control access to the code and establish a set of rules for how to control access. Once you break the threat/vulnerability pair like this, you'll no longer have a serious risk.

It's important to note that this is an *iterative* process, and you'll likely need to repeat the cycle more than once to fully mitigate any issues. Each time you go through the cycle, you take into account the knowledge and experience you gained from your previous mitigation efforts, allowing you to adjust your solution for an even greater level of security. You'll also need to revisit this process when your environment changes and new factors arise.

If you're familiar with risk management, you might have noticed that the operations security cycle lacks a step that evaluates the effectiveness of the countermeasures. I believe this step is implied throughout the entire operations security process. However, the process is certainly not set in stone, and you can include this step if you see the benefits of doing so.

Laws of Operations Security

Kurt Haase, a former employee of the Nevada Operations Office of the Department of Energy, distilled the operations security process into three rules, called the *laws of OPSEC*. These laws are another way of thinking about the cycle discussed earlier, and while not necessarily the most *important* parts of the process, they do serve to highlight some of operation security's main concepts.

First Law: Know the Threats

The first law of operations security is "If you don't know the threat, how do you know what to protect?"[1] In other words, you need to be aware of both the actual and potential threats facing your critical data. This law maps directly to the second step in the operations security process.

Ultimately, as discussed earlier, each piece of information could be susceptible to its own threat. Threats might even depend on your location. This is particularly true when it comes to cloud-based services. For example, even if you've enumerated all the threats facing your critical data for a location, you might encounter new threats if you replicate that data across multiple storage areas, in multiple countries. That's because different parties may have easier access in one area, or the relevant laws may differ significantly from one location to another.

Second Law: Know What to Protect

"If you don't know what to protect, how do you know you are protecting it?"[2] This law of operations security points to the need to evaluate your information assets and determine what exactly you might consider to be your critical information. This second law maps to the first step in the operations security process.

Most government environments mandate the identification and classification of information. Each item of information—perhaps a document or file—is assigned a label, like *classified* or *top secret*, that identifies the sensitivity of its contents. Such labeling makes the task of identifying your critical information considerably easier, but unfortunately, few people outside the government use that system.

Some organizations in the business world might have information classification policies, but, in my experience, they usually implement such labeling sporadically. A few civilian industries, such as those that deal with data that has federally mandated requirements for protection, like financial or medical data, do classify information, but these are the exceptions rather than the rule.

Third Law: Protect the Information

The third and last law of operations security is "If you are not protecting [the information], . . . THE DRAGON WINS!"[3] This law addresses the necessity of the operations security process overall. If you don't take steps to protect your information from the dragon (your adversaries or competitors), they win by default.

Cases of the "dragon" winning are unfortunately common. Security breaches show up constantly in the news and on websites that track breaches, such as Privacy Rights Clearinghouse (*https://www.privacyrights.org/*). In many cases, a breach was the result of simple carelessness and noncompliance with the most basic security measures.

This is true for the breach of the California-based email marketing company SaverSpy discovered by a security researcher in September 2018. The breach contained more than 43GB of user data, including the names, email addresses, physical addresses, and gender of more than 10 million Yahoo users.[4]

I'd like to think that hackers broke into the system and stole this information in the dark of night. But in fact, the researcher discovered the data while sifting through compromised servers on Shodan,[5] a search engine; it turned out the servers containing this data were wide open and unprotected on the internet. To add insult to injury, the database also contained a table with a ransom note from an attacker who had found the exposed servers earlier.

The operations security process would have quickly identified critical data sets such as these, giving you a much better chance of avoiding such a situation. The security measures needed to prevent breaches are neither complex nor expensive and can save you a great deal of reputational and financial damage in the long run.

Operations Security in Our Personal Lives

The operations security process can be useful not only in both business and government but also in our personal lives. You may not consciously work through all the parts of the operations security cycle to protect your personal data, but you still use some of the methods discussed.

For example, if you're going on vacation for several weeks and leaving behind an empty house, you might take steps to ensure some level of security while you're gone. You might start by making the following list of indicators that the house is unoccupied and vulnerable:

- No lights on at night
- No noise coming from the house
- Newspapers building up in the driveway
- Mail building up in the mailbox
- No car in the driveway
- No people coming and going

You might then take steps to ensure that you don't show your vulnerabilities so obviously to burglars or vandals. For example, you could set timers on your lights so that they turn on and off at various times throughout the house. You may also set a timer on the television or radio so that you can generate noise that makes it seem like someone is home. To solve the problem of mail and newspapers stacking up, you can suspend their delivery while you're gone. To make the house appear occupied, you might also have a friend drop by every few days to water the plants and perhaps move a car in and out of the garage every now and then.

OPERATIONS SECURITY AND SOCIAL MEDIA

In the age of social networking tools, you see personal operations security violations on a disturbingly regular basis. Many of these tools are now equipped with location awareness functionality that allows our computers and portable devices to report our physical locations when we update our statuses.

Additionally, people often post that they're going to lunch, leaving on vacation, and so on. In both instances, we've given the general public a very clear signal of when we might not be home or when we might be found at a particular location—a bad practice from an operational security standpoint.

Although you won't enforce these OPSEC measures to your personal data as strictly as the US government, the process is the same. When it comes to your logical assets, taking these approaches is especially important.

Your personal information travels through a staggering number of computer systems and networks. Although you might take steps to mitigate security threats by being careful about where and how you share your personal information over the internet, or perhaps by shredding mail that contains sensitive information before throwing it away, you're unfortunately not in control of all the ways your personal information might be exposed.

As you saw with the SaverSpy breach earlier in this chapter, you can't always trust organizations to handle your information carefully. That said, if you make plans to secure your personal data before breaches occur, you can at least mitigate the issue to a certain extent. For instance, you can put monitoring services in place to watch your credit reports, and you can file fraud reports with these same agencies in the case of a breach. You can also watch your financial accounts carefully. Although such steps might not be complex or terribly difficult to carry out, they can make a big difference if implemented before the problem has occurred.

Origins of Operations Security

Although the operations security process as implemented in the US government may be a recent idea, its foundational concepts are ancient. You can point to nearly any military or large commercial organization in any period in history and find the principles of operations security present. In this section, I'll cover a few examples that were important to the development of modern operations security.

Sun Tzu

Sun Tzu was a Chinese military general who lived in the sixth century BCE. For some, Sun Tzu's work *The Art of War* is a kind of bible for conducting military operations. *The Art of War* has spawned countless spin-offs, many of which apply the principles it preaches to a variety of situations, including information security. The text documents some of the earliest examples of operations security principles. Let's look at just a couple of these.

The first passage is, "If I am able to determine the enemy's dispositions while at the same time I conceal my own, then I can concentrate and he must divide."[6] This is a simple admonition to discover information held by our opponents while protecting our own.

The second passage is, "(When) making tactical dispositions, the highest pitch you can attain is to conceal them; conceal your dispositions, and you will be safe from prying of the subtlest spies, from the machinations of the wisest brains."[7] Here, Sun Tzu is saying we should conduct our strategic planning in an area that is difficult for our opponents to observe—in this case, the highest point we can find. Again, he recommends protecting our planning activities so that they don't leak to those that might oppose our efforts.

Although written a long time ago, both these passages agree closely with the laws of operations security that we discussed earlier in the chapter—namely, know the threats, know what to protect, and then protect it.

George Washington

George Washington, the first president of the United States, was an astute and skilled military commander who promoted good operational security practices. He is known in the operations security community for having said, "Even minutiae should have a place in our collection, for things of a seemingly trifling nature, when enjoined with others of a more serious cast, may lead to valuable conclusion,"[8] which means that even small items of information, which are worthless individually, can be of great value in combination.

A modern example of this idea is the three main items of information that constitute an identity: a name, an address, and a Social Security number. Individually, these items are completely useless. You could take any one of them in isolation and put it up on a billboard for the world to see and not be any worse for having done so. In combination, however, these three items are sufficient for an attacker to steal your identity and use it for all manners of fraudulent activities.

Washington is also quoted as having said, "For upon Secrecy, Success depends in most Enterprizes of the kind, and for want of it, they are generally defeated."[9] In this case, he was referring to an intelligence gathering program and the need to keep its activities secret. He is often considered to have been very well informed on intelligence issues and is credited with maintaining an extensive organization to execute such activities, long before any such formal capabilities existed.

Vietnam War

During the Vietnam War, the United States realized that information regarding troop movements, operations, and other military activities was being leaked to the enemy. Clearly, in most environments, military or otherwise, having our opponents gain knowledge of our activities is a bad thing, particularly when lives may be at stake. To stop the leak, authorities conducted a study, code-named Purple Dragon,[10] to discover its cause.

Ultimately, the study reached two main conclusions: first, in that environment, eavesdroppers and spies abounded, and second, the military needed a survey to reveal the extent of the information loss. The survey asked questions about the information itself and how vulnerable the information was. The team conducting these surveys and analyses coined the term *operations security* and its acronym *OPSEC*. Additionally, they saw the need for an operations security group to serve as a body that would espouse the principles of operations security to the different organizations within the government and work with them to get them established.

Business

In the late 1970s and early 1980s, some of the operations security concepts used in military and government began to take root in the commercial world. Industrial espionage—spying on business competition to gain a competitive advantage—is an old practice, but as the concept became more structured in the military world, it became more structured in the business world as well. In 1980, Michael E. Porter, a professor at Harvard Business School, published a book titled *Competitive Strategy: Techniques for Analyzing Industries and Competitors*. This text, now nearing its 60th printing, set the groundwork for what we now call competitive intelligence.

Competitive intelligence is generally defined as conducting intelligence gathering and analysis to support business decisions. The counterpart of competitive intelligence, *competitive counterintelligence*, includes the operations security principles that were laid out by the government only a few years previously and is an active part of conducting business to this day. You can see these principles at work in many large corporations, as well as in groups such as the Strategic and Competitive Intelligence Professionals (SCIP)[11] professional organization and the Ecole de Guerre Economique (or Economic Warfare School), located in Paris.

Interagency OPSEC Support Staff

After the end of the Vietnam War, the group that conducted Purple Dragon and developed the government OPSEC principles tried to get support for an organization that would work with the various government agencies on operations security. They had little success in interesting the military institutions and were unable to gain official support from the US National Security Agency. Fortunately, through the efforts of the US Department of Energy and the US General Services Administration, they garnered sufficient backing to move forward. At this point, they drafted a document to put in front of then-first-term-President Ronald Reagan.

These efforts were delayed due to Reagan's reelection campaign, but shortly afterward, in 1988, he signed the Interagency OPSEC Support Staff (IOSS) into being with the National Decision Security Directive 298.[12] Today, the IOSS is responsible for a wide variety of OPSEC awareness and training efforts, such as the Naval Operations Security poster shown in Figure 7-2.[13]

Figure 7-2: OPSEC awareness poster

Summary

The origins of operational security stretches far back into recorded history. You can find such principles espoused in the writings of Sun Tzu in the sixth century BCE, in the words of George Washington, in writings from the business community, and in the US government's methodologies. Although formalized operations security processes are a much more recent creation, the principles on which they are founded are ancient indeed.

The operations security process consists of five major steps. First, you start by identifying your most critical information so that you know what you need to protect. You then analyze your situation to determine what threats and vulnerabilities exist in your environment. Once you know your threats and vulnerabilities, you can attempt to determine what risks you might face. You have a risk whenever your threats and your vulnerabilities match. When you know the risks, you can plan countermeasures to mitigate your risks.

To summarize this process, you can also look to the laws of OPSEC penned by Kurt Haase. His three laws cover some of the high points of the process you might want to internalize.

You also use the operations security principles used in business and in government in your personal life, even though you may not do so in a formal manner. It's important to identify your critical information and plan measures to protect it, especially with the sheer volume of personal information shared through systems and networks.

Exercises

1. Why is it important to identify your critical information?

2. What is the first law of OPSEC?

3. What is the function of the IOSS?

4. What part did George Washington play in the creation of operations security?

5. In the operations security process, what is the difference between assessing threats and assessing vulnerabilities?

6. Why might you want to use information classification?

7. When you have cycled through the entire operations security process, are you finished?

8. From where did the first formal OPSEC methodology arise?

9. What is the origin of operations security?

10. Define competitive counterintelligence.

8

HUMAN ELEMENT SECURITY

In information security, we refer to people as the "weak link" of security programs. Regardless of the security measures you set, you have little control over your employees who might click dangerous links, send sensitive information via unprotected channels, hand over passwords, or post important data in conspicuous places.

Worse yet, attackers can take advantage of these tendencies to conduct *social engineering attacks* that manipulate people to gain information or access to facilities. These attacks usually rely on the willingness of people to help others, particularly when faced with someone who appears to be in distress, someone intimidating (such as a high-up manager), or someone who seems familiar.

That said, you can take measures to protect your organization from these attacks by setting appropriate policies and teaching your employees to recognize danger. In this chapter, you'll learn about the kind of data attackers might collect, several types of social engineering attacks, and how to set up an effective security training program to inform your staff.

Gathering Information for Social Engineering Attacks

To protect your organization, you'll need to know how social engineers collect data. People can gather information about individuals and organizations more quickly today than ever before. A staggering wealth of information exists in online databases, public records, and social media sites, and in many cases, this data is free for the taking. Many people post detailed personal information regarding their day-to-day activities for the entire world to see.

Once an attacker collects information about internal processes, people, or systems, they can use it to conduct sophisticated attacks. If an attacker called a company and flat-out asked for a report containing sensitive sales data, the person on the other end would likely refuse. On the other hand, if an attacker used social engineering techniques by calling in a panicked voice and asked for a copy of the latest TPS-13 report from the sales directory on the SalesCom server because they have a meeting with Mr. Kurosawa in 15 minutes and their laptop just crashed, they're more likely to succeed. (This is a social engineering attack known as pretexting. I'll discuss it in more detail later in this chapter.)

It's worth knowing what kind of information attackers might use in cases such as the one just discussed. When protecting people and commercial organizations, you should look at two primary sources of information: human intelligence and open source intelligence.

Human Intelligence

A chief tool for military and law enforcement organizations across the world, *human intelligence (HUMINT)* is data gathered by talking to people. HUMINT data might include personal observations, people's schedules, sensitive information, or any of a number of other similar items. You can collect HUMINT with hostile techniques such as torture or by tricking participants with subtle scams. Security professionals focus on the latter.

For example, you might use HUMINT as the basis for conducting other social engineering attacks. You could observe the traffic going in and out of an office building and notice that the office receives frequent package deliveries and that a shift change happens at 8 AM every morning, causing many people to enter and exit the building at the same time. You'd have a much better chance of entering the facility in an unauthorized manner during this busy time, while dressed in a familiar delivery uniform.

Open Source Intelligence

Open source intelligence (OSINT) is information collected from publicly available sources, such as job postings and public records. This publicly available data can reveal an enormous amount of useful data, including the technologies in use in a particular organization, the organization's structures, and the specific names of people and their positions. OSINT is one of the primary sources of information on which to base social engineering attacks.

Résumés and Job Postings

In résumés, you might find work histories, skill sets, and hobbies, which an attacker can use to set up social engineering attacks based on the target's skills or interests. In job listings, companies often expose information that they would otherwise consider sensitive, including office and data center locations, network or security infrastructure details, and the software in use. Recruiters might consider it necessary to post this information for the hiring process, but attackers can also use it to plan attacks or add focus to future surveillance efforts.

For example, if you collect information about a company and determine it runs Windows servers in its cloud hosting environment and uses CompanyX antivirus software, you've just dramatically reduced the number of variables you must consider when planning attacks against the company. If you collect additional information about the location and members of their information security team, you might also be able to predict the skill level and timing of any responses to your attack, making your attack more effective.

Social Media

Attackers can easily collect OSINT using social media tools, such as Facebook and Twitter, by following someone's activities, finding their friends and other social contacts, and even tracking their physical location. They can use this information to monitor people or take more direct action, such as blackmail. In many cases, younger people tend to document questionable activities more willingly and may provide a richer source for this type of information.

Attempts to manipulate the outcome of the 2016 US presidential election provide an example of how attackers can take advantage of social media tools. In the months preceding the election, the Russian-based company Internet Research Agency purchased approximately 3,500 Facebook ads intended to incite tensions among targeted groups of voters by touching on themes such as race, policing, and immigration. In February 2018, a US federal grand jury indicted 13 Russians working for Internet Research Agency for these activities.[1] This is a classic example of social engineering, which I'll discuss in detail later in this chapter.

Public Records

Public records can provide a wealth of information about a target, including evidence of mortgages, marriages, divorces, legal proceedings, and parking tickets. Attackers often use this data to conduct additional searches and locate even more information.

What exactly constitutes a public record can vary based on the geographical location of the record and the agency that holds it. In the United States, the laws in each state differ, so information that you may access legally in one state may be illegal in another.

Google Hacking

Google and other search engines are an excellent resource for information gathering, particularly when attackers make use of advanced search operators, such as the following:

site Limits results to a specific site (site:nostarch.com)

filetype Limits results to a specific file type (filetype:pdf)

intext Finds pages containing a words or words (intext:security)

inurl Finds pages containing a word or words in the URL (inurl:security)

You can combine these operators into a single search to retrieve specific results. For instance, entering **site:nostarch.com intext:andress security** into a search should return the publisher's page for this book, as shown in Figure 8-1.

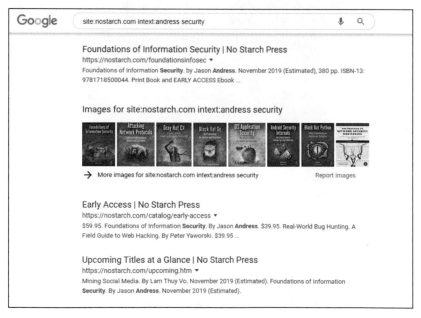

Figure 8-1: Google search operators at work

The Google Hacking Database (*https://www.exploit-db.com/google-hacking -database/*), shown in Figure 8-2, contains canned Google searches that make use of advanced search operators to find specific vulnerabilities or security issues, such as files that contain passwords or vulnerable configurations and services.

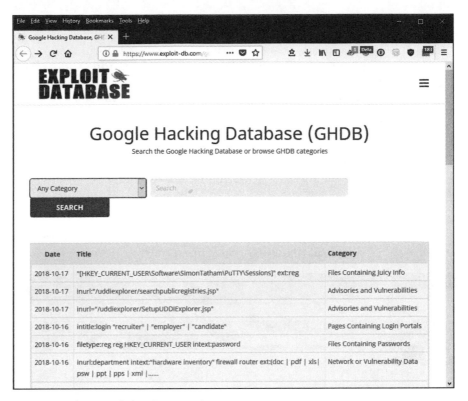

Figure 8-2: The Google Hacking Database

Not only does this provide a set of preassembled searches that you can click easily, but it also demonstrates some of the more complex ways that you can use search operators. For example, the bottom search in Figure 8-2 shows you a combination of three different operators (inurl:, intext:, and ext:). You could easily switch out the terms to repurpose the search for your own use.

File Metadata

Metadata is the data about data found in almost any file that can reveal not only mundane information such as timestamps and file statistics but also more interesting data such as usernames, server names, network file paths, and deleted or updated information. File metadata provides data for searches, sorting, file processing, and so on, and it generally isn't immediately visible to users. Many professional forensic tools, such as EnCase (*https://www.guidancesoftware.com/encase-forensic/*), have specific features to quickly and easily recover these data types in forensic investigations.

Image and video file metadata, called *EXIF data*, includes information such as the camera settings and hardware. You can view and edit EXIF data with ExifTool (*https://www.sno.phy.queensu.ca/~phil/exiftool/*), a great cross-platform tool that works with a wide variety of file types. Especially in document files that have been around for a while and edited by multiple people, the amount of metadata that they contain may surprise you. Try downloading and using it to analyze a few documents or image files.

Image files produced by devices containing Global Positioning System (GPS) information might also contain location coordinates; many smartphones embed users' location information into image files if they've enabled the location setting on the camera, which means uploading these images to the internet could leak sensitive data.

A multitude of tools exist to assist with information gathering from OSINT (and other) sources. Two of the more common and well-known among these tools are Shodan and Maltego.

Shodan

Shodan, shown in Figure 8-3, is a web-based search engine that looks for information saved on internet-connected devices.

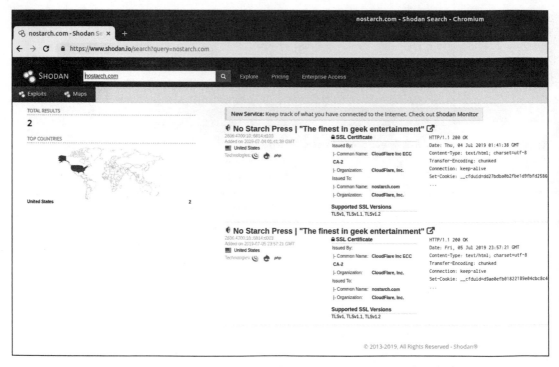

Figure 8-3: Shodan

Shodan allows you to search for specific information, such as particular hardware, software, or open ports. For example, if you knew of a vulnerable version of a specific File Transfer Protocol (FTP) service, you could ask Shodan for a list of all its instances in its database. Likewise, you could ask Shodan for everything that it knows about a domain or server and instantly see where specific vulnerabilities might be present.

Maltego

Maltego (*https://www.paterva.com/*), shown in Figure 8-4, is an intelligence-gathering tool that uses relationships between particular points of data, called *transforms*, to discover information related to information that you already have.

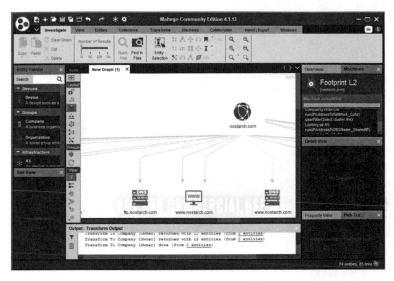

Figure 8-4: Maltego

For example, you might start by giving Maltego a website's domain name and then use a transform to find names and email addresses listed on the website. From these names and email addresses, you could find other addresses and names based on the same mail format elsewhere on the internet. You could also find the server Internet Protocol (IP) addresses that host the domain and then find other domains hosted on the same server.

Maltego displays the results of your search on a graph that shows the links between each of the items discovered. You can use the graph to conduct additional searches on specific items by clicking them and selecting a new transform.

Other Kinds of Intelligence

OSINT and HUMINT are by no means the only kinds of intelligence you can gather. You may also see references to these other types:

Geospatial intelligence (GEOINT)   Geographical information, typically from satellites.

Measurement and signature intelligence (MASINT)   Measurement and signature data from sensors, such as optical or weather readers. MASINT contains some sensor-specific kinds of intelligence, such as RADINT, or information collected from radar.

Signals intelligence (SIGINT)   Data gathered by intercepting signals between people or systems. You may also see this called communications intelligence (COMINT) when referring to communications between people and electronic intelligence (ELINT) when referring to communications between systems.

Technical intelligence (TECHINT)   Intelligence about equipment, technology, and weapons, often collected with the purpose of developing countermeasures.

Financial intelligence (FININT)   Data about the financial dealings and transactions of companies and individuals, often acquired from financial institutions.

Cyber intelligence/Digital network intelligence (CYBINT/DNINT) Intelligence gathered from computer systems and networks.

Most other types of intelligence will fit into one of these categories.

Types of Social Engineering Attacks

This section discusses some of the social engineering attacks a person could conduct with the information gathered in the previous section.

Pretexting

In *pretexting*, attackers use information they've gathered to assume the guise of a manager, customer, reporter, co-worker's family member, or other trusted person. Using a fake identity, they create believable scenarios that convince their targets to give up sensitive information or perform actions they wouldn't normally do for strangers.

An attacker could use pretexting in face-to-face encounters or over some communication medium. Direct interactions require a heightened level of attention to details such as body language, while indirect encounters, such as those conducted over the phone or through email, require a stronger focus on verbal mannerisms. Both types require good communication and psychological skills, specialized knowledge, and a quick mind.

Pretexting gives social engineers an advantage. For example, if the social engineer can drop names, provide details about the organization, and give the target sufficient cause to believe that they're entitled to the information or access for which they're asking—or, for that matter, that they already have it—their chances of success increase substantially.

Phishing

Phishing is a social engineering technique in which an attacker uses electronic communications such as email, texting, or phone calls to collect the target's personal information or install malware on their system, often by convincing the target to click a malicious link.

The fake sites used in web-based phishing attacks typically resemble well-known websites, such as banking, social media, or shopping sites. Some look obviously fake, with poor imitations of the company's logo and terrible grammar, while others are extremely difficult to distinguish from the legitimate page. Fortunately, many browsers have improved security in recent years and now render phishing attacks more difficult by showing warnings like the one in Figure 8-5.

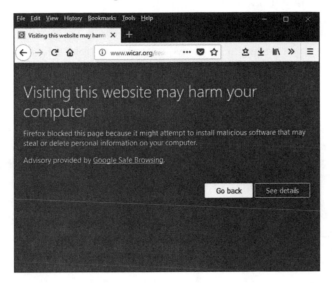

Figure 8-5: A phishing warning

Even without these warnings, however, most phishing attacks fail unless the target has an account on the site being faked; someone who doesn't have a MyBank bank account won't fall for a phishing attack that redirects to a fake MyBank bank website. Even if the target does have an account, people have become more cautious of unsolicited emails from their banks or other websites. In general, phishing attacks rely on a lack of attention to detail on the recipient's part, and their rate of success remains low.

To achieve higher rates of success, attackers may turn to *spear phishing*, or targeted attacks against specific companies, organizations, or people. A spear phishing attack requires advanced reconnaissance so that the message appears to come from someone the target would trust, such as human resources staff, a manager, the corporate IT support team, a peer, or a friend.

While a normal phishing attacks might appear clumsy and poorly constructed, aimed at tricking a small percentage of a large pool of recipients, spear phishing attacks take the opposite approach. For example, spear attackers typically send clean emails containing the expected logos, graphics, and signature block, and they'll disguise any malicious links present. If the attack exists to steal credentials for a site or service, the attacker may even use the freshly stolen credentials to log the target into the real site, leaving no error message or broken session to clue them in that something strange took place.

Tailgating

Physical *tailgating*, or piggybacking, is the act of following someone through an access control point, such as secure door, instead of using the credentials, badge, or key normally needed to enter. The authorized person may let you in intentionally or accidentally.

Tailgating happens in almost any place that uses technical access controls, partly because of the carelessness of authorized users and partly because most people tend to avoid confrontation. A few tricks of equipment, such as knowing which props to use, and the use of psychology to allow attackers to play on the sympathies of others will aid them in their tailgating efforts.

FURTHER RESOURCES ON SOCIAL ENGINEERING

Visit Chris Hadnagy's website *https://www.social-engineer.com/* and his excellent book *Social Engineering: The Science of Human Hacking* for more information about social engineering. Hadnagy goes into much greater depth than I do here about what social engineering attacks can do.

Building Security Awareness with Security Training Programs

To protect your organization, you'll have to build security awareness in your users by instituting a security training program. These programs often consist of instructor-led or computer-based lessons conducted during the new-employee onboarding process, followed up with mandatory quizzes. You might also repeat the training at regular intervals so the employee retains the information.

This section outlines some of the topics you should typically cover in these training programs.

Passwords

Although you can use technical tools to make sure users choose strong passwords, you can't easily control what users will do with those passwords. An employee could write their password down and stick it to the underside of their keyboard, for example, or share it with other users for convenience's sake.

Another kind of harmful behavior is using the same password for multiple accounts. Even if you force a user to create a strong password on a given system in the workplace, the user might manually synchronize all other systems in the organization to the same password (including their virtual private network credentials allowing external access to the organization's networks) and then proceed to go home and do the same with their internet forum credentials, email, and online gaming passwords to make their life easier. Unfortunately, if an attacker compromises the password database for their forum and publishes the user's email address and decrypted password, the attacker gains access to a disturbing amount of information—possibly including instructions for connecting to the company VPN that the user emailed to their home address.

Poor password hygiene is, unfortunately, a difficult problem to solve by technical means, and education is one of the best ways of tackling it. You should push users to create strong passwords even when they're not directly forced to do so, tell them not to leave or record their passwords where they might easily be compromised, and ask them not to use the same password repeatedly across multiple systems or applications.

Social Engineering Training

Training users to recognize and respond to social engineering attacks can be an incredibly arduous task because such attacks take advantage of our behavioral norms and tendencies. Thankfully, public awareness about phishing emails and fraud in general has grown.

Broadly, you should teach your users to be suspicious of anything that seems unusual, including atypical requests or emails in their inboxes and strangers in their working environments, even when these occurrences seem wrapped in a layer of normalcy.

Ask people to *trust but verify* when faced with even the slightest doubt. Your users may flood your security operations center with calls and emails, but at least they won't wire thousands of dollars to someone in a foreign country claiming to be the company vice president who was mugged while on a sales trip and is in dire need of funds to return home.

Network Usage

You should discuss proper network usage with your users. As I'll cover in Chapter 10, people today have access to a variety of networks, both wired and wireless, from relatively restricted ones in the workplace to wide-open networks in homes, coffee shops, and airports.

An uneducated user might assume that connecting a laptop to the network in a conference room at work is the same as connecting to the wireless network in a hotel, which is also the same as connecting to a network in an airport. Generally, people treat accessing networks in the same way they treat accessing any utility, like the power provided by a wall outlet or the light given off by a lamp; they expect it to be there and to function as expected. Beyond this, most people don't think too much about the risks present.

You should guide users toward behaviors that will protect the enterprise network. That means you shouldn't typically allow foreign devices to connect to it. Users need to know they can't allow vendors to plug in a device in a conference room and that they shouldn't connect their iPads to the production network, for example. You should instead provide a proper alternative network that outside devices can use, like a guest wireless network, and make sure that users know how to connect to it, as well as the parameters within which they can use it.

Also, you should restrict the use of corporate resources on outside networks, a problem that has bitten many organizations badly over time. If you load your laptop with sensitive data and then connect to the network at the local coffee shop or hotel, you may accidentally share this data with everyone else on the network.

An easy technical solution to this problem is to implement a VPN that allows users to access the corporate network. You should configure the VPN client to automatically connect the device to the VPN whenever it finds itself on a foreign network. Additionally, you should teach your users to avoid connecting devices containing sensitive information to insecure networks.

Malware

Educating users about malware generally involves teaching them not to indiscriminately click things. While they're surfing the web, opening email attachments, navigating social networks, and using smartphones, they should look out for the following common red flags:

- Email attachments from people they don't know
- Email attachments containing file types that are potentially executable and could contain malware, such as EXE, ZIP, and PDF
- Web links using shortened URLs such as *http://bit.ly/* (if in doubt, they can verify the destination of shortened URLs with tools like *https://linkexpander.com/* or *http://unshorten.me/*)
- Web links with names that differ slightly from those you expect (*myco.org* instead of *myco.com*, for example)
- Smartphone applications from nonofficial download sites
- Pirated software

If you instill a healthy sense of paranoia in your users, they'll call your help desk or security team to ask questions before immediately clicking suspicious links.

Personal Equipment

You should set rules for when and how employees can use personal equipment in the workplace. Typically, you might allow them to use it at the *border* of the organization's network; that means you'd let them bring their laptops to work and attach them to a guest wireless network but not to the same network as the company's production systems.

You should also be sure to communicate that these policies apply to devices such as vendor laptops or mobile devices that can connect to networks.

Clean Desk Policies

A *clean desk policy* states that sensitive information shouldn't be left unattended on a desk for any significant period of time, such as overnight or during a lunch break. When introducing such a policy, you should also discuss how to properly dispose of sensitive data stored on physical media, such as paper or tape, by using shred bins, data destruction services, and media shredders.

Familiarity with Policy and Regulatory Knowledge

Last, but certainly not least, if you expect your users to follow the rules, you need to communicate them effectively. You probably won't actually educate them if you just send an email to all users containing a link to a lengthy policy and then have them attest to having read it. Instead, you might try condensing the most critical part of your policy into a kind of crib notes or highlights reel to make sure users retain the key points.

Also, if you're creating a training presentation, you can try to make it more engaging. For instance, if you have an hour allotted to conducting security awareness training for newly hired employees, you might shorten your lecture portion to 30 minutes and then spend the second half of the time conducting an interactive quiz show–style game on the material you just covered. Once you've added an element of competition by dividing the class into teams and adding an incentive (such as prizes for the winners), you'll have created a more interesting environment.

You can also get your users' attention with posters, giveaways of pens or coffee mugs, and newsletters. If you present the information through repeated and varied avenues, you're more likely to educate users in the long term.

Summary

In this chapter, you explored a variety of issues concerning the human element of information security: the security issues that you can't address by technical means alone. Whether because of mere carelessness or targeted social engineering attacks, the people who staff your organizations pose a security challenge that you can't directly address with technical controls.

I discussed types of social engineering attacks, and you saw how attackers put these techniques to use to solicit information or coerce unauthorized actions from people in your organizations. I also covered how to build security awareness and training programs. Common issues to discuss with users include protecting passwords, recognizing social engineering attacks and malware, using networks and personal equipment safely, and adhering to a clean desk policy. If you make your security awareness and training programs engaging, this information is more likely to stick with users over time.

Exercises

1. Why are people the weak link in a security program?
2. Define tailgating. Why is it a problem?
3. How can you more effectively reach users in your security awareness and training efforts?
4. Why shouldn't you allow employees to attach personal equipment to your organization's network?
5. How might you train users to recognize phishing email attacks?
6. Why is it important not to use the same password for all your accounts?
7. What is pretexting?
8. Why might using the wireless network in a hotel with a corporate laptop be dangerous?
9. Why might clicking a shortened URL from a service such as bit.ly be dangerous?
10. Why is it important to use strong passwords?

9

PHYSICAL SECURITY

In this chapter, I'll discuss physical security, which is the set of security measures that we put in place to protect our people, equipment, and facilities. In most places, you'll find physical security measures such as locks, fences, cameras, guards, and lighting. In higher-security environments, you might also notice iris scanners, mantraps (an access control that requires you to step through two locking doors to enter a building, similar to a phone booth with two entrances), or identification badges equipped to store certificates.

Physical security involves the protection of three main categories of assets: people, equipment, and data. Your primary goal, of course, is to protect people. People are valuable in their own right and are also more difficult to replace than equipment or data, particularly when they're experienced in their field and uniquely familiar with the processes and tasks they perform.

Although I'll discuss the protection of people, data, and equipment as separate concepts in this chapter, the security of each is closely integrated. You generally can't—and shouldn't—develop security plans that protect any of these categories in isolation from the others.

Many larger organizations protect their assets by implementing sets of policies and procedures collectively referred to as business continuity planning (BCP) and disaster recovery planning (DRP). *Business continuity planning* refers to the plans you put in place to ensure that critical business functions can continue in a state of emergency. *Disaster recovery planning* refers to the plans you put in place to prepare for a potential disaster, including what exactly to do during and after a disaster strikes, such as evacuation routes posted on maps throughout the facility or signage indicating meeting places in the case of an evacuation.

Identifying Physical Threats

Before you can implement any physical security measures, however, you have to identify the threats. Physical security threats generally fall into a few main categories, as shown in Figure 9-1.

Movement	Smoke and fire	Toxins	People	Energy anomalies
Extreme temperature	Gases	Liquids	Living organisms	Projectiles

Figure 9-1: Categories of physical threats

Donn Parker defined seven of these categories—extreme temperature, gases, liquids, living organisms, projectiles, movement, and energy anomalies—in his book *Fighting Computer Crime*, where he also introduces the Parkerian hexad discussed in Chapter 1. (Although written more than a decade ago, I still consider Parker's book a must-read for security practitioners.)

As you move through the sections in this chapter on protecting people, equipment, and data, I'll discuss how these threats can affect each asset, if at all.

Physical Security Controls

Physical security controls are the devices, systems, people, and methods you put in place to ensure your physical security. There are three main types of physical controls: deterrent, detective, and preventive. Each has a different focus, but none is completely separate from the others, as I'll discuss shortly. Additionally, these controls work best when used in concert. No single one of them is sufficient to ensure your physical security in most situations.

Deterrent Controls

Deterrent controls are designed to discourage people who might seek to violate your other security controls, and they generally indicate the presence of other security measures. Examples of deterrent controls include signs in public places that announce that video monitoring is in place as well as yard signs with alarm company logos in residential areas, as shown in Figure 9-2.

Figure 9-2: Deterrent controls

The signs themselves do nothing to prevent people from acting in an undesirable fashion, but they do point out the potential consequences for doing so. These measures help keep honest people honest.

Detective Controls

Detective controls, like burglar alarms and other physical intrusion detection systems, serve to sense and report undesirable events. These systems typically check for indicators of unauthorized activity, such as doors or windows opening, glass breaking, movement, and temperature changes. You could also use them to check for undesirable environmental conditions such as flooding, smoke and fire, electrical outages, or contaminants in the air.

Detective systems might also include human or animal guards, whether they're physically patrolling an area or monitoring it secondhand using cameras or other technology, as shown in Figure 9-3.

Figure 9-3: Detective controls

Monitoring using guards has both pros and cons. Unlike technological systems, living beings may become distracted, and they'll have to leave their posts for meals and bathroom breaks. On the other hand, guards are able to make inferences and judgment calls that can render them more efficient or perceptive than technological solutions.

Preventive Controls

Preventive controls use physical means to keep unauthorized entities from breaching your physical security. Mechanical locks are an excellent example of preventive security because they're used almost everywhere to secure businesses, residences, and other locations against unauthorized entry, as shown in Figure 9-4.

Figure 9-4: Preventive controls

Other preventive controls include high fences, bollards, and, once again, guards and dogs, which are both detective and preventive. These controls might focus specifically on people, vehicles, or other areas of concern, depending on the environment in question.

Using Physical Access Controls

Preventive controls generally make up the core of our security efforts. In some cases, they may be the only physical security control in place. For example, many houses have locks on the doors but no alarm systems or messages that might deter a criminal.

In commercial facilities, you're much more likely to see all three types of controls implemented, usually with locks, alarm systems, and signs indicating the presence of the alarm systems. Following the principles of defense in depth, the more physical security layers you put in place, the better off you'll be.

You should also implement a level of physical security that is consistent with the value of your asset, as discussed in Chapter 7. If you have an empty warehouse, it doesn't make sense to protect it with high-security locks, alarm systems, and armed guards. Likewise, if you have a house full of expensive computers and electronics, it doesn't make sense to equip it with cheap locks and forgo an alarm system entirely.

Protecting People

Physical security primarily aims to protect the individuals who keep your business running. In many cases, you can restore your data from backups, you can build new facilities if the old ones become destroyed or damaged, and you can buy new equipment, but replacing experienced people within a reasonable period of time is difficult, if not impossible.

Physical Concerns for People

Compared to equipment, people are rather fragile. They're susceptible to nearly the entire scope of physical threats outlined in Figure 9-1.

Extreme temperatures, or even not-so-extreme temperatures, can quickly become uncomfortable, as can the absence or presence of certain *liquids*, *gases*, or *toxins*. Even water, in excessive quantities, can cause harm, like in the massive flooding that took place in the southern United States during Hurricane Florence in 2018.

Likewise, the lack of a gas such as oxygen, or too much of it, can become deadly to people very quickly. Certain chemicals benefit us when they're used in small amounts to filter the water in your facilities but are harmful if the chemical ratios or mixtures change.

A variety of *living organisms*, from larger animals to nearly invisible molds, fungi, or other microscopic organisms, can be dangerous to people. Animals might bite or sting people; mold might cause breathing problems.

Significant *movement* is harmful to people, particularly when it comes from an earthquake, mudslide, avalanche, or a building's structural issue. *Energy anomalies* are also very dangerous to people. For example, equipment with poorly maintained shielding or insulation, or mechanical or electrical faults, could expose people to microwaves, electricity, radio waves, infrared light, radiation, or other harmful emissions. The consequences of such exposures may be immediately obvious in the case of an electric shock, or they may have long-term effects in the case of radiation.

Other *people* can be one of the most severe threats against people. Someone could physically attack your employees in a dark parking lot. In certain parts of the world, you might encounter civil unrest. You could be susceptible to social engineering attacks, like those discussed in Chapter 8, in which the attacker extracts information from your personnel to gain unauthorized access to facilities or data.

Smoke and fire can cause burns, smoke inhalation, and temperature issues (people don't function well when overheated generally), among other problems. Particularly in large facilities, smoke and fire can render the physical layout of the area confusing and make it difficult for people to navigate their way to safety. The problem could worsen if your supplies, your infrastructure, or the fabric of the building itself reacts to the heat and releases toxins, collapses, or produces any of the other threats discussed in this section.

Ensuring Safety

Because many data centers use dangerous chemicals, gases, or liquids to extinguish fires, facilities managers often equip fire suppression systems with safety overrides that prevent them from going off if there are people in the area. Such measures prioritize protecting human life over equipment and data.

Evacuation

Likewise, during an emergency, you should prioritize evacuating people from the facility, not saving the equipment. Planning evacuation procedures is one of the best ways to keep people safe. The main principles to consider when planning an evacuation are where, how, and who.

Where

Consider in advance where you'll be evacuating to. You need to get everyone to the same place to ensure that they're at a safe distance from the event and that you can account for everyone. If you don't do this in an orderly and consistent fashion, you may not be able to ensure everyone's safety. Commercial buildings often display their evacuation meeting places with signs and evacuation maps.

How

Also of importance is the route you'll follow to reach the evacuation meeting place. When planning your routes, you should consider the location of the nearest exit in each area, as well as an alternate trajectory, in case some passages become blocked during an emergency. You should also avoid crossing any potentially dangerous or unusable areas, such as elevators or rooms blocked off automatically by closing fire doors.

Who

The most vital part of the evacuation, of course, is ensuring that you get everyone out of the building and that you can account for everyone at the evacuation meeting place. This process typically requires at least two designated people: one person to ensure that everyone in the group has left the premises and another at the meeting place to ensure that everyone has arrived safely.

Practice

Particularly in large facilities, a full evacuation can be a complicated prospect. In a true emergency, if you don't evacuate quickly and properly, a great number of lives may be lost.

As an example, consider the 2001 attacks on the World Trade Center in the United States. A study conducted in 2008 determined that only 8.6 percent of the people in the buildings evacuated when the alarms sounded. The rest remained inside, gathering belongings, shutting down computers, and performing other such tasks.[1] It's important that you train your personnel to respond quickly and properly when the signal to evacuate has been given.

Administrative Controls

Most organizations will also have a variety of administrative controls in place to protect people. Administrative controls may be policies, procedures, guidelines, regulations, laws, or similar rules instituted by any authority, from companies to the federal government.

A common administrative control is background checks companies use to screen potential candidates for a job. These investigations typically involve checks for criminal history, verification of previous employment and education, credit checks, and drug testing, depending on the position being pursued.

A company may also conduct a variety of reoccurring checks, like drug tests, on employees. When a person leaves a job, employers often conduct an exit interview to ensure that the employee has returned all company property and that any accesses to systems or areas have been revoked. The company may also ask the individual to sign paperwork agreeing not to pursue legal action against the company or to sign additional nondisclosure agreements (NDAs).

Protecting Data

Second only to the safety of your personnel is the safety of your data. As discussed in Chapter 5, the primary way to protect data is by encrypting it. Even so, encryption alone isn't sufficient; an attacker might access the data by breaking an encryption algorithm or obtaining the encryption keys. Also, encryption won't protect data from various physical conditions.

Following the concept of defense in depth covered in Chapter 1, you should add additional layers of security to keep your physical storage media safe against attackers, unfavorable environmental conditions, and other threats.

Physical Concerns for Data

Adverse physical conditions, including temperature changes, humidity, magnetic fields, electricity, and physical impact, can harm the integrity of physical media. Moreover, each type of physical media has strengths and weaknesses.

Magnetic media, such as hard drives, tapes, and floppy disks, uses a combination of movement and magnetically sensitive material to record data. Strong magnetic fields can harm the integrity of data stored on magnetic media, especially if the media lacks any metal casing, like magnetic tapes.

Additionally, jolting magnetic media while it's in motion (being read from or written to) can render the media unusable.

Flash media, or media that stores data on nonvolatile memory chips, is hardier. If you avoid impacts that might directly crush the chips that store the data and if you protect the chips from electrical shocks, they'll generally withstand conditions that many other types of media wouldn't. They're not terribly sensitive to temperature, so long as the temperature isn't extreme enough to destroy the media's housing, and they'll often survive brief immersion in liquid, if properly dried afterward. Some flash drives are designed specifically to survive extreme conditions that would normally destroy other media.

Optical media, such as CDs and DVDs, is fragile, as anyone with a small child can attest to. Even small scratches on the surface of the media may render it unusable. It's also highly temperature sensitive, since it's constructed largely of plastic and thin metal foil. Outside of a protected environment, such as a purpose-built media storage vault, any of a variety of threats may destroy optical media.

When storing media over an extended period, you should consider technical obsolescence. For example, Sony stopped producing floppy diskettes in March 2011. Prior to that, the company produced 70 percent of all new floppy diskettes.[2] Today, few new computers come equipped with drives to read them, and in a few short years, finding hardware to read these disks will become difficult indeed.

Accessibility of Data

Not only do you have to protect the physical integrity of your data, you must also ensure that the data is available when you need to access it. This generally means that both your equipment and your facilities must remain in functioning condition and that the media containing your data must be usable. Any of the physical concerns I mentioned can render your data inaccessible as well as unusable.

Some availability issues relate to infrastructure. For example, during an outage, whether it's related to network, power, computer systems, or other components, you may not be able to access your data remotely. Many businesses operate globally today, so it's possible that losing the ability to access data from afar, even temporarily, could have serious impacts.

To ensure availability of your data, back up the data itself and the equipment and infrastructure used to provide access to the data. Use *redundant arrays of inexpensive disks (RAID)*, or RAID array, in a variety of configurations for your backups. RAID is a method of copying data to more than one storage device to protect the data if any one device is destroyed. You can read the original paper describing the basic concept, "A case for redundant arrays of inexpensive disks (RAID)," at the Association for Computing Machinery (ACM) Digital Library.[3]

You can also replicate data from one machine to another over a network or make copies of data onto backup storage media, such as DVDs or magnetic tapes.

Residual Data

On the flipside of being able to access data when you need it, you must be able to render data inaccessible when you no longer need it. For instance, you'd likely remember to shred a stack of paper containing sensitive data before you throw it away. But people often forget about the data stored on electronic media.

In 2016, Blancco conducted a study on 200 used hard drives purchased from eBay and Craigslist. When researchers analyzed the contents of the disks, they discovered that many of them still contained sensitive data, including corporate information, emails, customer records, sales data, pictures, and Social Security numbers. In many cases, nobody had attempted to erase the data from the disks at all; in other cases, they had done so ineffectively.[4]

In addition to the devices that obviously contain storage and hold potentially sensitive data, you might find residual data in machines such as copiers, printers, and fax machines, which may contain volatile or nonvolatile internal storage, often in the form of a hard drive. In the hard drive, you might find copies of any processed documents, including sensitive business data. When you retire these types of devices from service or send them for repair, be sure to remove the data from the storage media.

Protecting Equipment

Lastly, protect your equipment and the facilities that house it. This category falls last on the list because it represents the easiest and cheapest segment of assets to replace. Even if a major disaster destroyed your facility and all the computing equipment inside it, you could be back in working order very shortly, as long as you still had people to run your operation and access to your critical data.

Although it may take you some time to return to the state you were in before the incident, you can generally replace floor space or relocate to another area nearby relatively easily, and computing equipment is both cheap and plentiful.

Physical Concerns for Equipment

You will find fewer physical threats to equipment than to employees or data, although they're still numerous.

Extreme temperatures—especially heat—can harm your equipment. In environments that contain large numbers of computers and associated equipment, we rely on environmental conditioning equipment to keep the temperature down to a reasonable level, typically in the high-60s to mid-70s on the Fahrenheit scale. (Experts still debate the ideal range.)

Liquids, even in small quantities, like the water in humid air, could harm equipment. Depending on the liquid in question and the quantity present, it could cause corrosion in a variety of devices, short-circuits in electrical equipment, and other harmful effects. Clearly, in extreme cases like flooding, any immersed equipment will often become completely unusable.

Living organisms might also damage equipment, although in more minor ways. Insects and small animals in your facility could cause electrical shorts, interfere with cooling fans, chew on wiring, and generally wreak havoc.

DON'T BUG ME

People started using the term *bug* to indicate problems in computer systems in September 1947, when someone discovered a moth shorting two connections in a system together, causing the system to malfunction. When workers removed the moth, they described the system as having been debugged.[5] You can see the actual "bug" in question in Figure 9-5.

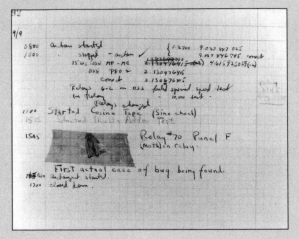

Figure 9-5: The first computer bug

Movement, in the earth and in the structure of your facilities, can hurt your equipment. An earthquake is an obvious example of this. *Energy anomalies* can be extremely harmful to any type of electrical equipment, especially if the power is absent or sends the wrong amount of voltage. Good facility design will provide some measure of protection against such threats, but you generally can't mitigate the effects of severe electrical issues, such as lightning strikes.

Smoke and fire are bad for your equipment, as they introduce extreme temperatures, electrical issues, movement, liquids (electronics don't function well when wet, generally), and a variety of other problems. Efforts to extinguish fires, depending on the methods used, may cause as much harm as the fire itself.

Site Selection

When planning a new facility, take into account the facility's location. If the site is in an area prone to natural disasters, you may eventually find your facility to be completely unusable or destroyed. Other environmental threats could include civil unrest, unstable power or utilities, poor network connectivity, or extreme temperature conditions.

With proper facility design, you may be able to compensate for some problems by installing power filtering and generators to counteract power problems, for instance. But others, such as the local temperature, may ultimately be out of our control. For certain types of facilities, such as data centers, it's important to have a problem-free environment, and if you encounter significant environmental issues, you may want to look elsewhere.

Securing Access

When securing access to equipment or facilities, use the concept of defense in depth by placing security measures at multiple areas, both inside and outside the facility. Again, the appropriateness of the barriers you enforce depends on the context. A military installation may have the highest level of security available; a small retail store may have the lowest level.

Often, you'll see physical security measures implemented on the perimeter of the property. Minimal measures might control vehicle traffic to make sure it doesn't enter undesirable places. For example, this can take the form of *security landscaping*, which can include trees, large boulders, and cement planters, placed in front of buildings or next to driveways to prevent vehicle entry. More secure facilities might also have fences, concrete barriers, and other more obvious measures. Such controls are generally deterrents but may be preventive, as well.

The entrance to the facility will likely have locks, whether mechanical or electronic, on the doors to the building. A typical arrangement for non-public buildings is to keep the main entrance unlocked during business hours and station a security guard or receptionist inside. More secure facilities might keep the doors locked at all times and require a badge or key to enter the building.

Once inside the facility, physical access controls could include locks on internal doors or individual floors of the building to keep visitors or unauthorized people from freely accessing the entire facility. Often, facilities will restrict access to computer rooms or data centers to only those who specifically need to enter them for business reasons. You may also find more complex physical access controls in place in such areas, such as biometric systems.

Environmental Conditions

When it comes to the equipment within your facilities, maintaining proper environmental conditions is crucial to continued operations. Computing equipment can be sensitive to changes in power, temperature, and humidity, as well as electromagnetic disturbances. In areas with large quantities of equipment, maintaining the proper conditions can be challenging, to say the least.

People constructing such facilities generally equip them with sources of emergency electrical power, like generators, as well as systems that can heat, cool, and moderate the humidity as required. Unfortunately, these controls are expensive, and smaller facilities might not be appropriately equipped.

Summary

In this chapter, you learned how to mitigate physical security issues using deterrent, detective, and preventive measures. Deterrents aim to discourage those who might violate your security, detective measures alert you to potential intrusions, and preventive controls physically prevent intrusions from taking place. None of these controls is a complete solution by itself, but together, they can put you on stronger footing.

Protecting people should be your foremost concern in physical security. Although you can generally replace data and equipment, you can't replace people. One of the best ways to protect them is to remove them from dangerous situations quickly. You can also implement a variety of administrative controls to keep them safe in their working environments.

Protecting data should be the next priority in a technology-based business. Make sure your data is available when you need it and that it's completely deleted when you no longer need it. Ensure its availability by keeping backups, whether by using RAID to protect against storage media failures or with removable devices, such as DVDs or magnetic tape.

Protecting your equipment, although the lowest of your priorities, is still a vital task. When selecting the location of your facility, consider relevant threats and take steps to mitigate them. Take the necessary steps to secure access to and within your facility. Lastly, maintain the environmental conditions appropriate for your equipment.

Exercises

1. What are the three major concerns for physical security, in order of importance?
2. What are the three main kinds of physical security measures?
3. Why might you want to use RAID?
4. What is physical security's most important concern?
5. What type of physical access control might you put in place to block access to a vehicle?
6. Can you give three examples of physical controls that work as deterrents?
7. Can you give an example of how a living organism might constitute a threat to your equipment?
8. Which category of physical control might include a lock?
9. What is residual data, and why is it a concern when protecting the security of your data?
10. What is your primary tool for protecting people?

10

NETWORK SECURITY

A computer network is a group of computers or other devices that are connected to
facilitate the sharing of resources. You likely
depend on a variety of networks to function
daily. Networks control and enable modern automo-
biles, airplanes, medical devices, refrigerators, and
countless other devices. Networks provide the ability
for you to communicate, navigate road systems, go to school, play games,
watch TV, and listen to music. Without a secure and stable system of networks, many of the daily conveniences that you enjoy would be made considerably more difficult to interact with or just fail to function entirely.

Your networks may face threats from attackers; they may also suffer from
misconfigurations of their infrastructure or network-enabled devices, or even
from simple outages. Most of the world is network dependent, so losing network connectivity and the services it provides can suffocate you. At worst, it
can devastate your business.

In January 2017, civil unrest in Cameroon reached a high point when large-scale protests erupted over the dominance of French in a country where both French and English are official languages. In what appears to have been an attempt to rein in the protestors, the government deliberately disconnected large, primarily English-speaking areas of the country from the global networks that comprise the internet. These regions remained offline for 93 days before the government restored access.[1] These types of outages can have wide-reaching impacts across industries, disrupting medical care, communications, employment, education, shopping, and many other aspects of people's lives.

Although the situation in Cameroon may be an extreme example, smaller network outages and other malfunctions cause serious impacts all over the world every day. Some of these problems may result from technical issues. Others may result from the specific *distributed denial-of-service (DDoS) attacks* (DoS attacks that originate from many distributed sources) I'll discuss in this chapter, or from temporary causes entirely unknown to the network users.

This chapter will cover the infrastructure and devices you can put in place to secure your networks and the methods you can use to protect the network traffic itself. You'll also learn about tools that can help verify your security.

Protecting Networks

You can use two methods to protect your networks and network resources. One option is to design your networks securely by laying them out so they're resistant to attack or technical mishap. You can also implement a variety of devices, such as firewalls and intrusion detection systems, in and around your networks.

Designing Secure Networks

By designing your networks properly, you can prevent some attacks entirely, mitigate others, and, when you fail, fail in a graceful way.

One strategy for reducing the impact of attacks is *network segmentation*. When you segment a network, you divide it into multiple smaller networks called *subnets*. You can control the flow of traffic between subnets, allowing or disallowing it based on a variety of factors or even blocking the flow of traffic entirely if necessary. Properly segmented networks can boost network performance by containing certain traffic to the portions of the network that need to see it, and they can help you localize technical network issues. Additionally, network segmentation can prevent unauthorized network traffic or attacks from reaching particularly sensitive portions of the network.

You can also secure your networks by funneling traffic through *choke points*, or locations where you can inspect, filter, and control the traffic. The choke points might be the routers that move traffic from one subnet to another, the firewalls that filter traffic through your networks or portions of your networks, or the application proxies that filter the traffic for applications such as web or email. I'll discuss some of these devices at greater length in the next section of this chapter.

Creating redundancies when designing your networks can also help mitigate issues. Certain technical failures or attacks may render portions of your technology—including networks, network infrastructure devices, or border devices such as firewalls—unusable. For example, if one of your border devices is subjected to a DDoS attack, you can't do much to stop it. You can, however, switch to a different internet connection or route traffic through a different device until you can come to a longer-term solution.

Using Firewalls

A *firewall* is a mechanism for maintaining control over the traffic that flows in and out of networks. One of the first papers to discuss the idea was "Simple and Flexible Datagram Access Controls," written in 1989 by Jeffrey Mogul,[2] then at Digital Equipment Corporation. In 1992, Digital Equipment Corporation created first commercial firewall, the DEC SEAL.[3]

You typically place firewalls at points where the level of trust changes, like the border between an internal network and the internet, as shown in Figure 10-1. You may also install a firewall on your internal network to prevent unauthorized users from accessing network traffic of a sensitive nature.

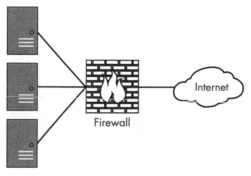

Figure 10-1: Firewall placement

Many of the firewalls in use today work by examining the *packets* (blocks of data) moving through the network to determine which ones it should allow in or out. They base their decision on a variety of factors. For example, they might allow or disallow traffic depending on the protocol being used to let web and email traffic pass but block everything else. I'll go over the types of firewalls in this section.

Packet Filtering

In packet filtering, one of the oldest and simplest firewall technologies, the firewall looks at the contents of each packet in the traffic individually and either allows or disallows it based on the source and destination IP addresses, the port number, and the protocol being used.

Since the packet filtering firewall examines each packet individually and not in concert with the rest of the packets making up the traffic, an attacker could slip attacks through this type of firewall by sending attack traffic that spans more than one packet. To find these, you need to employ more complex methods of detection.

Stateful Packet Inspection

Stateful packet inspection firewalls, or stateful firewalls, function on the same general principle as packet filtering firewalls, but they can keep track of the traffic at a granular level. While a packet filtering firewall examines an individual packet out of context, a stateful firewall can watch the traffic over a given connection. A connection is defined by the source and destination IP addresses, the ports being used, and the already existing network traffic.

A stateful firewall uses a state table to keep track of the connection state (the normal sequence of traffic) and allows traffic that is part of a new or already established connection only. This can help to prevent some intentionally disruptive attack traffic that doesn't resemble a proper and expected connection. Most stateful firewalls can also function as packet filtering firewalls, and they often combine the two forms of filtering. In addition to packet filtering features, stateful firewalls might also identify and track the traffic related to a user-initiated connection to a website, and they'll know when the connection has been closed, meaning no further legitimate traffic would be present.

Deep Packet Inspection

Deep packet inspection firewalls add yet another layer of intelligence to your firewall capabilities because they can analyze the actual content of the traffic that flows through them. While packet filtering firewalls and stateful firewalls can look at only the structure of the network traffic to filter out attacks and undesirable content, deep packet inspection firewalls can reassemble the contents of the traffic to see what it will deliver to the application for which it's destined.

To use an analogy, when you ship a package, the parcel carrier will look at the size and shape of the package, how much it weighs, how it's wrapped, and the sending and destination addresses. This is generally what packet filter firewalls and stateful firewalls do. In deep packet inspection, the parcel carrier would do all of this as well as open the package, inspect its contents, and then make a judgment about whether to ship it.

Although this technology has great promise for blocking many attacks, it also raises privacy concerns. In theory, someone in control of a deep packet inspection device could read every one of your email messages, see every web page exactly as you saw it, and easily listen in on your instant messaging conversations.

Proxy Servers

Proxy servers are special kinds of firewall that pertain specifically to applications. These servers provide security and performance features, generally for an application, such as mail or web browsing. Proxy servers can provide a layer of security for the devices behind them by serving as choke points, and they allow you to log the traffic that goes through them for later inspection. They are a single source for requests.

Many companies rely on proxy servers to keep spam from reaching their users' email accounts and lowering productivity, to keep employees from visiting websites that might have objectionable material, and to filter out traffic that might indicate the presence of malware.

DMZs

A *demilitarized zone* (DMZ) is a layer of protection that separates a device from the rest of a network. You accomplish this by using multiple layers of firewalls, as shown in Figure 10-2. In this case, the internet-facing firewall might allow traffic through to a web server sitting in the DMZ, but the internal firewall would not allow traffic from the internet through to the internal servers.

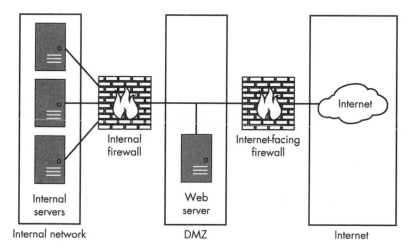

Figure 10-2: A DMZ

The DMZ creates a zone that allows public-facing servers to be accessed from the outside while both providing a measure of protection for them and restricting traffic from those servers from penetrating the more sensitive portions of your network. This helps to prevent the scenario where attackers compromise your public-facing servers and use them to attack the other servers behind them.

Implementing Network Intrusion Detection Systems

Intrusion detection systems (IDS) are hardware or software tools that monitor networks, hosts, or applications for unauthorized activity. You can classify IDS based on the way they detect attacks: signature-based detection and anomaly-based detection.

Signature-based IDS work like most antivirus systems. They maintain a database of the signatures that might signal an attack and compare incoming traffic to those signatures. In general, this method works well—except when an attack is new or has been specifically constructed to not match existing attack signatures. One of the large drawbacks to this method is that if you don't have a signature for the attack, you may not see it at all. In addition to this, the attacker crafting the traffic may have access to the same IDS tools you're using and may be able to test the attack against them to specifically avoid your security measures.

Anomaly-based IDS typically work by determining the normal kinds of traffic and activity taking place on the network. They then measure the present traffic against this baseline in order to detect patterns that aren't present in the traffic normally. This method can detect new attacks, or attacks that have been deliberately assembled to avoid IDS, very well. On the other hand, it may produce a larger number of false positives than a signature-based IDS because it might flag legitimate activity that causes unusual traffic patterns or spikes in traffic.

You can, of course, install an IDS that uses both the signature-based and anomaly-based methods, giving you some of the advantages of each type of detection. This would detect attacks more reliably, although it would perhaps operate a bit more slowly and cause a lag in detection.

You typically attach a network IDS to a location where it can monitor the traffic going by, but you need to place them carefully so the quantity of data to examine won't overloaded it. Putting a network IDS behind another filtering device, such as a firewall, can eliminate some of the obviously unwanted traffic.

Since network IDS typically examine a large amount of traffic, they can generally do only a relatively cursory inspection of it, and they may miss some types of attacks, especially those that are specifically crafted to pass through such inspections. *Packet crafting attacks* use packets of traffic that carry attacks or malicious code but are designed to avoid detection by IDS, firewalls, and other similar devices.

Protecting Network Traffic

In addition to protecting your networks from intrusion, you need to separately protect the traffic that flows over them. When you send data over networks that aren't secure or trusted, an eavesdropper can glean a large amount of information from what you send. If you use applications or protocols that don't encrypt the information they're sending, you may end up giving away your login credentials, credit card numbers, banking information, and other data to anyone who happens to be listening.

Attackers can intercept data from both wired and wireless networks, often with little effort, depending on the design of the network. But although insecure networks are a security problem, they're not an insurmountable one, if you have the right tools.

Using Virtual Private Networks

Virtual private networks (VPNs) can help you send sensitive traffic over insecure networks. Often called a tunnel, a *VPN connection* is an encrypted connection between two points. You usually create the connection using a VPN client application on one end and a device called a *VPN concentrator* on the other end—a client and server, in simple terms. The client uses the VPN client application to authenticate to the VPN concentrator, usually over the internet. Once you've established a connection, all traffic exchanged from the network interface connected to the VPN flows through the encrypted VPN tunnel.

VPNs can allow remote workers to access the internal resources of their organization; in that case, the worker's device acts as though it were connected directly to the organization's internal network.

You could also use VPNs to protect or anonymize the traffic you're sending over untrusted connections. Companies such as StrongVPN (*https://strongvpn.com/*) sell their services to the public for exactly such purposes. You might use these to keep your internet service provider from logging the contents of your traffic, stop people on the same network from eavesdropping on your activity, or obscure your geographical location and bypass location-oriented blocking. People who use peer-to-peer (P2P) file-sharing services to share pirated media sometimes hide their traffic and IP addresses with VPNs.

Protecting Data over Wireless Networks

If you use wireless networks to send your data, you face several specific security risks. Today, a wide variety of places provide free wireless internet access. In general, public wireless networks are set up without a password or encryption of any kind—measures you'd normally put in place to protect the confidentiality of the traffic flowing over the network. Even in cases where accessing a network does require a password, like in a hotel, everyone else connected to the hotel's network could potentially see your data. The present record for the range of an unamplified 802.11 wireless connection is about 238 miles.[4]

In addition, it's possible for someone to attach wireless devices to your network without your knowledge. Unauthorized wireless access points, commonly known as *rogue access points*, present a serious security issue. For example, if you worked in an area that banned wireless connections, such as a secure government facility, an enterprising individual could decide to bring in an access point of his own and install it under his desk to provide wireless access to a nearby outdoor smoking area. Although he might have good intentions, his simple action might have invalidated an entire set of carefully planned network security measures.

If the rogue access point were set up with poor security or no security at all, the well-intentioned access point installer would provide anyone within range with an easy path directly into the network that bypassed any border security in place. It's possible that a network IDS might pick up the activity from the rogue access point, but you can't guarantee that it will. A better solution to finding rogue equipment is to carefully document the legitimate devices that are part of the wireless network infrastructure and regularly scan for additional devices using a tool such as Kismet, which I'll discuss later in this chapter.

When it comes to the legitimate and authorized devices on your network, your chief method of protecting the traffic that flows through them is with encryption. You can separate the encryption used by 802.11 wireless devices—the most common family of wireless network devices—into two major categories: Wired Equivalent Privacy (WEP) and Wi-Fi Protected Access (WPA, WPA2, and WPA3). WPA3 is the current standard. Compared to the other common encryption types, WPA3 makes it easier to set up client devices and offers stronger encryption, improving protections against brute-force attacks and eavesdropping.[5]

Using Secure Protocols

One of the simplest and easiest ways you can protect your data is by using secure protocols. Many of the more common and older protocols, such as File Transfer Protocol (FTP) for transferring files, Telnet for interacting with remote machines, and Post Office Protocol (POP) for retrieving email, handle data insecurely. Such protocols often send sensitive information, such as logins and passwords, in cleartext (unencrypted data) over the network. Anyone listening on the network can pick up the traffic from such protocols and easily glean the sensitive information.

Many insecure protocols have secure equivalents, as I'll discuss at greater length in Chapter 13. In brief, you can often find a secure protocol for the type of traffic you want to carry. Instead of operating over the command line with Telnet, you can use Secure Shell (SSH), and instead of transferring files with FTP, you can use Secure File Transfer Protocol (SFTP), which is based on SSH.

SSH is a handy protocol for securing communications because you can send many types of traffic over it. You can use it for file transfers and terminal access, as mentioned, and to secure traffic in a variety of other situations, such as when connecting to a remote desktop, communicating over a VPN, and mounting remote file systems.

Network Security Tools

You can use a broad variety of tools to improve your network security. Attackers rely on many of the same tools to penetrate networks, so by using them to locate security holes in your networks, you can preemptively keep the attackers out.

An enormous number of security tools are on the market today, and many of them are free or have free alternatives. Many run on Linux operating systems and can be a bit difficult to configure. Fortunately, you can use these tools without having to set them up by installing one of the Security Live CD distributions, which are versions of Linux that come with all the tools preconfigured. One of the better-known distributions is Kali, available for download at *https://www.kali.org/*.

As I discussed in earlier chapters, the key to assessing vulnerabilities is to conduct assessments thoroughly and regularly enough that you can find the holes before the attackers do. If you perform penetration testing only on an occasional and shallow basis, you'll likely not catch all the issues present in your environment. Additionally, as you update, add, or remove the various network hardware devices and the software running on them, the vulnerabilities present in your environment will change. It's also worth noting that most of the tools you're likely to use will be capable of finding only known issues. New or unpublished attacks or vulnerabilities, commonly known as *zero-day attacks*, can still take you by surprise.

Wireless Protection Tools

As I discussed earlier in the chapter, attackers who can access your network via a wireless device could bypass all your carefully planned security measures. If you don't take steps to protect against unauthorized wireless devices, such as rogue access points, you could allow a large hole in your network security and never know it.

You can use several tools to detect wireless devices. One of the best-known tools for detecting such devices is called Kismet. It runs on Linux and macOS and can also be found on the Kali distribution. Penetration testers commonly use Kismet to detect wireless access points and can find them even when they're well-hidden.

Other tools enable you to break through the different kinds of encryption in use on wireless networks. A few of the more common ones, for cracking WEP, WPA, and WPA2, include coWPAtty and Aircrack-NG.

Scanners

Scanners, mainstays of the security testing and assessment industry, are hardware or software tools that enable you to interrogate devices and networks for information. You can divide scanners into two main categories: port scanners and vulnerability scanners. These types sometimes overlap, depending on the specific tool.

In network security, people tend to use scanners as tools for discovering the networks and systems in an environment. One of the more famous port scanners is a free tool called Nmap, short for network mapper. Although generally considered a port scanner, Nmap can also search for hosts on a network, identify the operating systems those hosts are running, and detect the versions of the services running on any open ports.

Packet Sniffers

A network or protocol analyzer, also known as a packet sniffer or just plain sniffer, is a tool that can intercept (or sniff) traffic on a network. The sniffer listens for any traffic that your computer or device's network interface can see, whether you were intended to receive it or not.

Sniffer (with a capital S) is a registered trademark of NetScout (previously Network General Corporation). I use the term sniffer in the generic sense in this book.

To use a sniffer, you have to place it on the network in a position that allows you to see the traffic you'd like to sniff. In most modern networks, the traffic is segmented in such a way that you'll likely not be able to see much of it at all (other than the traffic you generate from your own machine). That means you'll likely need to gain access to one of the higher-level network switches and may need to use specialized equipment or configurations to access your target traffic.

A classic sniffer invented in the 1980s, Tcpdump, is a command-line tool. It has a few other key features, such as the ability to filter traffic. Tcpdump runs only on UNIX-like operating systems, but Windows systems can run a version of the tool called WinDump.

Previously known as Ethereal, Wireshark is a fully featured sniffer capable of intercepting traffic from a wide variety of wired and wireless sources. It has a graphical interface, shown in Figure 10-3, and includes many filtering, sorting, and analysis tools. It's one of the more popular sniffers on the market today.

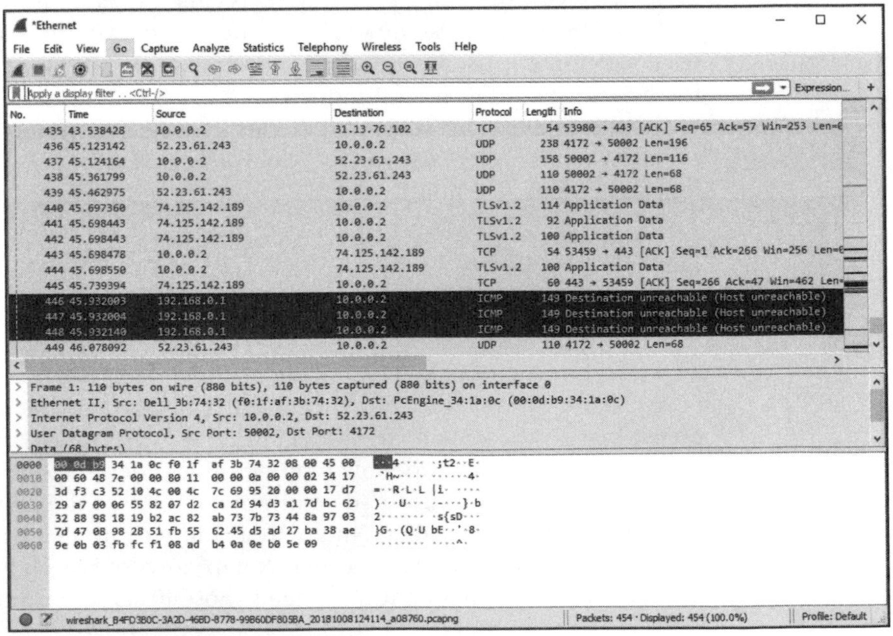

Figure 10-3: Wireshark

You can also use Kismet, a tool discussed earlier in this chapter, to sniff from wireless networks.

Packet sniffers also come in hardware form, such as the OptiView Portable Network Analyzer from Fluke Networks. Although well-equipped portable analyzers such as this may provide benefits, such as increased capture capacity and capabilities, they're often expensive, well beyond the budget of the average network or security professional.

Honeypots

A somewhat controversial tool in the network security arsenal, a honeypot is a system that can detect, monitor, and sometimes tamper with the activities of an attacker. You configure them to deliberately display fake vulnerabilities or materials that would make the system attractive to an attacker, such as an intentionally insecure service, an outdated and unpatched operating system, or a network share named "top-secret UFO documents."

When attackers access the system, the honeypot monitors their activity without their knowledge. You might set up a honeypot to provide an early warning system for a corporation, to discover an attacker's methods, or as an intentional target to monitor the activities of malware in the wild.

You can also expand honeypots into larger structures by creating networks of them, called *honeynets*. A honeynet connects multiple honeypots with varying configurations and vulnerabilities, generally with some sort of centralized instrumentation for monitoring all the honeypots on the network. Honeynets can be particularly useful for understanding malware activity on a large scale since you can reproduce a variety of operating systems and vulnerabilities.

An excellent resource for more information on honeypots and honeynets is the Honeynet Project at *https://www.honeynet.org/*. The Honeynet Project provides access to a variety of resources, including software, the results of research, and numerous papers on the subject.

Firewall Tools

In your kit of network tools, you may also find it useful to include tools that can map the topology of firewalls and help you locate vulnerabilities in them. Scapy (*https://github.com/secdev/scapy/*) is a well-known and useful tool for such efforts. It can construct specially crafted Internet Control Message Protocol (ICMP) packets that evade some of the normal measures put in place to prevent you from seeing the devices that are behind a firewall and may allow you to enumerate some of them. You can also script Scapy's abilities to manipulate network traffic and test how firewalls and IDS respond, which could give you an idea of the rules on which they're operating.

You could use some of the other tools I've discussed in this section to test the security of your firewalls, as well. You can use port and vulnerability scanners to look at them from the outside to find any ports that are unexpectedly open or any services running on your open ports that are vulnerable to known attacks. You can also use sniffers to examine the traffic that is entering and leaving firewalls, presuming that you can get such a tool in place in a network location that will enable you to see the traffic.

Summary

When you protect your networks, you should do so from a variety of angles. You should use secure network design to ensure that you've properly segmented your networks, that you have choke points to monitor and control traffic, and that you create redundancies where you need them. You should also implement security devices such as firewalls and IDS to protect yourself both inside and outside the networks.

In addition to protecting the networks themselves, you also need to protect your network traffic. To do this, you can use VPNs to secure your connections when using untrusted networks, implement security measures specific to wireless networks, and apply secure protocols.

A variety of security tools can help you keep your networks secure. When working with wireless networks, you can use Kismet. You can also listen in on network traffic with Wireshark or Tcpdump, scan for devices on your networks with Nmap, and test your firewalls using Scapy and other similar utilities. You can also place devices called honeypots on your networks specifically to attract the attention of attackers and then study them and their tools.

Exercises

1. For what might you use the tool Kismet?
2. Explain the concept of segmentation.
3. What are the three main types of wireless encryption?
4. What tool might you use to scan for devices on a network?
5. Which tools can you use to sniff traffic on a wireless network?
6. Why would you use a honeypot?
7. Explain the difference between signature and anomaly detection in IDS.
8. What would you use if you needed to send sensitive data over an untrusted network?
9. What would you use a DMZ to protect?
10. What is the difference between a stateful firewall and a deep packet inspection firewall?

11

OPERATING SYSTEM SECURITY

When you seek to protect your data, processes, and applications against concerted attacks, you're likely to find weaknesses on the operating system that hosts all of these. The *operating system* is the software that supports the basic functionality of the device. The primary operating systems in current use are several varieties of Linux and the server and desktop operating systems offered by Microsoft and Apple. If you don't take care to protect your operating systems, you have no basis for getting to a strong security footing.

You can mitigate threats to the operating system in several ways. One of the easiest methods is *operating system hardening*, or the process of decreasing the number of openings through which an attacker might reach you. You can use this technique when you're configuring hosts (individual computers or network devices) that might face hostile action.

You can also add applications to your operating system designed to combat some of the tools attackers might use against you. The most common and obvious of these, particularly on internet-facing devices, are the anti-malware tools that protect you from malicious code. The software firewalls and host-based intrusion detection systems discussed in earlier chapters can also block unwanted traffic or alert you when it passes through your systems.

Other security tools can detect potentially vulnerable areas on your hosts by finding services that you didn't know were running, locating network services known to contain exploitable flaws, and generally inspecting your systems.

By applying the concept of defense in depth and combining these efforts, you can mitigate many of the security issues on the hosts for which you're responsible.

Operating System Hardening

A relatively new concept in information security, operating system hardening is a technique that aims to reduce the number of available avenues through which your operating system might be attacked. We call the sum of these areas the *attack surface*.[1] The larger your attack surface is, the greater chance an attacker has of successfully penetrating your defenses.

You can decrease your attack surface in six main ways, as shown in Figure 11-1.

Hardening		
Remove unnecessary software	Remove unneeded services	Alter default accounts
Use principles of least privilege	Perform updates	Implement logging and auditing

Figure 11-1: The six primary means of operating system hardening

I'll walk you through each of these strategies.

Remove All Unnecessary Software

Each piece of software installed on your operating system adds to your attack surface. If you're seeking to harden your operating system, you should take a hard look at the software you load onto it and ensure that you're installing the bare minimum.

If you're preparing a web server, for instance, you'll need to install the web server software, any libraries or code interpreters needed to support the web server, and any utilities that involve the administration and maintenance of the operating system, such as backup software or remote access tools. You have no reason to install anything else.

Problems begin to arise once you install other software on the machine, even with the best of intentions. For example, let's say that one of your developers logs into the server remotely. They need to make a change to a web page, so they install the web development software they need. Then they need to evaluate the changes, so they install their favorite web browser and the associated media plug-ins, such as Adobe Flash and Acrobat Reader, as well as a video player to test some video content. Soon, not only does the system contain software that shouldn't be there, but the software quickly becomes outdated since it isn't patched or updated as a result of not being officially supported and maintained by the IT department. At this point, you have a relatively serious security issue on an internet-facing machine.

Remove All Unessential Services

In the same vein, you should also remove or disable unessential *services* (software that loads automatically when the system starts). Many operating systems ship with a wide variety of services to share information over the network, locate other devices, synchronize the time, allow you to access or transfer files, and perform other tasks. Various applications might also install some services to provide the tools and resources they need to function.

Attempting to turn off services can be a frustrating exercise, and it might take some experimentation. In many cases, the services' names don't indicate their actual function, and tracking down what each of them does may require a bit of research. One of the best ways to start is to determine the network ports on which the system is listening for network connections, as this can often give you a clue as to what might be on the back end of the open port. For instance, if the system is listening on port 80, you're likely looking for a web server service. Many operating systems have built-in utilities that allow you to do this, such as netstat on Microsoft operating systems or Nmap, discussed in Chapter 10.

In addition to locating the devices on your networks, Nmap can allow you to determine network ports on which a given system is listening. (To install Nmap, download it from *https://nmap.org/*.) Run the following Nmap command in your system's command line:

```
nmap <IP address>
```

Replace <IP address> with your device's IP address. You'll see results like those shown in Figure 11-2.

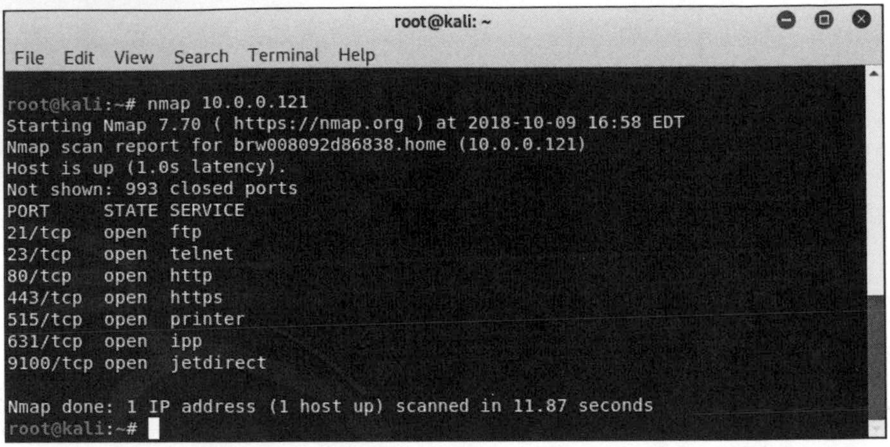

```
root@kali: ~                                    ⊖ ⊡ ⊗
File  Edit  View  Search  Terminal  Help

root@kali:~# nmap 10.0.0.121
Starting Nmap 7.70 ( https://nmap.org ) at 2018-10-09 16:58 EDT
Nmap scan report for brw008092d86838.home (10.0.0.121)
Host is up (1.0s latency).
Not shown: 993 closed ports
PORT     STATE SERVICE
21/tcp   open  ftp
23/tcp   open  telnet
80/tcp   open  http
443/tcp  open  https
515/tcp  open  printer
631/tcp  open  ipp
9100/tcp open  jetdirect

Nmap done: 1 IP address (1 host up) scanned in 11.87 seconds
root@kali:~# ▮
```

Figure 11-2: Locating services using Nmap

Figure 11-2 reveals several common services running on the system, listed here:

Port 21   File Transfer Protocol (FTP), which allows files to be transferred

Port 23   Telnet, which allows remote access to the device

Port 80   Hypertext Transfer Protocol (HTTP), which serves web content

Port 443   Hypertext Transfer Protocol Secure (HTTPS), which serves web pages secured with Secure Sockets Layer (SSL) or Transport Layer Security (TLS)

Several other ports are open as well, running services that indicate that the device in the example is a printer. You can use this information as a starting place for closing undesirable services. For example, if you didn't intend to allow remote access to the system or serve web content, you'd want to take note of the fact that ports 21, 23, 80, and 443 are open. From there, you could attempt to reconfigure it in order to not run the unneeded services.

Alter Default Accounts

Many operating systems come with standard accounts. These usually include the equivalent of a guest account and an administrator account. There might also be others, such as accounts intended for support personnel or to allow specific services or utilities to operate.

In some cases, the default accounts may come equipped with excessively liberal permissions regulating the actions they can carry out, which can cause a great deal of trouble when an informed attacker gains access to them. The default accounts might have a standard password or no password at all. If you allow these accounts to remain on the system with their default settings, attackers might be able to stroll right in and make themselves at home.

To mitigate these security risks, you should first decide whether you need these default accounts at all and disable or remove any you won't be using. You can usually turn off or remove guest accounts and support accounts without causing problems. In the case of administrative accounts, which often have names such as *administrator, admin,* or *root,* you may not be able to safely remove them from the system without causing it to malfunction, or the operating system may prevent you from doing so. However, you might be able to rename these accounts to confound attackers who attempt to make use of them. Lastly, you shouldn't leave a default password on any account, no matter its status, since those passwords are often documented and well known.

Apply the Principle of Least Privilege

As discussed in Chapter 3, the principle of least privilege dictates that you should allow a party only the absolute minimum permission needed for it to carry out its function. Operating systems may put this concept into practice to varying extents.

Most modern operating systems separate tasks into those that require administrative privileges and those that don't. In general, normal operating system users can read and write files, and perhaps execute scripts or programs, but they can do so only within a certain restricted portion of the file system. They generally can't modify the way hardware functions, make changes to the files on which the operating system itself depends, or install software that can change or affect the entire operating system. You typically need administrative access to perform those activities.

The administrators of UNIX and Linux-like operating systems tend to strictly enforce these roles. Although the administrators could allow all users to act with the privileges of an administrator, they rarely do so. On Microsoft operating systems, the exact opposite is typically true. Administrators of a Windows operating system are typically more apt to give users administrative rights. While Microsoft has gotten better at making its operating systems usable by, and useful for, nonadministrative users, there is still a large difference in mind-set between the two camps of administrators.

When you allow the average system user to regularly function with administrative privileges, you leave yourself open to a wide array of security issues. If the user executes a malware-infected file or application, they do so as the administrator, which means that the program has considerably more freedom to alter the operating system and other software installed on the host. If an attacker compromises a user's account and that account has been given administrative rights, the attacker now has keys to the entire system. Nearly any type of attack, launched from nearly any source, will have more impact when allowed access to administrative rights on a host.

If, instead, you limit the privileges on your systems to the minimum needed in order for users to perform their required tasks, you'll go a long way toward mitigating many security issues. In many cases, attacks will fail entirely when an attacker attempts to run them from a user account with a limited set of permissions. This is a cheap and easy security measure you can put in place, and it's simple to implement.

Perform Updates

To maintain strong security, you must perform regular and timely updates to your operating systems and applications. Researchers publish new attacks on a regular basis, and if you don't apply the security patches released by the operating system and application vendors to mitigate those vulnerabilities, you'll likely fall victim to attacks quickly.

To see an example of this in action, take a look at the news regarding malware propagating over the internet at any given time.[2] Many pieces of malware continue to spread by exploiting known vulnerabilities that have long since been patched by the software vendors. Although it pays to be prudent when planning to install software updates and it's a good idea to test them thoroughly before doing so, it's generally unwise to delay updating for long.

One of the most crucial times to ensure that your system is properly patched is directly after you've finished installing it. If you connect a newly installed and completely unpatched system to your network, it may become compromised in short order, even on internal networks, because it lacks the latest patches and secure configurations. The best practice in such a situation is to download the patches onto removable media and use this media to patch the system before you connect it to a network.

Turn On Logging and Auditing

Last, but certainly not least, you should configure and turn on the appropriate logging and auditing features for your system, such as those that record failed login attempts. Although the steps for configuring such services may vary slightly depending on the operating system in question and its intended use, you generally need to be able to keep an accurate and complete record of the important processes and activities that take place on your systems. You should log significant events, such as administrative privileges being exercised, users logging in to and out of the system (or failing to log in), changes made to the operating system, and similar activities.

You may also want to include additional features to supplement the tools built into the operating system for these purposes. You could install monitoring tools that alert you to issues with the system itself or anomalies that might show in the various system or application logs. You could also install supplementary logging architecture to monitor the activities of multiple machines or simply to maintain duplicate remote copies of logs outside the system to help ensure that you have an unaltered record of all activities.

It's also important to note that reviewing the logs is a vital part of the process. If you collect logs but never review them, you might as well not collect them at all.

Protecting Against Malware

A mind-boggling amount of malware exists on the world's networks, systems, and storage devices. Using these tools, attackers can disable systems, steal data, conduct social engineering attacks, blackmail users, and gather intelligence, among other attacks.

One particularly complex and impactful example of recent malware is Triton. First discovered in November 2017, it apparently attempted to subvert the mechanisms in industrial systems that respond to abnormal operating conditions and then potentially cause direct harm to them.[3] The device that Triton targets exists in a variety of systems, including nuclear facilities, and has the potential to cause catastrophic damage.

To protect your operating systems from malware, you can use some of the tools outlined here.

Anti-malware Tools

Like the intrusion detection systems discussed in Chapter 10, most anti-malware applications detect threats by either matching a file to a signature or detecting unusual activities. Anti-malware tools tend to depend more heavily on signatures than on anomaly detection (often called *heuristics* in the anti-malware field), largely because signatures are easier to write and detect more reliably. The application vendor typically updates malware signatures at least once a day, or more often if the need arises, because malware changes quickly.

When a tool finds malware, it might respond by killing any associated processes and either deleting the detected files or quarantining them so that they're not able to execute. Other times, it may simply leave the files alone. Anti-malware tools sometimes detect other security tools or files that aren't malware, which you'll want to leave alone and ignore in the future.

People generally install anti-malware tools on individual systems and servers as a matter of course or to comply with a policy. You might also find them installed on proxy servers to filter malware out of the incoming and outgoing traffic. This is common on proxies for email, as malware often uses email to propagate. The tool might reject the email entirely, strip the malware out of the message body, or remove the offending attachment.

Executable Space Protection

Executable space protection is a technology that prevents the operating system and applications from using certain portions of the memory to execute code. This means that classic attacks, such as buffer overflows (discussed in the "What Is a Buffer Overflow?" box on the next page), which depend on being able to execute their commands in hijacked portions of memory, may not function at all. Many operating systems also use *address space layout randomization (ASLR)*, a technique that shifts the contents of the memory in use around so that tampering with it is even more difficult.[4]

WHAT IS A BUFFER OVERFLOW?

A buffer overflow attack works by inputting more data than an application is expecting—for example, by entering 10 characters into a field that was expecting only 8, as shown in Figure 11-3.

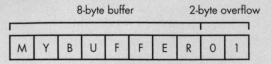

Figure 11-3: An example of buffer overflow

Depending on the application, the extra two characters might be written somewhere into memory, perhaps over memory locations used by other applications or the operating system. It's sometimes possible to execute commands by specifically crafting the excess data.

Executable space protection requires two components to function: a hardware component and a software component. The two main CPU chip manufacturers, Intel and AMD, have executable space protection components. Intel calls it the Execute Disable (XD) bit, and AMD calls it Enhanced Virus Protection.

Many common operating systems, including Microsoft's, Apple's, and several Linux distributions, implement the executable space protection software component.

Software Firewalls and Host Intrusion Detection

I've already discussed using firewalls and intrusion detection systems on the network to detect and filter out undesirable traffic. You can also add a layer of security at the host level by implementing a similar set of tools there. Although network firewalls and intrusion detection systems are usually purpose-built appliances implemented at the network, the actual functions they perform take place via specialized software resident on the devices. You can install similar software directly onto the hosts residing on your networks. In addition, using firewalls and IDS both on and off your hosts can increase your layers of security.

Properly configured software firewalls add a useful layer of security to the hosts residing on your networks. These firewalls generally contain only a subset of the features you might find on a large firewall appliance, but they're often capable of similar packet filtering and stateful packet inspection. They can range from the relatively simple versions that are built into common operating systems to large versions, intended for use on corporate networks, that include centralized monitoring and considerably more complex rules and management options.

Host-based intrusion detection systems analyze the activities on or directed at a host's network interface. They have many of the same advantages as network-based intrusion detection systems but with a considerably reduced scope of operation. As with software firewalls, these tools may range from simple consumer models to much more complex commercial versions.

A potential flaw in centrally managed host intrusion detection systems is that, for the software to report an attack to the management mechanism in real time, the information needs to be communicated over the network. If the host in question is under attack via the same network, the software may not be able to do this. You can attempt to mitigate this issue by sending a regular beacon from the device to the management mechanism, allowing you to assume that there's a problem if the beacon doesn't appear, but this might not be a complete approach, as no news doesn't always equal good news.

Operating System Security Tools

Many of the same tools you can use to evaluate your network security (discussed in Chapter 10) can help you assess the security of your hosts. For example, you can use scanners to examine how your hosts interact with the rest of the devices on the network, or you could use vulnerability assessment tools to help point out particular areas that might contain applications or services that are vulnerable to attack—or tools already in your environment that someone might use against you to subvert your security. The tools I will discuss in this section aren't an exhaustive list, but I'll hit a few of the highlights.

Scanners

You can use the scanning tools mentioned in Chapter 10 to detect security flaws in your hosts. For example, you could look for open ports and versions of services that are running, examine banners that services display upon connection to give you information about things such as the version of the software, or examine the information your systems display over the network.

Earlier in this chapter, when I discussed operating system hardening, you learned how to use Nmap to discover ports that had services listening on them. Nmap has many uses, and it can give you considerably more information—for example, specific vendor or version information. Figure 11-4 shows the results of an Nmap scan directed against a network printer using the following command:

```
nmap -sS -sU -A -v 10.0.0.121
```

```
                                    root@kali: ~                    ● ● ●
File  Edit  View  Search  Terminal  Help
| ----------    1 root      printer     0 Sep 28  2001 Sleep-----------
23/tcp  open  telnet    Brother/HP printer telnetd
80/tcp  open  http      Debut embedded httpd 1.20 (Brother/HP printer http admin)
| http-methods:
|_  Supported Methods: GET
| http-robots.txt: 1 disallowed entry
|_/
| http-server-header: debut/1.20
| http-title: Brother HL-L8350CDW series
|_Requested resource was /general/status.html
443/tcp open  ssl/http Debut embedded httpd 1.20 (Brother/HP printer http admin)
| http-methods:
|_  Supported Methods: OPTIONS
| http-title: Brother HL-L8350CDW series
|_Requested resource was /general/status.html
| ssl-cert: Subject: commonName=Preset Certificate
| Issuer: commonName=Preset Certificate
| Public Key type: rsa
| Public Key bits: 2048
| Signature Algorithm: sha1WithRSAEncryption
| Not valid before: 2000-01-01T00:00:00
| Not valid after:  2049-12-30T23:59:59
| MD5:    0012 4fc0 c0f5 f13a 8e48 e541 dcbe d76a
|_SHA-1: fbba 7f11 4078 edb6 2d6f c650 bc29 1abe 71c4 ce04
515/tcp open  printer
631/tcp open  http      Debut embedded httpd 1.20 (Brother/HP printer http admin)
| http-methods:
|   Supported Methods: GET HEAD POST TRACE OPTIONS
|_  Potentially risky methods: TRACE
| http-robots.txt: 1 disallowed entry
|_/
|_http-server-header: debut/1.20
| http-title: Brother HL-L8350CDW series
|_Requested resource was /general/status.html
Device type: bridge|general purpose
Running (JUST GUESSING): Oracle Virtualbox (96%), QEMU (94%)
OS CPE: cpe:/o:oracle:virtualbox cpe:/a:qemu:qemu
```

Figure 11-4: Nmap results

In this case, I used -sS to run a TCP SYN port scan and -sU to run a UDP
port scan. I enabled OS detection, version detection, and script scanning (-A),
and I enabled verbose output as it ran (-v). If you try this command, you'll
notice that it takes considerably longer to complete than the one I ran earlier.

In Figure 11-4, the port listing displays several extra ports, as well as quite
a bit of information about the specific services and versions that are running.
The http-title returned tells you that this is a Brother HL-L8350CDW series
printer. Armed with this information, you might have a much better chance
of successfully attacking the device in question.

YOU FOUND A WHAT?

When scanning with Nmap with OS detection enabled, you may notice that it
reports the device fingerprints found as running something odd or even wrong
entirely. Sometimes Nmap's OS fingerprints can be a little skewed, so it's often
best to verify the output from Nmap with another tool if something looks odd.

In addition to the many features built into Nmap, you can create custom Nmap functionality of your own using the Nmap Scripting Engine, which is a custom language and scripting engine that enables you to add functionality to Nmap. Nmap is a capable tool with a dizzying array of switches, features, and capabilities. Fortunately, there is also a great set of documentation to refer to at *https://nmap.org/book/man.html*.

Vulnerability Assessment Tools

Vulnerability assessment tools, which often include many of the same features found in a tool such as Nmap, attempt to find and report network services on hosts that have known vulnerabilities.

One such well-known scanning tool is OpenVAS (*http://www.openvas.org/*). You can use OpenVAS from the command line, but it also has a convenient graphical interface called Greenbone, shown in Figure 11-5. OpenVAS can conduct a port scan on a target and then attempt to determine what services (and which versions) are running on any ports it finds open. OpenVAS will then report back with a specific list of possible vulnerabilities for a given device.

Figure 11-5: The OpenVAS interface

OpenVAS includes a port scanner, which finds the listening services so you can identify vulnerabilities in them.

Exploit Frameworks

Exploits are small bits of software that take advantage of flaws in other software to cause them to behave in ways that their creators didn't intend. Attackers commonly use exploits to gain access to systems or get additional privileges on those systems. As a security professional, you can also use these tools and techniques to assess the security of your own systems so that you can fix any issues before attackers find them.

An *exploit framework* is a collection of prepackaged exploits and tools, such as network mapping tools and sniffers. These frameworks make exploits simple to use, and they give you access to a large library of them. Exploit frameworks gained popularity in the first few years of the 2000s and are still going strong. Some notable ones include Rapid7's Metasploit (shown in Figure 11-6), Immunity CANVAS, and Core Impact.

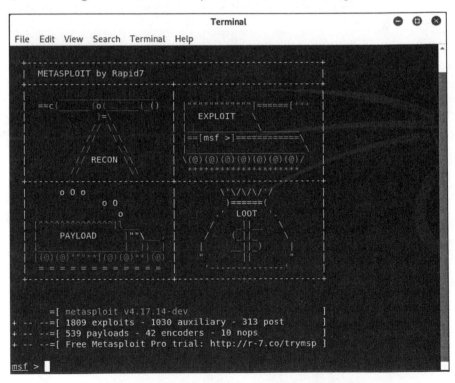

Figure 11-6: The Metasploit framework

Many exploit frameworks are graphically interfaced tools that you can run in much the same way as any other application functions. You can even configure some tools to automatically seek out and attack systems, spreading further into the network as they gain additional access.

Summary

To secure your operating systems, you can start by hardening it. Hardening involves removing all unnecessary software and services, altering the default accounts on the system, applying the principle of least privilege, updating software often, and conducting logging and auditing.

You can also implement additional software to secure your operating systems. Anti-malware tools can detect, prevent, and remove malware, and you can put firewall technology to use directly on your hosts to filter out undesirable traffic as it enters or exits your network interfaces. You can also install host intrusion detection systems to detect attacks as they come at you over the network.

Finally, you can make use of a variety of security tools to find security flaws. Several scanning tools, like Nmap, can give you information about your systems and the software running on them. Vulnerability assessment tools such as OpenVAS can locate specific security flaws in your services or network-enabled software. Additionally, you can use exploit frameworks like Metasploit to attack systems to gain access to them or to elevate your privilege levels. Using some of the same techniques that attackers use can help you to find and mitigate security issues.

Exercises

1. What does address space layout randomization do?
2. What is an exploit framework?
3. What is the difference between a port scanner and a vulnerability assessment tool?
4. Explain the concept of an attack surface.
5. Why might you want a firewall on your host if one already exists on the network?
6. What is operating system hardening?
7. What is the XD bit, and why do you use it?
8. What does executable space protection do for you?
9. How does the principle of least privilege apply to operating system hardening?
10. Download Nmap from *https://www.nmap.org/* and install it. Conduct a basic scan of *scanme.nmap.org* using either the Zenmap GUI or the command line (`nmap <IP address>` is a good place to start). What ports can you find open?

12

MOBILE, EMBEDDED, AND INTERNET OF THINGS SECURITY

So far, I've assumed that you'll be protecting information contained on traditional desktop or laptop computers. However, you'll also find vulnerable devices in your pockets, heating and air conditioning systems, security systems, hospital rooms, cars, and a dizzying array of other places. That's why your security program should include mobile devices, Internet of Things devices, and embedded devices. Internet of Things devices, such as cameras or medical devices, are any internet-connected devices that don't run a full desktop operating system. Embedded devices are computers that run inside some other device, such as the controller in a car. These technologies are often small and go unnoticed, but they densely litter our world.

In many cases, people overlook security concerns related to these devices because the devices are either ubiquitous, such as smartphones, or rarely thought about, such as medical devices. However, when they're compromised, the consequences can range from embarrassing to fatal. If attackers compromise these systems, they could steal our photo libraries, cause rolling power outages that black out half the country, or increase the dosage on our insulin pumps to issue a fatal dose.

Each of the areas I'll discuss in this chapter has its own specific security issues, some of which resemble those discussed in other chapters and some of which are entirely unique.

Mobile Security

As mobile devices become more prevalent, they also grow increasingly vulnerable to security issues. These devices have powerful hardware resources and capabilities, and they're generally connected to some kind of network at all times. They move in and out of environments with regularity and store and transmit data without notice—and don't necessarily comply with the basic security measures considered normal on standard, nonmobile computers.

Mobile devices include smartphones and tablets most likely running iOS or Android operating systems, as well as a variety of head-mounted devices and smartwatches. People use mobile devices to send and receive email, surf the web, edit documents, play videos or games, and listen to music—in short, most of the same functions as nonmobile computers.

The line between mobile devices and computers has become considerably blurred. On the one hand, some of our smartphones rival the processing power and storage capacity of computers and have similarly capable operating systems. On the other hand, some computers, like small ultrabooks and devices such as the Raspberry Pi, run on minimal hardware and use little power. Some even run mobile operating systems, such as Android. Since distinguishing between these devices becomes a question of design philosophy rather than physical capability, we should treat them the same from a security perspective.

Protecting Mobile Devices

That said, people protect mobile devices in a few specific ways. Usually, businesses will use both software and some sort of policy to maintain mobile device security.

Mobile Device Management

Many devices used in organizational environments have well-established sets of tools and features allowing you to centrally manage them. Being *centrally managed* means that these devices are under the control of one main system that maintains them. Central management lets you automatically patch vulnerabilities and upgrade software, force users to change their passwords at regular intervals, regulate and track installed software, and adjust a device's settings to a standard dictated by a particular policy.

For mobile devices, you can generally accomplish these tasks through an external management solution, a category referred to as *mobile device management*, enterprise mobility management, or unified endpoint management, depending on slight differences in features and vendors' preferences. Over time, these solutions have expanded to include desktop and server operating systems.

The exact architecture of a management solution will vary from one vendor to another, but most use an agent (a piece of software) on the mobile device to enforce a certain configuration on the device. These agents typically regulate access to a business's resources, such as email, calendaring, or network resources, and can discontinue a client's access if it becomes noncompliant, if the device is stolen, or if the user's employment is terminated. Additionally, many management solutions let you remotely wipe a device, either completely or just corporate data, or disable it entirely.

As the distinction between mobile and nonmobile devices becomes narrower, vendors of management solutions have begun to support some traditionally nonmobile devices, allowing you to remotely manage both mobile and nonmobile devices using the same tools and techniques.

Deployment Models

Most organizations have a bring-your-own-device (BYOD) policy regulating the use of personal and corporate devices in the workplace. The policy might allow only corporate-owned devices to interact with enterprise resources, personal devices only, or something in between.

Allowing only corporate-owned mobile devices can make it easier for the organization to centrally manage them. Using a mobile device management solution, you might ban the use of personal email and file-sharing apps, for instance, and disable a user's ability to install non-business-related apps. You can also force users to install updates or security patches and change their password regularly, leading to a more secure mobile environment. We typically call corporate-owned mobile devices either *corporate-owned business only (COBO)* or *corporate-owned personally enabled (COPE)*, depending on whether you can use them for personal reasons or not.

If, on the other hand, you allow personal devices only and don't manage them with mobile device management, you won't have many of these capabilities. Certain tools also provide some additional security functionality, such as allowing you to delete data remotely without actively monitoring them, but a savvy technical user may be able to subvert such measures. While a small organization with minimal resources might use this method to administer a complex mobile infrastructure, this probably wouldn't be optimal for a large enterprise.

Many organizations allow a mix of personal and corporate-owned devices and sometimes restrict some of the personal devices' capabilities. You could allow the more secure and trusted devices access to a greater set of resources, while still letting people access basic services, such as email, on their personal devices, providing they agree to have these devices managed by a management tool and accept a reasonable set of security features.

Mobile Security Issues

Mobile devices face several specific security issues. While this section is by no means exhaustive, it outlines some of the more common areas of risk.

The Baseband Operating System

Every modern mobile device contains an operating system underneath the one you can see, called the *baseband operating system*. This tiny operating system runs on its own processor and generally handles the phone's hardware, like radios, universal serial bus (USB) ports, and global positioning system (GPS). The type of baseband operating system varies based on the processor it runs on, and the operating systems are generally proprietary to the manufacturer of the device. This lack of standardization, coupled with infrequent device updates (I'll return to this momentarily), can cause vulnerabilities that last for years, often for the life of the device.

Given that the baseband operating systems work outside the view of the device's "normal" operating system, attackers can use them to carry out a variety of attacks. For example, in October 2018, attackers spied on US President Trump's cell phones via the Signaling System No. 7 (SS7) protocol[1] used by the baseband operating system and cell phone carriers for routing calls and text messages, among other things. The SS7 protocol was developed in 1975, in an era where security was not a design goal.

Unfortunately, short of an update from the device manufacturers, you can't do much to directly fix these vulnerabilities other than putting additional controls in place to compensate for them, such as additional encryption or application segmentation on the device.

Jailbreaking

Jailbreaking, or rooting, a mobile device means modifying it to remove restrictions that the device manufacturer placed on it. You typically do this to open normally inaccessible features, such as administrative access, and to install apps the device vendor hasn't approved.

Typically, you accomplish a jailbreak by conducting a series of exploits to bypass the security features of the device. For the jailbreak to persist through a reboot, you often have to disable these security features or patch the files on the device to remove them entirely. Mobile devices typically have many layers of security in place, and a persistent jailbreak typically requires punching a permanent hole all the way through to the kernel that is the core of the operating system. This, of course, leaves the device open to malicious apps and outside attacks.

When vendors release new operating systems, they include fixes to patch the holes that allowed the last jailbreak to take place. The jailbreak developers then start working on a new generation of jailbreaks as the vendor releases the next beta version of its operating system, and the cycle continues.

To stop jailbreaking on a device, you could attach it to an external management solution, which installs its own apps to provide additional security layers. Some might be able to prevent jailbreaking entirely or at least alert you about attempts to jailbreak the device. Mobile anti-malware apps may provide a measure of protection as well.

Malicious Apps

Malicious apps can compromise the security of mobile devices. Mobile apps often request a great number of privileges when they're installed; often, they can access sensitive information, log into other apps, read email, and use the network connection.

You might think you're safe if you use an unjailbroken device and download apps from the standard operating system app store, but this isn't the case. The measures that vendors put in place to keep malicious apps out of their stores are by no means foolproof. In January 2018, researchers from RiskIQ analyzed thousands of apps in the Apple and Google app stores and found hundreds of malicious cryptocurrency apps designed to steal coins from users.[2]

Worse still are apps designed especially for jailbroken devices, sourced from the shadowy back alleys of the internet. While the normal vendor app stores have security measures in place and at least some level of vetting for the apps in them, these back-alley apps have no such protections. They could do nearly anything in the background, out of site of the user interface, and you'd have no way of knowing at all.

To protect against malicious apps, you should stick to the standard app stores and avoid jailbroken devices. Apps from Apple's app store are typically more secure than those from others because Apple has a higher standard for the apps it accepts. You could also use an anti-malware app for additional protection.

Updates (or Lack Thereof)

Lastly, updates to mobile devices and their apps can cause major security problems—specifically when they don't happen.

People depend on the device manufacturer to issue updates to the primary and baseband operating systems, but these updates don't always occur in a timely manner, or at all. Typically, a manufacturer will update a device consistently for two or three years and then release new updates infrequently, or never again, because it's more profitable to sell you a new device than keep older ones up-to-date.

Apple devices tend to fare slightly better than most, but even Apple's updates become less frequent after a few years. Google, with its looser licensing of the Android operating system, typically leaves updates up to the device's manufacturer, so the experience there can vary. Additionally, the descriptions of device updates often lack specific details, so smaller updates, such as those to fix specific security issues, may be difficult to learn more about.

App updates can also be problematic. Aside from the apps the device shipped with, you have no guarantee at all that an app's creator will update the app or fix security issues, especially when it comes to smaller apps.

You can, to a certain extent, manage the update issue yourself. By carefully selecting devices from vendors that have better track records for updates over time, you can keep these devices safer for longer. Currently, devices from Apple and those sold directly by Google receive more frequent updates and operating system upgrades. For apps, the same holds relatively true—apps from larger vendors have a higher likelihood of being updated over time.

Embedded Security

An embedded device is a computer contained inside in another device that typically performs a single function. Embedded devices include everything from the computer controlling the car wash you drove through the other day to the insulin pump keeping a diabetic person healthy. Even the drivers inside some newer LED flashlights are tiny embedded devices. These devices surround us, and you'd have to go to great extremes to avoid them.

Where Embedded Devices Are Used

I've talked a little bit already about where embedded devices can be found. Now let's look at some of the more common use cases for them.

Industrial Control Systems

Industrial control systems and supervisory control and data acquisition systems commonly use embedded devices. An *industrial control system* is any system controlling an industrial process. A *supervisory control and data acquisition system* is a kind of industrial control system that specifically monitors and controls systems over long distances, often those related to utilities and other infrastructure.[3]

These systems control our water systems, nuclear power plants, oil pipelines, and a variety of other critical infrastructure. If an attacker took control of or tampered with them, the effects could reach into the physical world. Triton, discussed in the previous chapter, targeted industrial control systems. The Stuxnet virus in 2007 is another excellent example of the impact of attacks against these types of systems. Believed to have been a joint project of the US and Israeli governments, Stuxnet specifically targeted the systems controlling Iran's facilities for enriching uranium.[4] The virus tampered with the controls of the centrifuges used in the facility, causing the rotors in them to spin faster, wobbling the centrifuges until they failed. At the same time, the virus prevented the sensors detecting this activity from communicating with the safety systems that would have prevented this unusual activity.[5]

While these devices ostensibly have high levels of security, much of it is security through obscurity, a concept I've discussed in previous chapters. Industrial control systems often run on proprietary real-time operating systems (RTOSs), similar to the baseband operating systems used in mobile devices, and have many of the same security issues, for many of the same reasons.

Frequently, these devices operate on *air-gapped networks*, which have no direct network connections to the outside. The Iranian control systems that Stuxnet attacked operated on just this type of network, and this didn't save them from infection. You can bypass these controls with an infected USB drive so long as the facility's staff lacks security education.

Medical Devices

Medical devices containing embedded systems can include anything from the vital signs monitors in hospitals to the pacemakers and insulin pumps directly attached to people. Like industrial control systems, these devices commonly run RTOSs, with either minimal user interfaces or specialized interface devices required to communicate with them.

Though the cardiac device implanted in your chest to keep your heart on track may not seem like a computer with the same set of security needs as the one on your desk, it is, in fact, more closely related than might make you comfortable. In October 2018, the US Food and Drug Administration (FDA) issued a warning for patients and doctors using the Medtronic Cardiac Implantable Electrophysiology Device, a kind of pacemaker.[6] The FDA found that the programmer for the device didn't communicate securely with the manufacturer when downloading updates, potentially leaving an opening for attackers to manipulate the settings of the programmer or the device itself, including sending it modified firmware.

Such an attack could be deadly. Unfortunately, just as with other devices, lack of standardization across the industry and, to some extent, the secretive and proprietary nature of these devices leads to less secure products than the battle-hardened desktop operating systems and apps we all use regularly. These devices don't have anywhere near the number of users that the more popular operating systems have, and they aren't as easily accessible for casual poking and prodding by attackers and security researchers. You can think of them as the delicate hothouse orchids of the operating system world.

Cars

Cars can have as many as 70 embedded devices communicating over a network to run a vehicle. The network on which these devices communicate is called a *controller area network bus*. First developed in the early 1980s, the controller area network (CAN) bus has seen several revisions since, as vehicles have grown more complex and computerized.

For example, a car's airbag system makes use of the CAN bus, as crash sensors all over the car watch for impacts and communicate these events across the network to the airbag control system. The airbag control system might also ask the car's occupant detection system which seats in the car are occupied and whether the occupant is of a safe size before deploying the airbags.

Car hacking began to heat up in the security industry a few years ago, thanks to the research of Charlie Miller and Chris Valasek, among others. Miller and Valasek succeeded in remotely controlling a hacked Jeep Cherokee. They caused it to accelerate, disabled the brakes, and even took control of the steering wheel, terrifying the reporter from *Wired* who was behind the wheel at the time, despite the reporter knowing what was going on.[7]

Clearly, the consequences of such attacks can be dire. Cars surround us every time we leave the house, and it takes only a single issue like this to put many people in danger.

For a much more in-depth discussion of the CAN bus and associated devices, their security, and how to hack them, I recommend *The Car Hacker's Handbook* by Craig Smith, which goes into a lot of technical depth I don't have the space to cover here.

Embedded Device Security Issues

Embedded devices face a few specific security issues, which I'll discuss further in this section.

Upgrading Embedded Devices

The process of upgrading embedded devices can pose an interesting set of challenges. In many cases, you can't upgrade embedded devices at all, or if you can, it's often difficult to do so. Since these devices aren't typically networked, you generally can't update them automatically.

You can update some devices, such as the pacemakers discussed earlier, with a specialized external device designed to communicate with them, but this can have its challenges also. You probably can't completely reset an embedded device or take it in for service if you have an issue, like you can with smartphones or desktop computers. In the case of a pacemaker, you likely wouldn't even want to frequently update the software controlling it, as the impact of a bad update could be heartbreaking (literally).

As for the hardware, engineers typically expect any embedded hardware to last the lifetime of the device it's part of. (There are a few exceptions to this, such as the devices in industrial control systems, which typically have the support necessary to be replaced.) Short of a safety recall or a warranty repair of the larger device containing it, you're unlikely to find many options for upgrading. To protect against this vulnerability, you should be sure to keep the hardware that depends on the embedded systems up-to-date, at least to the point that the manufacturer can still repair it, although it may be costly to do so.

Physical Impacts

Not only do embedded devices often lack the necessary protections, but a compromised embedded device can have huge impacts. Earlier, I discussed the cases of the hacked Jeep and the uranium centrifuges in Iran. Those could be the tip of the iceberg. Many devices might impact human safety, even though some industries, such as those related to vehicles, medical devices, and industrial control systems, have begun to harden their embedded systems against deliberate attacks. Because of the prevalence of such systems, there are many potential targets.

Adding to the device-specific and industry-specific issues, governments could use security issues involving embedded devices in nation-state attacks. Stuxnet was the first public example of this. As embedded devices control our power, heat, water, sanitation, food production, and countless other systems, they become likely targets when disagreements between nations escalate.

Recently, both vendors and governments have started to pay more attention to these devices. Many companies, such as SANS (*https://ics.sans.org/*), now offer security training for industrial control systems that used to be very specialized.

Unfortunately, you can't do much to protect the physical world from the impacts of embedded devices, short of updates or fixes from the manufacturer. In some cases, you can try to fit a compensating control of some type to a specific situation, such as adding intervening layers of security, such as a firewall, to protect the device.

Internet of Things Security

Internet of Things (IoT) devices are prevalent, and they're becoming more so—gradually creeping into our toasters, refrigerators, and other appliances so that we can reach them from the internet. With this, of course, comes a host of security issues.

What Is an IoT Device?

In 1999, Kevin Ashton coined the term *Internet of Things* while working with the Auto-ID Center.[8] The term referred what he saw as the increasing need to provide network connectivity to track and connect a wide variety of parts and devices. Today, we use the term to refer to any device with an internet connection that doesn't run a full desktop operating system.

The term is broad, and since the world of IoT is still a bit of a frontier, many of the concepts and ideas related to it are open to interpretation. Let's talk briefly about a few of the more common IoT devices.

Printers

Although common, network printers often go unnoticed in offices and homes. We often treat them as something along the lines of a toaster, when in reality, they're complex devices with operating systems like any other computer, capable of communicating on one or more networks, and with plenty of starting places for an attacker to attempt to gain a foothold. Printers generally use an RTOS on a small embedded device, which drives the printer hardware. Hewlett-Packard LaserJet printers run LynxOS operating systems.[9] These devices listen on a variety of ports and run common services, such as FTP, Telnet, SSH, and HTTP/HTTPS, along with several services peculiar to printing devices. Additionally, they'll typically have both wired and wireless network adapters. Printers also commonly come equipped with a reasonable amount of memory and storage to support the large print jobs sent to them.

While attacks on these devices are not terribly common, they do occasionally succumb to vulnerabilities. One of the more recent ones, the KRACK vulnerability, can allow attackers to eavesdrop on traffic sent wirelessly to one of these devices and to access sensitive documents.[10]

Surveillance Cameras

Networked surveillance cameras, another common type of device, are frequently full of vulnerabilities. Some vendors develop and maintain their camera models well, but others don't. You can put together a networked camera simply by running a few services on a lightweight platform (often Linux) at a low price. Certain manufacturers create these devices with little testing, developing their product by modifying the source code of other projects.

These devices often have simple default administrative credentials, backdoors enabling unauthorized use of the device, or hordes of security vulnerabilities and misconfigurations. Malware can easily take advantage of them to conduct attacks against other devices or to serve as an entry into deeper parts of the environment.

Physical Security Devices

Physical security devices include tools such as smart locks, which connect to a network (often Bluetooth or Bluetooth Low-Energy) and allow you to open and close a lock through a mobile app or other software.

Smart locks save you the inconvenience of having to carry around a key or remember a combination. In some cases, simply bringing your mobile device within range of the lock will open the lock; you don't have to take any direct action at all. As you might expect, this doesn't always help the security of the device.

In July 2018, the company Pen Test Partners undertook research on the Tapplock (*https://tapplock.com/*) smart padlock, which you open through a mobile app. The company discovered that the unlock code sent to the device was static and replayable, meaning that, even without the associated app, you could just tell the device to unlock directly via Bluetooth and it would do so. They also learned that the unlock code relied on the MAC address broadcast by the device and could be easily calculated by an attacker.[11] To add insult to injury, another researcher discovered vulnerabilities in the API behind the Tapplock that allowed attackers to attach any lock to their account, retrieve the physical location where the app last unlocked the lock, and unlock the lock via the app.[12]

If you try to make every device into an IoT device, you'll likely face vulnerabilities such as these. Although you gain convenience from the smart lock, putting a device like a lock behind an open API literally accessible to anyone with a computer on the internet causes serious vulnerabilities. Even when you put a great deal of effort into strong security, there will always be vulnerabilities present and someone will always be there to exploit them.

THE DIFFERENCE BETWEEN EMBEDDED AND IOT DEVICES

The line between an embedded device and an Internet of Things device is a bit of a fuzzy one, and people often disagree about the definitions of each. There are, however, a few relatively high-level differences.

Embedded devices generally aren't designed for regular interactions with a person. Both devices are often wrapped up inside another device, which may have a user interface of some kind, but the embedded one usually hides behind the scenes, and it tends to have simpler interfaces that allow you to turn it on or off or make adjustments to its settings.

Also, embedded devices aren't typically connected to the internet, although some embedded devices, such as the embedded devices found in cars, are connected to internal networks. Some people might argue that providing an embedded device with an internet connection would move it into the IoT device category.

IoT Security Issues

IoT devices, of course, face several specific security issues stemming from their network connections.

Lack of Transparency

Often, you won't know exactly what your IoT devices are doing. Although they have limited user interfaces, they typically contain similar sets of features as your mobile device and desktop computer. When your IoT device is idling on the network, it could be communicating with anyone. You won't always be able to tell if it's doing something unusual or unexpected.

Unless you put specific instrumentation in place to discover what these devices are doing, you don't really have any way of answering those questions. An advanced user might be able to log into a command line interface on the device and interrogate it slightly further, but you might not be able to glean much additional information aside from tidbits of data from the file system and logs.

One way of discovering what exactly an IoT device is doing is to connect the device to a virtual private network to isolate the device (making its traffic easier to distinguish) and force it to communicate through a monitorable choke point and then use a tool such as mitmproxy (*https://mitmproxy.org/*) to eavesdrop on it and see who exactly the device is trying to talk to and what data is being sent or received. You can find this tool and accompanying scripts in the Data-Life project on GitHub (*https://github.com/abcnews/data-life/*). If the device is sufficiently chatty on the network, you'll have to sift through many results to identify the devices on the other end of the connection. You can expect to see most IoT devices communicating with a variety of other devices under normal operation. They might, for example, ask for updates from the vendor, talk to APIs, and check the time against time servers.

Everything Is an IoT Device

All sorts of appliances now ship with "smart" capabilities and network connectivity of some variety. Even lightbulbs and exercise machines talk to the internet. As I've discussed, devices have their own specific security failings, but they also face issues that arise from just having such a large mass of devices on the internet.

In October 2016, an enormous distributed denial-of-service (DDoS) attack left massive swaths of the internet unusable, including services from large providers such as Amazon Web Services, Twitter, Netflix, and CNN. These outages stemmed from DDoS attacks against Dyn, the company controlling many of the root DNS servers forming the infrastructure of the internet. The attack against these servers had a rate of 1.2 terabytes per second, at the time the largest DDoS attack ever witnessed, and came from more than 100,000 devices, almost all of which were IoT devices.[13]

The attack was possible because malware called Mirai recruited vulnerable IoT devices into a *botnet* (a network of compromised systems) and made them accessible for the controllers of the botnet to use for DDoS attacks. The malware didn't perform a complex attack; it simply looked for devices on the network and attempted to access them using their default administrative password.

Of course, users could have prevented this problem by changing the administrative password when they first configured the device, but unfortunately, users rarely do so. When wireless access points first became common, they faced similar issues. Manufacturers will likely resolve this vulnerability the same way they resolved the vulnerabilities in the wireless access points: by shipping devices in a secure state by default.

Outdated Devices

In addition to the large number of vulnerable devices on the market, the many old devices on the market cause security problems. IoT devices of some variety have existed for about 20 years now. Even if no insecure devices left any factory starting today, these old devices could remain in operation for at least the next decade.

It's not easy to add security measures to older devices. You could update the firmware to patch holes in certain devices, but this would require performing updates, which most devices don't automatically download. The many nontechnical people with IoT devices in their homes are unlikely to understand both why these devices need to be updated and how to do so.

Summary

In this chapter, I discussed mobile devices, embedded devices, and IoT devices. Each of these categories faces a particular set of potential security issues, which you can mitigate to varying extents.

When it comes to mobile devices, the baseboard operating system, jailbreaking, and malicious apps can threaten your security. However, you can take certain steps to manage mobile devices and, to a certain extent, control how people use them, particularly in corporate environments. Embedded devices, which are present in many critical systems, have the potential to cause physical impacts well beyond the device itself, while IoT devices, or devices with a network connection, are particularly difficult to monitor and secure.

From a security perspective, these devices are just as important as traditional computers, even if they're rarely considered.

Exercises

1. What is the difference between an embedded device and a mobile device?

2. What does the baseband operating system in a mobile device do?

3. How can embedded devices impact the physical world?

4. What did the Mirai botnet do?

5. What is the difference between a supervisory control and data acquisition system and an industrial control system?

6. What are the dangers of jailbreaking a mobile device?

7. What problems might you see when updating embedded devices?

8. What is the difference between an embedded device and an IoT device?

9. What common types of network connectivity might you see in an IoT device?

10. What solutions might you use to prevent a mobile device from being jailbroken?

13

APPLICATION SECURITY

In Chapters 10 and 11, I discussed the
importance of keeping your networks and
operating systems secure. Part of keeping
attackers from interacting with your networks
and subverting your operating system security is
ensuring the security of your applications.

In December 2013, the Target Corporation, a retailer operating more
than 1,800 stores throughout the United States, reported a breach of
customer data that included 40 million customer names, card numbers,
card expiration dates, and card security codes.[1] A month later, Target
announced that an additional 70 million customers had had their personal data breached.[2]

This breach didn't originate in Target's systems at all, but rather those of a vendor, Fazio Mechanical, that was connected to Target's network. Experts believe the attack to have occurred as follows:[3]

1. Attackers compromised the systems of Fazio Mechanical with a trojan (a type of malware), using a phishing attack to get it in place.

2. Because of poor network segmentation practices, the attackers were able to use Fazio's access to Target's network to gain access to other portions of the Target network.

3. Attackers installed the credit card harvesting BlackPOS malware on the Target point-of-sale (POS) systems (cash registers, basically) and used the malware to collect information from payment cards scanned by the POS.

4. Attackers moved the collected credit card numbers to compromised File Transfer Protocol (FTP) servers on the Target network and then sent them outside of the company, where they eventually ended up on a server in Russia.

5. Attackers then sold the stolen credit card and personal data on the black market.

A variety of issues at several levels allowed this attack to take place. Any one of these missing or lapsed controls—the lack of network segmentation, the lack of anti-malware tools, and the lack of data loss prevention tools— could have prevented the attack from succeeding. In this chapter, you'll look at application vulnerabilities introduced during software development, vulnerabilities commonly found in web applications, and vulnerabilities that affect the databases that applications use. I'll also discuss tools you can use to protect your applications.

Software Development Vulnerabilities

Many common software development vulnerabilities can lead to security issues in your applications. These include buffer overflows, race conditions, input validation attacks, authentication attacks, authorization attacks, and cryptographic attacks, as shown in Figure 13-1. I'll go over each kind of vulnerability in this section.

You can avoid all these vulnerabilities with relative ease when developing new software by simply not using the programming techniques that enable them to exist. The Computer Emergency Response Team at Carnegie Mellon University publishes a set of documentation that defines secure software development standards for several programming languages, and it's a good overall resource for further investigation into secure coding in general.[4]

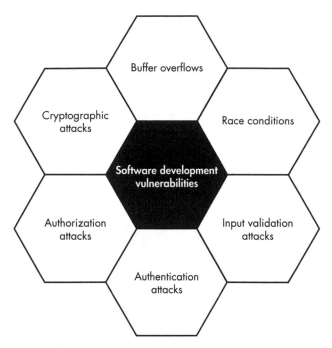

Figure 13-1: Software development vulnerabilities

Buffer Overflows

Buffer overflows, or buffer overruns, occur when you don't properly account for the size of the data input into your applications. If an application accepts data, most programming languages will require you to specify the amount of data you expect to receive and then set aside storage for that data. If you don't set a limit on the amount of data you take in (a process called *bounds checking*), you may receive 1,000 characters of input when you had allocated storage for only 50 characters.

In this case, the excess 950 characters of data may overwrite other areas in memory that are used by other applications or the operating system. Attackers might exploit this technique to tamper with other applications or cause the operating system to execute their own commands.

Proper bounds checking can nullify this type of attack entirely. Some languages, such as Java and C#, implement bounds checking automatically.

Race Conditions

Race conditions occur when multiple processes (or multiple threads within a process) control or share access to a resource and the correct handling of that resource depends on the proper ordering or timing of transactions.

For example, if you're making a $20 withdrawal from your bank account via an automatic teller machine (ATM), the process might go as follows:

1. Check the account balance ($100).
2. Withdraw funds ($20).
3. Update the account balance ($80).

If someone else starts the same process at roughly the same time and tries to make a $30 withdrawal, you might end up with a bit of a problem.

User 1	User 2
Check the account balance ($100).	Check the account balance ($100).
Withdraw funds ($20).	Withdraw funds ($30).
Update the account balance ($80).	Update the account balance ($70).

Because two users share access to the resource, the account ends up recording a balance of $70 where you should see only $50. The two users "race" to access the resource, and undesirable conditions occur. (Note that most actual banks implement measures to keep this from happening.)

Race conditions can be difficult to detect in existing software, as they're hard to reproduce. When you're developing new applications, you can generally avoid these issues if you carefully handle the way users access resources to avoid dependencies on timing.

Input Validation Attacks

If you're not careful to *validate* the input to your applications—in other words, make sure any input that users submit, such as the answers to forms, arrives in an acceptable format—you might fall victim to problems such as a format string attack.

In *format string attacks*, attackers use certain print functions within a programming language that are meant to format the output but instead allow the attacker to manipulate or view an application's internal memory. In some languages, such as C and C++, you can insert certain characters into the input, such as %f, %n, and %p, to apply formatting to the data you're printing to the screen. Attackers could, for example, include the %n (write an integer into memory) parameter in a specially crafted input to write a value into a location in memory that they might not normally be able to access. They could use this technique to crash an application or cause the operating system to run a command, potentially compromising the system.

To solve this attack, you should validate your input by filtering it for unexpected or undesirable content. In the case of the format string attack, you may be able to remove the offending characters from the input, or you could put error handling in place to ensure that you anticipate and compensate for such issues so that they don't cause a problem.

Authentication Attacks

Authentication attacks are those that attempt to gain access to resources without the proper credentials to do so. Putting strong authentication mechanisms in place in your applications will help resist these kinds of attacks.

If you require users of applications to create strong passwords, you'll help keep attackers out. If you use an eight-character, all-lowercase password, such as *hellobob*, a reasonably powerful machine may be able to break the password almost instantaneously. If you use a ten-character, mixed-case password that also includes numbers and a symbol, such as *H3lloBob!1*, the time needed to crack it increases to more than 20 years.[5] Furthermore, your applications should not use passwords that are built-in and impossible to change (often called *hard-coded* passwords).

Additionally, you should avoid performing authentication on the client side (the end user's machine), because you'd then place such measures where they may easily be attacked. As with most security measures, when you give attackers direct access to your controls to manipulate them as they please, you largely remove the effectiveness of the control.

If you depend on a local application or script to perform authentication steps and then simply send the "all clear" message to the server end, nothing prevents an attacker from repeating this message to your back end directly, without completing the authentication. Authentication efforts should always be placed as far out of reach of attackers as you can make them, and entirely on the server side, if possible.

Authorization Attacks

Authorization attacks are attacks that attempt to gain access to resources without the appropriate authorization to do so. Like authentication mechanisms, placing authorization mechanisms on the client side is a bad idea. Any process performed in a space where it might be subject to direct attack or manipulation by users is almost guaranteed to be a security issue at some point. You should instead authenticate against a remote server or on the hardware of the device if the device is portable, which gives you considerably more control.

When you're authorizing a user for some activity, you should do so using the principle of least privilege, as discussed in Chapter 3. If you're not careful to allow the minimum permissions required, both for your users and for your software, you may leave yourself open for attack and compromise.

Additionally, whenever a user or process attempts an activity that requires privileges, you should always check again to ensure that the user is indeed authorized for the activity in question, each time it's attempted. If you have a user who, whether by accident or by design, gains access to restricted portions of your application, you should have measures in place that stop the user from proceeding.

Cryptographic Attacks

Cryptography is easy to implement badly, and doing so can give you a false sense of security. One of the big mistakes when implementing cryptography in your applications is to develop your own cryptographic scheme. The major cryptographic algorithms in use today, such as Advanced Encryption Standard (AES) and Rivest-Shamir-Adleman (RSA), have been developed and tested by thousands of people who are very skilled and make their living developing such tools. Additionally, these algorithms are in general use because they have been able to stand the test of time without serious compromise. Although it's possible that your homegrown algorithm may have some security benefit, you probably shouldn't test it on software that stores or processes sensitive data.

In addition to using known algorithms, you should plan for the possibility that the mechanisms you select will become obsolete or compromised in the future. This means you should design the software in such a way to support the use of different algorithms or at least design your applications in such a way that changing them is not a Herculean task. You should also make it possible to change the encryption keys the software uses, in case your keys break or become exposed.

Web Security

Attackers can use an enormous variety of techniques to target web applications and compromise your machines, steal sensitive information, and trick you into carrying out activities without your knowledge. You can separate these attacks into two main categories: client-side attacks and server-side attacks.

Client-Side Attacks

Client-side attacks either take advantage of weaknesses in the software loaded on the user's clients or rely on social engineering to fool the user. There are many such attacks, but I'll focus specifically on some that use the web as an attack vehicle.

Cross-site scripting (XSS) is an attack carried out by placing code written in a scripting language into a web page, or other media like Adobe Flash animation and some types of video files, that is displayed by a client browser. When other people view the web page or media, they execute the code automatically, and the attack is carried out.

For example, the attacker might leave a comment containing the attack script in the comments section of an entry on a blog. People visiting the web page with their browsers would execute the attack.

Cross-site request forgery and clickjacking, two attacks mentioned in Chapter 3, are also client-side attacks. In a cross-site request forgery attack, the attacker places a link, or links, on a web page in such a way that they'll execute automatically. The link initiates an activity on another web page or application where the user is currently authenticated, such as adding items to their shopping cart on Amazon or transferring money from one bank account to another.

If you're browsing several pages and are still authenticated to the page the attack is intended for, you might execute the attack in the background and never know it. For example, if you have several pages open in your browser, including one for *MySpiffyBank.com*, a common banking institution, and you're still logged in to that page when you visit *BadGuyAttackSite.com*, the links on the attack page may automatically execute to get you to transfer money to another account. Although attackers most likely won't know which websites a user is authenticated to, they can make educated guesses, such as banks or shopping sites, and include components to target those specifically.

Clickjacking is an attack that takes advantage of your browser's graphical display capabilities to trick you into clicking something you might not click otherwise. Clickjacking attacks work by placing another layer of graphics or text over the page, or portions of the page, to obscure what you're clicking. For example, the attacker might hide a Buy Now button under another layer with a More Information button.

These types of attacks are, for the most part, thwarted by the newer versions of common browsers, such as Internet Explorer, Firefox, Safari, and Chrome. The most common attacks discussed in this section will be blocked by these automatically, but in many cases, new attack vectors simply allow for new variations of old attacks. Additionally, many clients are running on outdated or unpatched software that remain vulnerable to attacks that are years old. Understanding how the common attacks work and protecting against them not only gives you an additional measure of security but also helps you understand how attackers develop newer attacks.

It's important to keep up with the most recent browser versions and updates, as the vendors that produce them regularly update their protections. Furthermore, some browsers let you apply additional tools to protect you from client-side attacks. One of the better known of these tools is NoScript (*http://noscript.net/*) for Firefox. NoScript blocks most web page scripts by default and requires you to specifically enable those you'd like to run. When used carefully, script-blocking tools such as these can disable many of the web-based threats you're likely to encounter.

Server-Side Attacks

Several vulnerabilities on the server side of web transactions may cause problems, as well. These threats and vulnerabilities can vary widely depending on your operating system, web server software and its versions, scripting languages, and many other factors. However, these vulnerabilities are typically caused by a few common factors.

Lack of Input Validation

As discussed earlier in the chapter, software developers often neglect to properly validate user input, and some of the most common server-side web attacks use this weakness to carry out their attacks.

Directory traversal attacks present a strong example of what might happen if you don't validate input to your web applications. Attackers can use these attacks to gain access to the file system outside of the web server's structure where content is stored by using the ../ character sequence, which moves up one level of a directory to change directories. For example, browsing to *https://www.vulnerablewebserver.com/../../../etc/passwd* on a vulnerable server would display the contents of the */etc/password* file. To break this down further, this URL asks the web server to move in the file system in this fashion:

1. From */var/www/html* (where web content is normally stored)
2. To */var/www*
3. Then to */var*
4. Then to / (the root directory)
5. Then back down to */etc*
6. Then to display the contents of */etc/passwd*

If you're careful to validate the input you accept into your web applications and filter out characters that might be used to compromise your security, you can often fend off such an attack before it even begins. In many cases, filtering out special characters, such as the ones described and *, %, ', ;, and / will defeat such attacks entirely.

Improper or Inadequate Permissions

Assigning improper user permissions can often cause problems with web applications and internet-facing applications of most any kind. Web applications and pages often use sensitive files and directories that will cause security issues if they're exposed to general users.

For example, one area that might cause trouble is the exposure of configuration files. Many web applications that make use of databases (which is a clear majority of applications) have *configuration files* that hold the credentials the application uses to access the database. If these files and the directories that hold them aren't properly secured, attackers may simply read your credentials from the file and access the database as they please. For applications that hold sensitive data, this could be disastrous.

Likewise, if you don't take care to secure the directories on your web servers, you may find files changed in your applications, new files added, or the contents of some files deleted entirely. Insecure applications that are internet-facing don't tend to last long before being compromised.

Extraneous Files

When a web server moves from development into production, developers often forget to clean up any files not directly related to running the site or application, or files that might be artifacts of the development or build process.

If you leave archives of the source code from which your applications are built, backup copies of your files, text files containing your notes or credentials, or any such related files, you may be handing attackers exactly the materials they need to compromise your system. One of the final steps when rolling out a web server should be to make sure all such files are cleaned up or moved elsewhere if they're still needed. This is also a good periodic check to ensure that, during troubleshooting or upgrading, these items haven't been left behind where they're visible to the public.

Database Security

Many websites and applications in use today rely on databases to store the information they display and process. In some cases, the database applications may hold very sensitive data, such as tax returns, medical information, or legal records, or they may contain only the contents of a knitting discussion forum. In either case, the data is important to the owners of the application, and they'd be inconvenienced if it were damaged or manipulated in an unauthorized manner.

Several issues can harm the security of your databases. The canonical list includes the following:[6]

- Unauthenticated flaws in network protocols
- Authenticated flaws in network protocols
- Flaws in authentication protocols
- Unauthenticated access to functionality
- Arbitrary code execution in intrinsic SQL elements
- Arbitrary code execution in securable SQL elements
- Privilege escalation via SQL injection
- Local privilege escalation issues

Although this may seem like a horribly complex set of issues to worry about, you can break them down into four major categories, as shown in Figure 13-2. I'll cover each of these categories in detail in this section.

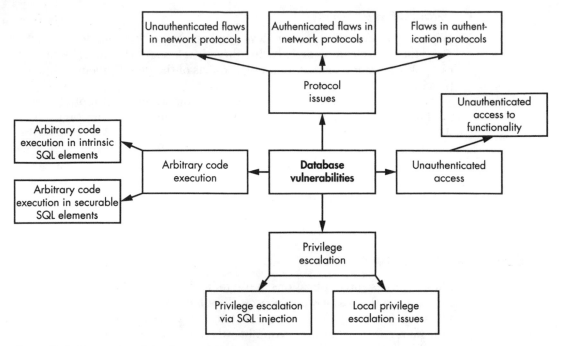

Figure 13-2: Categories of database vulnerabilities

Protocol Issues

Vulnerabilities might exist in the protocols used by any given database. This includes the network protocols used to communicate with the database. The vulnerabilities in these protocols often involve common software development issues, such as the buffer overflows discussed earlier in this chapter.

To mitigate *known* protocol issues, you should use the most current software version and patches for the database software in question, as discussed in Chapter 11. To protect your databases from *unknown* issues (issues that haven't been discovered yet), you should limit access to your databases, either by limiting who is able to connect to the database over the network, by using some of the methods discussed in Chapter 10, or by limiting the privileges and accounts you make available for the database itself, following the principle of least privilege.

You may also discover issues in the protocols used to authenticate to your database, depending on the specific software and version in use. In general, the older and more out-of-date your software becomes, the more likely it is that you're using an authentication protocol that isn't robust. Many older applications will use authentication protocols known to have been broken at some point or to have obvious architectural flaws, such as sending login credentials over the network in plaintext, which Telnet (a tool remotely accessing to a device) does. Again, the best defense here is to ensure that you're using the most current versions of all software.

Unauthenticated Access

When you give a user or process the opportunity to interact with your database without supplying a set of credentials, you create the possibility for security issues. For example, some simple queries to the database through a web interface might accidentally expose information contained in the database; or you might expose information about the database itself, such as a version number, giving an attacker additional material with which to compromise your application. You might also experience a wide variety of issues related to the secure software development practices discussed at the beginning of the chapter.

If, instead, the user or process is forced to send a set of credentials to begin a transaction, the transaction can be monitored and appropriately restricted, based on those credentials. If you allow access to part of your application or toolset without requiring credentials, you may lose visibility and control over the actions taking place.

Arbitrary Code Execution

Arbitrary code execution (also known as *remote code execution* when conducted over the network) is the ability for attackers to execute any commands on a system that they choose, without restriction. When it comes to database security, attackers are able to do this because of security flaws related to the languages you use to talk to databases. Structured Query Language (SQL) is the language used to communicate with many of the common databases currently on the market. It contains several built-in elements that can create these security risks, some of which you can limit the use of and some of which you can't.

These language elements can help facilitate bugs in the software you're using, or they can create issues if you use insecure coding practices, such as allowing attackers to execute arbitrary code within the application. For example, if the server was not appropriately and securely configured, anyone could read from and write to the file system of the server (with the load_file and outfile functions), a common ability in many database systems. Once you're able to interface with the operating system itself, you have a foothold to conduct further attacks, steal data, and so on.

Your best defenses against such attacks are twofold. From the consumer side, you should use the current versions and patch levels of all software. From the vendor side, you should mandate secure coding practices, in all cases, to eliminate the vulnerabilities in the first place, as well as conduct internal reviews to ensure that such practices are being followed.

Privilege Escalation

The last kind of major database security issue is privilege escalation. *Privilege escalation attacks* are those that increase your level of access above what you're authorized to have on the system or application. Privilege escalation is aimed at gaining administrative access to the software to carry out other attacks that need a high level of access.

You can often conduct privilege escalation through *SQL injection*, an attack in which input containing SQL commands is submitted to the application. For example, one of the more common SQL injection examples is to send the string ' or '1'='1 as the input in a username field for an application. If the application has not filtered the input properly, this string may cause it to automatically record that you've entered a legitimate username, because you have set up a condition that always evaluates to true, 1 = 1. This allows you to potentially escalate your level of privilege.

Privilege escalation in your databases can also occur if you fail to properly secure your operating system. Database applications run on the operating system, using the credentials and privileges of an operating system user, just like a web browser or any other. If you're not careful to protect your operating systems and the user accounts that run on them, as discussed in Chapters 10 and 11, any database security measures you put in place might have no effect. If attackers gain access to the account under which the database software is running, they'll likely have privileges to do anything they care to do, including deleting the database itself, changing passwords for any of the database users, changing the settings for the way the database functions, manipulating data, and so on.

Your best defenses against operating system issues such as these are the set of hardening and mitigation steps discussed in Chapter 11. If you can keep attackers from compromising your system in the first place, you can largely avoid this concern.

Application Security Tools

You can use tools to assess and improve the security of your applications. I discussed some of them, such as sniffers, in Chapters 10 and 11. Others are less familiar and more complex, such as fuzzers and reverse engineering tools. Some also require a certain amount of software development experience and familiarity with the technologies concerned to use effectively.

Sniffers

You can use sniffers to watch the specific network traffic that is being exchanged with an application or protocol. In Figure 13-3, I'm using Wireshark to examine Hypertext Transfer Protocol (HTTP) traffic specifically.

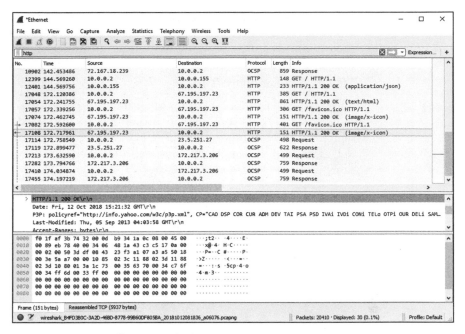

Figure 13-3: HTTP traffic in Wireshark

In some cases, you can also use tools specific to certain operating systems to get additional information from sniffing tools. A good example of this is Linux's network monitoring tool EtherApe, which enables you to not only sniff the network traffic but also easily associate the traffic you see with network destinations or specific protocols, as shown in Figure 13-4.

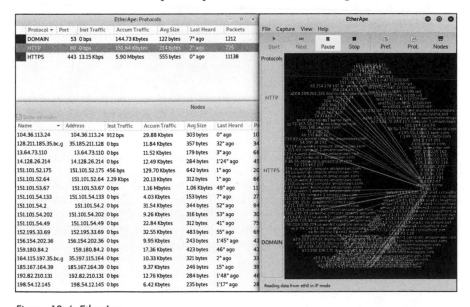

Figure 13-4: EtherApe

Often, graphical representations such as these allow you to parse data more intuitively and easily discern patterns of traffic that might otherwise go unnoticed.

Web Application Analysis Tools

A great number of tools exist for analyzing web pages or web-based applications, some of them commercial and some of them free. Most of these tools search for common flaws, such as XSS or SQL injection vulnerabilities, as well as improperly set permissions, extraneous files, outdated software versions, and many other security issues.

OWASP Zed Attack Proxy

OWASP Zed Attack Proxy (ZAP), shown in Figure 13-5, is a free and open source web server analysis tool that performs checks for many of the common vulnerabilities mentioned in this chapter.

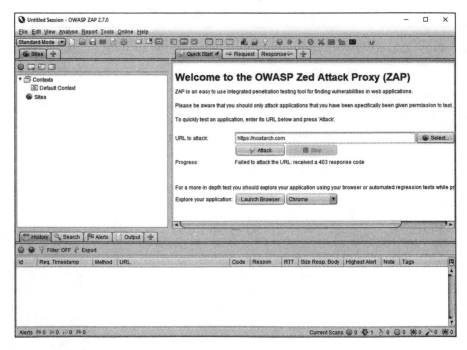

Figure 13-5: ZAP

ZAP indexes all the files and directories it can see on the target web server, a process commonly referred to as *spidering*, and then locates and reports on any potential issues it finds.

TRUST BUT VERIFY

It's important to note, when using web analysis tools, that not everything the tool reports as a potential issue will be an actual security problem. These tools almost universally return a certain number of false positives, indicating a problem that doesn't actually exist. It is important to manually verify that the issue really exists before acting to mitigate it.

Burp Suite

You can also choose from quite a few commercial web analysis tools, which vary in price from several hundred dollars to many thousands of dollars. One such tool, Burp Suite (*https://portswigger.net/burp/*), tends toward the lower end of the cost scale for the professional version ($399 per year at the time of this writing) but still presents a solid set of features. Burp Suite runs in a GUI interface, as shown in Figure 13-6, and, in addition to the standard set of features found in any web assessment product, it includes several more advanced tools for conducting more in-depth attacks.

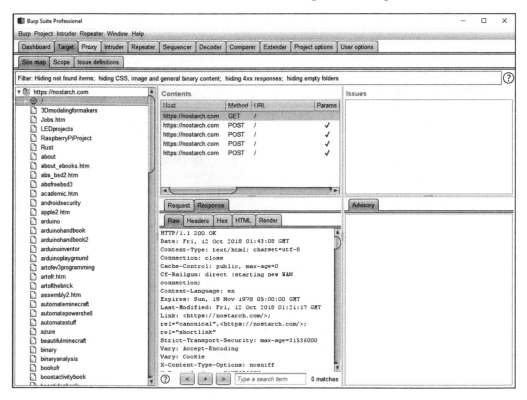

Figure 13-6: Burp Suite

Burp Suite is also available in a free community version that allows you to use the standard scanning and assessment tools but doesn't include access to the more advanced features.

Fuzzers

In addition to all the tools you can use to look over your software for various known vulnerabilities, there are tools that can help you find completely unexpected problems through a process referred to as *fuzz testing*. The tools used for this technique, called *fuzzers*, work by bombarding your applications with all manner of data and inputs from a wide variety of sources, in the hope that you can cause the application to fail or to perform some unexpected behavior.

The concept of fuzzing was first developed by Barton Miller for a graduate-level university operating system class in the late 1980s,[7] and it's become popular among security researchers and those conducting security assessments on applications. Miller's fuzzing web page at the University of Wisconsin is a great resource for further reading on fuzzing, and it includes the document that spawned this field of analysis. You can find it at *http:// pages.cs.wisc.edu/~bart/fuzz/*.

A wide variety of fuzzing tools are available; some have a specific focus, such as web applications or hardware devices, and some are more general. OWASP's fuzzing page (*https://www.owasp.org/index.php/Fuzzing*) lists many current fuzzing tools and materials.

Summary

Several common vulnerabilities, introduced during the software development process, can affect the security of your applications. You might encounter buffer overflows, race conditions, input validation attacks, authentication attacks, authorization attacks, and cryptographic attacks, just to name a few. Although such issues are common, you can resolve most of them with relative ease by following secure coding guidelines, either those internal to your organization or from external sources such as the National Institute of Standards and Technologies (NIST) or the United States Computer Emergency Readiness Team (US-CERT).

In terms of web security, you should look for client-side issues and server-side issues. Client-side issues involve attacks against the client software you're running or the people using the software. You can help mitigate these by ensuring that you're using the most current version of the software and any associated patches and sometimes by adding extra security tools or plug-ins. Server-side attacks are attacks directed against the web server itself. These attacks often take advantage of a lack of strict permissions, a lack of input validation, and the presence of leftover files from development or troubleshooting efforts. Fixing such issues requires scrutiny by both developers and security personnel.

Database security is a large concern for almost any internet-facing application. You should look out for protocol issues, unauthenticated access, arbitrary code execution, and privilege escalation. You can mitigate many of these problems by following secure coding practices, keeping up-to-date on your software versions and patches, and following the principle of least privilege.

Application security tools can help your applications resist attack. As with network and host security, you can put sniffers to use to examine the network data that enters and exits your applications. You can also use tools to examine how existing applications operate and determine what weaknesses they might have that a skilled attacker could exploit. In addition, fuzzing tools and web application analysis tools can locate vulnerabilities, whether known or unknown.

Exercises

1. What does a fuzzing tool do?
2. Give an example of a race condition.
3. Why is it important to remove extraneous files from a web server?
4. What does the tool Burp Suite do and in what situation might you use it?
5. Name the two main categories of web security.
6. Is a SQL injection attack an attack on the database or an attack on the web application?
7. Why is input validation important?
8. Explain a cross-site request forgery attack and what you might do to prevent it.
9. How might you use a sniffer to increase the security of your applications?
10. How can you prevent buffer overflows in your applications?

14

ASSESSING SECURITY

Once you've put your security measures in place, you need to make sure they're actually protecting your assets. As discussed in Chapter 6, complying with laws and regulations doesn't actually mean you're secure. Since that's the case, how can you assess the true level of your security? You have two primary vehicles for doing so: vulnerability assessment and penetration testing. In this chapter, I'll discuss these two methods.

Vulnerability Assessment

A *vulnerability assessment* is a process that uses a specially designed tool to scan for vulnerabilities. Two common vulnerability assessment tools are Qualys and Nessus. To create these tools, vendors must do a great deal of legwork to catalog vulnerabilities, determine which platforms and applications the vulnerabilities apply to, and classify them by severity. The vendors will also often provide additional information along with them about the potential impact of the vulnerabilities, how to fix them, and so on.

Because of the work that goes into keeping them up-to-date, some of these tools can be rather expensive. Since vulnerabilities are in a constant state of flux, vendors need to constantly keep up with changes to the vulnerabilities, patches being issued for them, new variants that appear, and a dizzying array of other factors in flux. Without these constant updates, these tools will quickly fall out of usefulness and be unable to detect new vulnerabilities or provide accurate information.

Ultimately, the results of a vulnerability assessment will give you only one bit of information about whether you're secure—namely, it will tell you whether there are specific known vulnerabilities existing on each of your hosts.

Conducting a vulnerability assessment takes several steps, outlined in this section.

Mapping and Discovery

To be able to scan for vulnerabilities, you need to know what devices you have in your environments. Typically, you conduct scans against groups or ranges of hosts, which change over time. If you don't have some method of keeping your lists of hosts up-to-date, you'll get incomplete scan results, or you may scan the wrong hosts entirely. This can be a particular issue with hosts in the cloud, which I'll come back to later in this chapter.

Mapping Environments

Start your vulnerability scanning efforts by creating a map of your environment that shows you what devices are present in your network. Most vulnerability scanning tools let you directly create such a map; otherwise, you can import host information from tools built specifically for this purpose, such as Nmap (*https://nmap.org/*).

Often, tools create these maps by interrogating every single IP address in the network range you're building a map for. For large network ranges, this can take a long time—perhaps more time than it will take for a host to appear and disappear again. For example, a *class A* internal network, commonly recognizable by having IP addresses in the 10.0.0.0 to 10.255.255.255 range, can hold more than 16 million IP addresses. Another common internal network scheme, a *class B* network, which commonly uses IPs that look like 192.168.0.0, can hold more than 65,000 hosts. It's not uncommon for an environment to use a class A and several class B networks for segmentation purposes. Since most tools take a second or two per IP to interrogate each address while discovering hosts, you'll be at it for a quite a while.

Performing these discovery scans can also be stressful to your network infrastructure if you're not careful to do so slowly. While mapping a network, it's entirely possible to overload network devices, such as routers and switches, to the point they become nonresponsive.

Discovering New Hosts

In addition to mapping to figure out what's there in the first place, you also need to keep your lists of hosts up-to-date. If you know the locations of any new devices on your networks, you can look in those specific places, but you may miss some hosts if they're not where you expect them to be—particularly if they've been placed somewhere odd in order to hide them.

You can actively or passively discover new hosts. *Active* discovery involves a process similar to the one used to map the network in the first place: you go IP by IP and interrogate each to see whether anything responds. This has many of the same limitations mapping does, but you could restrict these updates to portions of the network you know to contain devices, in the interest of being able to get through a network range more quickly and at shorter intervals.

You can also use *passive* scanning techniques to discover devices on the network. This often involves placing a device at network choke points, such as routers or switches, to eavesdrop on the traffic flowing through your infrastructure. In this way, you'll automatically discover devices as they talk on the network and can automatically add them to your lists of hosts to scan.

Scanning

Once you know what hosts you have, you can scan them for vulnerabilities. There are a few different types of scans you can conduct, as well as different methods you can use for each.

Unauthenticated Scans

A basic vulnerability scan of a host is typically an external and unauthenticated scan. These types of scans don't require any credentials for the host you're scanning or any access other than network connectivity to the host in question. This allows you to conduct the scan against almost any device. Depending on the settings of the scan, it will often show you what ports are open on the host in question, reveal the banner information for the services listening on those ports, and guess at the applications and operating systems in use, based on the other information gathered.

Authenticated Scans

You can also perform authenticated scans against hosts. An *authenticated scan* is one that is conducted using a valid set of credentials, generally administrative, for the system being scanned. Having credentials to log into a host will often let you collect internal information, such as what software is installed, the contents of configuration files, the permissions on files and directories, the vulnerability patches that the system needs but doesn't currently have, and other information. This gives you a considerably more thorough view of the device and its potential vulnerabilities than you can see from the outside, generating a considerably more accurate picture of the security of the device.

However, authenticated scans require you to keep your authentication credentials current, both on the vulnerability scanning tool end and on the hosts themselves. Some of the checks will also require administrative access to the device, and some system owners may be reluctant to give you credentials with this broad level of access.

Agented Scans

Agented scans can provide a means to get around some of the downsides of authenticated scans. An *agent* is a small piece of software installed on each host. The software runs as though it were a user on the system, so it's authenticated, but it doesn't require you to maintain a separate set of credentials on the device or in the vulnerability scanning tool.

Another benefit of using agents is that hosts configured with them typically report to the management devices on their own, thus removing some of the need to search for the devices individually on your networks. While it doesn't remove the need entirely, because some devices, such as network appliances, may not be able to run an agent, it should ease your burden quite a bit, as most or all the devices you expect to be present should identify themselves automatically.

Application Scanning

Some tools allow you to scan specific applications. For example, many well-developed scanners exist solely for scanning web applications. These types of scans are specific to web technologies and vulnerabilities and can search considerably more deeply in the application for issues than a scanner intended strictly for hosts would be able to find. You will often find web application scanners to be one of the more deeply developed application vulnerability scanners, and indeed there are many scanners that exist for this purpose alone. One common such scanner is Burp Suite (*https://portswigger.net/burp/*), mentioned in Chapter 13, which is a highly capable tool for both automated and manual testing of web applications.

Technological Challenges for Vulnerability Assessment

You'll likely run across a great number of technological challenges that will make it harder for you to instantiate and maintain vulnerability scanners. A few of the most common and frequent stumbling blocks are related to cloud and virtualization technologies.

The Cloud

Resources in the cloud put a bit of a twist in the tasks, processes, and technologies discussed here. As mentioned in Chapter 6, cloud providers may have some specific rules in place for what you can and can't do in their environments, and this can change from one cloud provider to the next.

When it comes to vulnerability scanning, some vendors may not want you to scan devices in their environments at all, particularly if they're using certain cloud deployment models. In most infrastructure as a service (IaaS) models, you'll likely be able to scan within certain boundaries and according to certain rules. In platform as a service (PaaS) environments, vendors may restrict you to scanning with agents, as the infrastructure itself probably won't be visible to you. In software as a service (SaaS) environments, the provider probably won't want you to scan at all.

Another consideration for cloud scanning is the fluctuating nature of the environment. Even in the case of an IaaS platform, the devices and IPs may change frequently behind the scenes, and you may accidentally find yourself scanning devices or networks no longer belonging to you. The traffic generated by external vulnerability scanning from an unknown entity is virtually indistinguishable from attack traffic, so you shouldn't accidentally point these tools at another company's resources without appropriate permission.

Containers

Another common and potentially problematic feature of cloud and virtualized environments is the container. A *container* is an entirely self-contained and ready-to-run virtualized instance, specifically designed to allow easy scaling up and down of portions of the environment seeing variable levels of load. For instance, your web server farm may see little load in the middle of the night and scale down to a few containers, as that's all they need to keep things running at that hour. In the middle of the day, the server farm may scale up to hundreds of instances and then scale up and down over the course of the day according to load.

As containers may exist one second and be gone the next, they don't work well with vulnerabilities scans on a schedule of any kind. Containers often require specialized vulnerability scanning tools to assess them for vulnerabilities.

Penetration Testing

Some people assume that vulnerability scanning is the same thing as penetration testing. While a penetration tester might use the results from a vulnerability scan, these are two different sets of activities, each with their own processes.

Penetration testing, also referred to as *pentesting* or *ethical hacking*, is the process of testing a system for vulnerabilities that an attacker could exploit. Penetration testing is a much more in-depth process than vulnerability scanning, and it's often done manually. While a vulnerability assessment may get you part of the way to assessing your security, it won't get you all the way there.

The goal of penetration testing is to find the holes in your security so you can fix them before attackers discover them. Penetration testers use the same tools and techniques as genuinely hostile hackers (called *black hat hackers*) do. But unlike black hat hackers, penetration testers have permission to conduct these activities, which means that a penetration test conducted against your own systems would, in every sense, be considered an act of cybercrime if directed against the assets of another company without their authorization.

You'll often see a penetration testing team referred to as a *red team,* a term of military origin. The red team plays the part of the attacker when evaluating the security of your systems as realistically as they can while keeping the test safe and reasonable.

The Penetration Testing Process

Penetration testing follows a relatively standard process: scoping, reconnaissance, discovery, exploitation, and reporting, as shown in Figure 14-1.

Figure 14-1: The penetration testing process

Although some descriptions of the penetration testing process might use slightly different terminology or contain more or fewer steps, the general concepts will almost always be the same.

Scoping

Before you can conduct a penetration test against anything, you need to know what it is you're testing against. The scope of your penetration test may be very open, such as "all assets of MyCompany," or it may list only individual IP addresses you can test against.

Also, the organization might restrict your testing to test or quality assurance (QA) environments only to prevent impacts on production systems. While penetration testers generally won't use intentionally damaging attacks, their tools and techniques could always have unforeseen side effects.

An organization might also provide *rules of engagement* as part of their scoping discussion. These rules may specify times of day in which testing must take place, procedures testers should follow if they uncover a severe vulnerability, and so on. These rules will vary greatly depending on the environment being tested and the specific organization.

Reconnaissance

Reconnaissance, or *recon,* is the research you conduct before attempting any attacks against a target. This can involve searching the internet for information about the target environment or company, looking through job listings for mentions of specific technologies, researching some technology you know the company to be using, and so on. Recon is often, but not always, a passive activity and falls just short of directing tools against the target environment.

Discovery

The discovery phase of the penetration test begins the active testing stage. Here, you'd likely run your vulnerability assessment tools, if you didn't already do so, and go over the results. In this step, you'd look for open ports and services on hosts to detect any running services that could be vulnerable to attack. Based on what you find here, you might conduct additional research and recon based on specific information you collected.

Exploitation

This phase involves attempting to exploit the vulnerabilities you detected in the earlier stages. This may include attacking vulnerabilities in the environment or even chaining multiple vulnerabilities together to penetrate deeper into the environment. Again, what you find here may prompt additional research and recon as you gain new information about the target or new targets become available.

Reporting

The last phase of penetration testing is reporting. Here, you carefully document what you discovered and what exact steps you need to reproduce the attacks you successfully carried out.

This step illustrates one of the key differences between vulnerability assessment and penetration testing. While vulnerability assessment may produce a potential list of vulnerabilities in the environment, the tools can't guarantee that an attacker will actually be able to exploit them. In penetration testing, the tester will report only the issues that resulted in an actionable attack against the system or have a high chance of being exploited.

Classifying Penetration Tests

You can classify penetration tests in several different ways. When testing, you can approach the test with differing levels of knowledge about the environment, from different starting places, or with different teams conducting specific portions of the test.

Black Box, White Box, and Gray Box

You'll often see penetration tests referred to as some color or level of opacity. This refers to the level of information the tester is provided with regarding the environment being tested.

In *black-box testing*, the tester has no knowledge of the environment other than the testing scope. This closely simulates a real-world attack, as presumably an outside attacker would start from this same place.

White-box testing gives the tester all the information about the environment available. This likely includes a list of all hosts, what software is in use, source code for applications and websites, and so on. While this isn't a realistic attack because an attacker likely wouldn't have access to all this information, it allows the tester to be considerably more thorough and potentially turn up issues that would have otherwise gone undiscovered.

Gray-box testing is a hybrid of the two testing types already mentioned. Here, the attacker is given some inside information about the environment, but not as much as they'd get if they were conducting a white-box test. This is one of the more common types of penetration test.

Internal vs. External

Penetration tests might also be called internal or external, which can have two different interpretations. *Internal* and *external* might refer to the kinds of access the tester is granted to the environment being tested. For example, if you give the testers access to the environment from the internet-facing portions of it only, you might call this an external pentest. Conversely, if the testers are on the same network as the environment, either physically or via a virtual private network (VPN) connection, you might call this an internal test. In this case, internal testing would probably provide a greater level of access to the environment because the testers would begin their tests inside some layers of security.

Internal and *external* might also indicate what kind of person or team is conducting the penetration test. External testing might refer to a third-party testing company hired to perform the pentest, while internal testing would likely refer to a penetration testing team working for your organization.

Targets of Penetration Tests

Penetration tests sometimes target specific technologies or environments, such as web applications, networks, or hardware. I'll discuss these in depth in this section.

Network Penetration Testing

Although the term *network penetration testing* might sound like it would apply to tests of specific network devices, such as routers or switches, it's often used as an overarching penetration testing term for the broad testing of hosts for vulnerabilities, issues specific to web applications, and even employees who might be vulnerable to social engineering attacks.

Network penetration tests tend to have broad scopes but often take place in limited time frames (also called being *time boxed*) and therefore tend to be a bit shallower than a specifically focused test because the testers might not have the time to dig into everything in the testing scope. This is one of the more common types of testing.

Application Penetration Testing

Application penetration testing, the other common type of testing, focuses directly on an application or application environment. Application testing generally involves a more specialized set of tools and skills on the part of the tester than those necessary for network penetration testing and is more focused. It can involve two differing approaches: static analysis and dynamic analysis.

Static analysis involves directly analyzing the application source code and resources. For instance, the tester might pore through the code, looking for issues such as logic errors or vulnerabilities that exist due to the specific lines of code and libraries in use. To perform static analysis, the tester must have a strong development background and grasp of the languages used.

Dynamic analysis involves testing the application while it's in operation—in other words, testing the compiled binary form or the running web application. While this doesn't give the tester the same insight into the code that static analysis does, it more closely resembles real attacks against the application.

Web application testing is common because of how often organizations use web applications and how often attackers are likely to target them. Mobile and desktop applications are also frequent targets for specific application testing, more often through static analysis techniques. These applications can make particularly easy targets for attackers, because large portions of applications and their resources sit on devices that the tester can control.

Physical Penetration Testing

Physical penetration testing involves directly testing physical security measures by, for example, picking locks or bypassing alarm systems. Like application testing, this kind of testing also requires a particular set of tools and skills to test well. It's also one of the less common kinds of test, because many organizations are more concerned with hackers penetrating their systems than they are with someone picking the lock on their office doors.

Testers often conduct physical penetration testing in conjunction with other penetration testing or to aid other testing. For example, if an attacker can get into a facility and enter a locked network closet, they may be able to plug a device into the network and leave it behind, which then allows them to perform attacks from the network itself without needing to be present.

As with any other type of penetration testing, you'll generally carry out physical penetration testing within a particular scope and with a specific goal in mind, whether you aim to get access to a data center or office or to plug your hostile device into the network.

Social Engineering Testing

Social engineering penetration testing uses the same techniques discussed in Chapter 8 and also often takes place in conjunction with other tests. Social engineering tests are so effective that the testers almost always succeed, and so many organizations refuse to allow them. To keep them from succeeding, the workplace generally needs careful preparation and good education (or they need to be paranoid).

Social engineering tests frequently involve phishing attacks, which are easy to set up and deliver to large numbers of employees. Impersonating employees and attempting to gain unauthorized access to facilities or resources are also common strategies. External audit teams often simply walk in the door of a secured area right behind someone without using a badge (remember that this is called *tailgating*). Once they've done this, they can bring a rogue piece of equipment into a building and leave it behind, as mentioned in the previous section. Many people won't ask questions about the "IT guy" who is plugging in and setting up a computer at an empty desk.

Hardware Testing

Hardware testing is a slightly more unusual kind of penetration test. It typically occurs in organizations that manufacture hardware devices, such as network gear, TVs, or IoT devices, which often make for fertile ground for penetration testers since many of their interfaces are inaccessible to common users and not terribly secure. In addition to testing the device, penetration testers often test the firmware on the device, associated mobile applications, and application program interfaces (APIs) the devices use to communicate with their associated servers.

You'll likely discover specific information about the hardware in the reconnaissance and discovery phases. This step might involve taking the device apart and looking at the markings on the components and chips inside. It's also often possible to find manufacturer specifications, which will sometimes let you access the hardware in ways the device manufacturer didn't intend.

Hardware devices are typically equipped with Universal Asynchronous Receiver/Transmitter (UART) or Joint Test Action Group (JTAG) debug ports, which are accessible on the circuit boards after you open the device. These will often provide terminal access to the device, in many cases without any sort of authentication, and you can use them to manipulate the device.

The discovery phase for hardware devices can be slightly more involved as well. Testers may investigate the firmware of the device itself, perhaps after dumping a copy of it from flash storage chips internal to the device, or they may test a module or application controlling the device or even an associated web application. The software portions of these devices can be quite complex to investigate, as they consist of the entire operating systems and all the applications running the device. Some devices, such as smartphones, may even have multiple layers of operating systems and software.

Bug Bounty Programs

In the last few years, many organizations have taken to using bug bounty programs as a kind of penetration testing. These follow essentially the same rules and process as a regular penetration test, with a slight twist.

In a *bug bounty program*, an organization offers rewards to people who discover vulnerabilities in their resources. The "bounties" typically vary based on the severity of the issues uncovered. They can range from an expression of thanks or a T-shirt to hundreds of thousands of dollars. As an example, in January 2018, Google paid a Chinese security researcher US $112,000 for a bug found in its Pixel smartphones.[1]

The organizations with bounty programs allow anyone to test within the scope they've set, and they pay the tester who finds a specific issue first according to the specified bounty. Allowing anyone in the world to hack your systems at any time might sound like a terrible idea, but these programs have enjoyed a high level of success. The risk is partly mitigated by the fact that the organizations are typically careful to spell out specific scopes for their programs, and they'll pay bounties only for issues reported within the scope specified. As a result, there typically isn't much of an incentive to conduct attacks outside of this—say, just for "joyriding."

Plenty of platforms manage bug bounty programs on behalf of other companies. Some of the better-known bug bounty platforms are HackerOne (*https://www.hackerone.com/*), Bugcrowd (*https://www.bugcrowd.com/*), and Synack (*https://www.synack.com/*). These platforms also make it easy for those wanting to participate in the programs to see what bounties are out there and what the scope and rewards are for each company.

Technological Challenges for Penetration Testing

Like for vulnerability analysis, technical challenges exist for penetration tests, which face many of the same issues.

The Cloud

The cloud also presents issues for penetration testing. One of the larger issues is that cloud providers generally don't like testers attacking their cloud infrastructure at will. Cloud providers run a tight ship from a resource perspective and don't tend to like surprise activities that use large amounts of their resources. Cloud providers will often require you to formally request permission to penetration test and conduct the test within a specific schedule, from known IP addresses, if they allow testing at all. Testers willy-nilly conducting attacks against cloud services will likely find their traffic blocked or, worse, the authorities involved.

Finding Skilled Testers

It's also often difficult to find skilled penetration testers. The difference between a highly skilled and experienced tester and a novice is huge in terms of the results you can expect. An unskilled tester may not get much further than reviewing the results the vulnerability scanning tool spit out, which will likely contain unverified false positives and miss major issues.

Getting a report from a penetration testing team with few results is often less a ringing endorsement for your amazingly tight security than a reflection of the skill level of the team doing the testing. Penetration testing skills take time and experience to develop, but penetration tests are in high demand. As a consequence, you may encounter tests conducted by testers who have no business doing so unsupervised.

Does This Really Mean You're Secure?

After you've assessed your vulnerabilities, conducted your penetration tests, and fixed all of your resulting issues and findings, are you really secure? Will the evil black hat hackers scrabble at the slick icy walls of your impenetrable security and then slink off, tails betwixt their legs? Well, probably not. There are a few caveats to everything I've discussed, and there's no such thing as being perfectly secure.

Realistic Testing

To get accurate results about your security, you need to perform realistic testing. That means you should conduct vulnerability assessments and penetration tests without impeding them or skewing the results. This is a taller order than it sounds like.

Rules of Engagement

When you set your rules of engagement for testing, they need to closely adhere to the conditions under which an outside attack would take place. The whole point of this exercise is to emulate what attackers do so you can do it first and fix what you find. If you set rules of engagement to artificially increase the level of your security, you're not doing yourself any favors. For instance, if you set a rule of engagement specifying no chaining of attacks (performing multiple attacks one after the other to penetrate more deeply), you've stopped short of exactly what an attacker would do to gain entry to the deeper portions of the environment.

Scope

For similar reasons, it's important to set a realistic scope. Yes, you must make sure that your tests don't impact production environments or degrade levels of service for customers, but organizations often use factors such as these as excuses to set an artificially narrow scope. If you're testing in a retail environment, for instance, and set the systems holding payment card data out of scope, you've just scoped out the exact thing attackers are trying to access.

In cases when you're making scoping decisions to protect production assets, you may be better off setting up a specific environment mirroring your production environment to test with impunity.

Testing Environment

If you're using a test environment for scanning or testing purposes, you should make sure it matches the production environment as close as possible. It is all too common for organizations to set up idealized, thoroughly patched, and well-secured environments for a penetration test, without taking any of the same measures in the actual production environment. Setting up a Potemkin village of an environment like this works counter to what you're trying to accomplish by performing these kinds of assessments and tests in the first place.

In these situations, it's often helpful to operate in a cloud environment. In many cases, you can exactly replicate an entire environment consisting of cloud-based hosts and infrastructure in its own segmented area, allowing you to test an environment that's identical to the production environment and then tear it down once you no longer need it.

Can You Detect Your Own Attacks?

Another way you can evaluate your level of security is to carefully watch your everyday security tools and alerting systems while running vulnerability tools and penetration tests. If you're correctly assessing your security, these activities should be almost indistinguishable from actual attacks. If you don't notice your testing taking place, you probably won't see the actual attacks coming in either. In many cases, penetration testers won't be as stealthy as attackers, so they should be even easier to catch.

The Blue Team and the Purple Team

Earlier in the chapter, we referred to penetration testers as the red team. The opposite of the red team is the *blue team*, tasked with defending the organization and catching the red team. The blue team should participate in the other side of the penetration test just as much as the red team is attacking. While you may not want to actively block attacks coming from the red team (interfering with testing is a bit of a religious discussion, as it can potentially taint the test results), you should definitely record and document the evidence of their activities. You should have evidence of every attack the red team gets through, or at least understand how it avoided your attention, so you can fix your security. The results of a penetration test make an excellent basis for requesting an additional budget for resources or tooling to cover these gaps.

You may also hear people talk about *purple teams*, which form the bridge between red teams and blue teams and help to ensure that both operate as efficiently as possible. In environments with small security teams, purple teams may also play the part of both the red team and the blue team at the same time.

Instrumentation

To catch penetration testers in the act, you must have appropriate instrumentation in place. If you don't have intrusion detection systems and firewalls you can use to watch for unusual traffic, anti-malware and file integrity monitoring (FIM) tools on systems, and so on, you'll have no source of data to watch for these kinds of attacks. The exact mix of tools that are reasonable to have in place will vary with your environment and security budget, but you can do a lot with a little if you need to do so.

At the least, you should run some of the many open source tools that function on minimal hardware and are possible to put in place with an extremely low expenditure. For example, the Security Onion distribution can get data from host intrusion detection, network intrusion detection, full-time packet capture, logs, session data, and transaction data—all on a shoestring budget.[2]

FIM TOOLS

FIM tools are used to monitor the integrity of the application and operating system files on a particular machine. Typically, you'd use FIMs to monitor only sensitive files, such as those that define configurations for the operating system or applications or hold particularly sensitive data. Once the file changes, an alert might notify someone of the changes, or in some cases, the file may automatically be reverted to its original state. FIM tools need to be carefully tuned, as they can produce a great deal of alerting "noise" if improperly configured.

Alerting

Also, of critical importance is proper alerting from your tools. You need to have good alerting so that you know when you've caught the testers. You don't want your tools muttering to themselves in the corner, completely ignored by the blue team. With proper alerting, you can respond to an attack or penetration test in close to real time.

You also need to be careful about the alerts you send. If you send too many alerts, particularly if they're false alarms, your blue team will start to ignore the alerts entirely. The common phrase for this, borrowed from the healthcare industry, is *alert fatigue*.[3] The answer to this is to carefully send actionable alerts (those that prompt a specific response) and to send as few alerts as possible.

Secure Today Doesn't Mean Secure Tomorrow

It's important to understand vulnerability assessments and penetration tests are a snapshot from a single point in time. Secure once doesn't mean secure always. You must iterate these processes regularly to maintain the usefulness of the information they produce.

Your Changing Attack Surface

An attack surface is the sum of all the points that an attacker can use to interact with your environment. It is your web servers, mail servers, hosted cloud systems, salespeople with laptops in hotel rooms, internal source code posted to public GitHub repositories, and hundreds of other similar issues. As your attack surface is composed of so many moving parts, it's in a constant state of flux. Your vulnerability assessment from a month ago or your penetration test from last year is probably no longer completely accurate— hence the need to update these at some regular interval.

Attackers Change, Too

Attackers are constantly evolving their attacks and tools, also. There are far more attackers than there are defenders, and many of the attackers have a direct monetary incentive to update their tools and techniques. Furthermore, attack tools are often sold to other hackers at a handsome profit. An entire cybercrime industry rides on keeping their tools current, at least as much as, if not more, than the security tool industry depends on defenders.

Putting in a security layer and expecting it to be just as solid and effective as the day it was installed years later is a bad bet. To cope with attackers changing, you need to change also. This cat-and-mouse game has driven the security industry for years and will continue to do so.

Technology Updates Under You

To make matters worse, your technology can change under you (and you may not even be aware of it). Many of the operating systems, mobile applications, cloud services, security tools, and code libraries you make use of regularly receive updates by those who create and maintain them. The operating system in your smart TV may have updated in the middle of last night, exposing you to attacks from the internet. It may be updated again tomorrow to fix the issue, and you probably won't know it then either.

You may find some of the security issues generated by updates during testing, or you may never know they existed at all. The best you can do in order to fend off this type of issue is to put multiple layers of security controls in place.

Fixing Security Holes Is Expensive

Finally, fixing holes in your security is expensive. It's expensive in terms of resources, the cost of purchasing and updating your security controls, and the development efforts needed to fix insecure code in your applications and websites. More often than you'd like to think, an organization will fail to prioritize security over business priorities. You might go to a great deal of effort to catalog vulnerabilities and write up penetration testing findings only to be told the critical issue you found won't be taken care of until some other work gets done. This happens often in the security world, and you'll likely find a way to put another control in place or fill the gap with a security tool. Things won't always be perfect, but you must still do what you can to make your organization secure.

Summary

In this chapter, I discussed vulnerability assessments and the tools you can use to suss out security issues in your hosts and applications. I also talked about how vulnerability assessments differ from penetration tests and why you should conduct both.

I covered penetration testing, the process of conducting one, and several of the specialized subareas of penetration testing, such as web application and hardware testing. I also talked about the challenges inherent in conducting penetration testing against cloud and virtualized environments.

Finally, I talked about whether you're really secure after going through all of the effort of vulnerability assessment and penetration testing and what it means to catch yourself testing (or not). Vulnerability assessment and penetration testing are representations of a point in time, meaning you must keep iterating over these to keep your data current.

Exercises

1. What methods can you use to detect new hosts in your environments?
2. What benefits does an agent provide when vulnerability scanning?
3. What challenges are there in vulnerability scanning for containers?
4. How is penetration testing different from vulnerability assessment?
5. How is a red team different from a blue team?
6. Why is scoping important for a penetration test?
7. What are the differences between static and dynamic analysis?
8. How is a bug bounty program different than a penetration test?
9. What impact does the environment on which you test have on your test results?
10. What is alert fatigue?

NOTES

A large portion of the articles and references in this list are freely available online through the links noted.

Chapter 1

1. Federal Information Security Modernization Act of 2002, 44 U.S.C. §3542.
2. Spafford, Eugene. "Quotable Spaf." Updated June 7, 2018. *https://spaf.cerias.purdue.edu/quotes.html.*
3. Parker, Donn B. *Fighting Computer Crime.* Hoboken, NJ: Wiley, 1998.
4. Munroe, Randall. "Password Strength." *xkcd: A Webcomic of Romance, Sarcasm, Math, and Language,* accessed July 2, 2019. *https://xkcd.com/936/.*

Chapter 2

1. Cisco, Talos Intelligence Group. "Email & Spam Data." Accessed July 2, 2019. *https://www.talosintelligence.com/reputation_center/email_rep*.

2. Pascual, Al, Kyle Marchini, and Sarah Miller. "2018 Identity Fraud: Fraud Enters a New Era of Complexity." Javelin Strategy, February 6, 2018. *https://www.javelinstrategy.com/coverage-area/2018-identity-fraud-fraud-enters -new-era-complexity/*.

3. Linux Screenshots. "Google Authenticator on Android." Flickr. July 5, 2014. *https://www.flickr.com/photos/xmodulo/14390009579/*.

4. Jain, Anil, Arun Ross, and Karthik Nandakumar. "Introduction." In *Introduction to Biometrics*, 1–49. New York: Springer, 2011.

5. Wolf, Flynn, Ravi Kuber, and Adam J. Aviv. "How Do We Talk Ourselves into These Things? Challenges with Adoption of Biometric Authentication for Expert and Non-Expert Users." Paper presented at the Association for Computing Machinery CHI Conference on Human Factors in Computing Systems, Montreal, Québec, April 21–26, 2018.

6. Eberz, Simon, and Kasper B. Rasmussen. "Evaluating Behavioral Biometrics for Continuous Authentication: Challenges and Metrics." In *Proceedings of the 2017 ACM on Asia Conference on Computer and Communications Security*. New York: ACM, 2017.

7. Greenberg, Andy. "OPM Now Admits 5.6M Feds' Fingerprints Were Stolen by Hackers," *Wired*, September 23, 2015. *https://www.wired .com/2015/09/opm-now-admits-5-6m-feds-fingerprints-stolen-hackers/*.

8. Kharitonov. "File:EToken NG-OTP.jpg." Wikimedia. August 11, 2009. *https://commons.wikimedia.org/wiki/File:EToken_NG-OTP.jpg*.

Chapter 3

1. Hardy, Norm. "The Confused Deputy: (Or Why Capabilities Might Have Been Invented)." *ACM SIGOPS Operating Systems Review* 22, no. 4 (October 1988): 36–38.

2. von Ahn, Luis, Manuel Blum, and John Langford, "Telling Humans and Computers Apart Automatically." *Communications of the ACM* 47, no. 2 (February 2004): 56–60.

3. LaPadula, Leonard J., and D. Elliott Bell. *Secure Computer Systems: Mathematical Foundations* (MITRE Technical Report 2547, Vol. 1). Bedford, MA: MITRE Corporation, March 1, 1973.

4. Biba, K.J. *Integrity Considerations for Secure Computer Systems* (MITRE Technical Report 3153). Bedford, MA: MITRE Corporation, 1975.

5. Lin, T.Y. "Chinese Wall Security Policy—An Aggressive Model." In *Proceedings of the Fifth Annual Computer Security Applications Conference*. Piscataway, NJ: IEEE, 1989.

Chapter 4

1. US Government Accountability Office. "DATA PROTECTION: Actions Taken by Equifax and Federal Agencies in Response to the 2017 Breach." August 30, 2018. *https://www.gao.gov/products/GAO-18-559*.

2. Kolodner, Jonathan S., Rahul Mukhi, Martha E. Vega-Gonzalez, and Richard Cipolla. "All 50 States Now Have Data Breach Notification Laws." Cleary Gottlieb, April 13, 2018. *https://www.clearycyberwatch .com/2018/04/50-states-now-data-breach-notification-laws/*.

3. Dictionary.com. s.v. "Audit." Accessed July 2, 2019. *http://dictionary .reference.com/browse/audit/*.

4. Scott & Scott, LLP. "BSA Audit Fine Calculator." Accessed July 2, 2019. *http://bsadefense.com/fine-calculator/*. (Registration is required to use the calculator.)

5. Business Software Alliance. "BSA End User Reward Program: Terms and Conditions." Accessed July 2, 2019. *https://reporting.bsa.org/r/report/ usa/rewardsconditions.aspx/*

6. Qualys home page. Accessed July 2, 2019. *https://www.qualys.com/*.

Chapter 5

1. US National Security Agency. "18th Century Cipher." Central Security Service, Digital Media Center, Cryptologic Machines Image Gallery. Accessed July 2, 2019. *https://www.nsa.gov/Resources/Everyone/ Digital-Media-Center/Image-Galleries/Cryptologic-Museum/Machines/ igphoto/2002138769/*.

2. US National Security Agency. "Enigma." Central Security Service, Digital Media Center, Cryptologic Machines Image Gallery. Accessed July 19, 2019. *https://www.nsa.gov/Resources/Everyone/Digital-Media-Center/ Image-Galleries/Cryptologic-Museum/Machines/igphoto/2002138774/*.

3. Crypto Museum. "Enigma-E: Build Your Own Enigma." Last modified October 15, 2017. *https://www.cryptomuseum.com/kits/enigma/index.htm*

4. Flash Enigma simulator. Accessed July 2, 2019. *https://www.enigmaco.de/*.

5. Petitcolas, Fabien. "Kerckhoffs' Principles from « La cryptographie mili-taire »." *The Information Hiding Homepage.* Accessed July 2, 2019. *http:// petitcolas.net/kerckhoffs/index.html*.

6. Jacobs, Jay. "Updating Shannon's Maxim." *Behavioral Security* (blog), May 28, 2010. *https://beechplane.wordpress.com/2010/05/28/updating -shannons-maxim/*.

7. Diffie, Whitfield, and Martin E. Hellman. "New Directions in Cryptography." *IEEE Transactions on Information Theory* IT-22, no. 6 (1976): 644–54. *https://ee.stanford.edu/~hellman/publications/24.pdf*.

8. Warburton, Dan. "Terror Threat as Heathrow Airport Security Files Found Dumped in the Street." *The Mirror,* October 29, 2017. *https://www .mirror.co.uk/news/uk-news/terror-threat-heathrow-airport-security-11428132*.

9. VeraCrypt homepage. Accessed July 2, 2019. *https://www.veracrypt.fr/*.

10. "Bitlocker." *Microsoft Docs*, January 25, 2018. *https://docs.microsoft.com/ en-us/windows/security/information-protection/bitlocker/bitlocker-overview/*.

11. Broz, Milan, ed. "DMCrypt." Updated June 2019. *https://gitlab.com/ cryptsetup/cryptsetup/wikis/DMCrypt/*.

12. Greenwald, Glenn, Ewen MacAskill, and Laura Poitras. "Edward Snowden: The Whistleblower behind the NSA Surveillance Revelations." *The Guardian*, June 11, 2013. *http://www.theguardian.com/world/2013/ jun/09/edward-snowden-nsa-whistleblower-surveillance/*.

Chapter 6

1. British Airways. "Customer Data Theft." Accessed July 2, 2019. *https://www.britishairways.com/en-gb/information/incident/data-theft/ latest-information/*.

2. FedRAMP. "FedRAMP Accelerated: A Case Study for Change within Government." Spring 2017, accessed July 2, 2019. *https://www.fedramp .gov/assets/resources/documents/FedRAMP_Accelerated_A_Case_Study_For _Change_Within_Government.pdf*.

3. FedRAMP. "FedRAMP PMO, The Federal Risk and Management Program Dashboard." Accessed July 2, 2019. *https://marketplace.fedramp .gov/#/products?sort=productName&status=Compliant*.

4. Segal, Troy. "Enron Scandal: The Fall of a Wall Street Darling." *Investopedia*, updated May 29, 2019. *https://www.investopedia.com/updates/ enron-scandal-summary/*.

5. Federal Deposit Insurance Corporation. "Privacy Act Issues under Gramm-Leach-Bliley." Updated January 29, 2009. *https://www.fdic.gov/ consumers/consumer/alerts/glba.html*.

6. InMobi. "InMobi—FTC Settlement, Frequently Asked Questions." Accessed July 2, 2019. *https://www.inmobi.com/coppa-ftc/*.

7. Davies, Jessica. "The Impact of GDPR, in 5 Charts." *Digiday*, August 24, 2018. *https://digiday.com/media/impact-gdpr-5-charts/*.

8. International Organization for Standardization. "All about ISO." Accessed July 2, 2019. *https://www.iso.org/about-us.html*.

9. Corkery, Michael, and N. Popper. "From Farm to Blockchain: Walmart Tracks Its Lettuce." *New York Times*, September 24, 2018. *https://www .nytimes.com/2018/09/24/business/walmart-blockchain-lettuce.html*.

Chapter 7

1. Haase, Kurt. "Kurt's Laws of OPSEC." *Viewpoints* 2 (1992). Wayne, PA: National Classification Management Society.

2. Haase.

3. Haase.

4. Cimpanu, Catalin. "MongoDB Server Leaks 11 Million User Records from E-marketing Service." *ZDNet*, September 18, 2018. *https://www.zdnet.com/article/mongodb-server-leaks-11-million-user-records-from-e-marketing-service/*.

5. Shodan home page. Accessed July 2, 2019. *https://www.shodan.io/*.

6. Tzu, Sun. *The Art of War*. Translated by Samuel B. Griffith. Oxford, UK: Oxford University Press, 1971.

7. Tzu.

8. Operations Security Professional's Association. "The Origin of OPSEC." Accessed October 3, 2018. *http://www.opsecprofessionals.org/origin.html* (Site discontinued).

9. Central Intelligence Agency. "George Washington, 1789–97." Center for the Study of Intelligence, March 19, 2007, updated July 7, 2008. *https://www.cia.gov/library/center-for-the-study-of-intelligence/csi-publications/books-and-monographs/our-first-line-of-defense-presidential-reflections-on-us-intelligence/washington.html*.

10. National Security Agency. *Purple Dragon: The Origin and Development of the United States OPSEC Program (Series VI, The NSA Period, Volume 2)*. Fort Meade, MD: National Security Agency, Center for Cryptologic History, 1993. Accessed July 2, 2019. *https://www.nsa.gov/news-features/declassified-documents/cryptologic-histories/assets/files/purple_dragon.pdf*.

11. SCIP home page. Accessed July 2, 2019. *https://www.scip.org/*.

12. The White House. "NSDD 298 National Operations Security Program." January 22, 1988, accessed July 2, 2019. *https://catalog.archives.gov/id/6879871/*.

13. Naval Operations Security Support Team. "Posters." US Navy, accessed July 2, 2019. *https://www.navy.mil/ah_online/opsec/posters.asp*.

Chapter 8

1. Penzenstadler, Nick, Brad Heath, and Jessica Guynn. "We Read Every One of the 3,517 Facebook Ads Bought by Russians. Here's What We Found." *USA Today*, May 11, 2018. *https://www.usatoday.com/story/news/2018/05/11/what-we-found-facebook-ads-russians-accused-election-meddling/602319002/*.

Chapter 9

1. McConnell, N.C., K.E. Boyce, J. Shields, E.R. Galea, R.C. Day, and L.M. Hulse. "The UK 9/11 Evacuation Study: Analysis of Survivors' Recognition and Response Phase in WTC1." *Fire Safety Journal* 45, no. 1 (2008): 21–34. *https://www.sciencedirect.com/science/article/pii/S0379711209001180/*.

2. Steven Musil. "Sony Delivers Floppy Disk's Last Rites." *CNET News*, April 25, 2010. *https://www.cnet.com/news/sony-delivers-floppy-disks-last-rites/.*

3. Patterson, David A., Garth Gibson, and Randy H. Katz. "A Case for Redundant Arrays of Inexpensive Disks (RAID)." In *SIGMOD'88: Proceedings of the 1988 ACM Sigmoid International Conference on Management of Data* (pp. 109–16). New York: Association for Computing Machinery. *https://dl.acm.org/citation.cfm?id=50214/.*

4. Blancco. *The Leftovers: A Data Recovery Study.* 2016. Accessed July 2, 2019. *htttps://www.blancco.com/resources/rs-the-leftovers-a-data-recovery-study/.*

5. Naval History and Heritage Command. "NJ 96566-KN The First 'Computer Bug.'" US Navy, accessed July 2, 2019. *https://www.history.navy.mil/content/history/nhhc/our-collections/photography/numerical-list-of-images/nhhc-series/nh-series/NH-96000/NH-96566-KN.html.*

Chapter 10

1. Kazeem, Yomi. "The Internet Shutdown in English-Speaking Parts of Cameroon Is Finally Over." *Quartz Africa*, April 20, 2017. *https://qz.com/africa/964927/caemroons-internet-shutdown-is-over-after-93-days/.*

2. Mogul, Jeffrey C. "Simple and Flexible Datagram Access Controls for Unix-Based Gateways." USENIX Conference Proceedings, 1989.

3. Higgins, Kelly Jackson. "Who Invented the Firewall?" *Dark Reading*, January 15, 2008. *https://www.darkreading.com/who-invented-the-firewall/d/d-id/1129238.*

4. Kanellos, Michael. "New Wi-Fi Distance Record: 382 Kilometers." *CNET News*, June 18, 2007. *https://www.cnet.com/news/new-wi-fi-distance-record-382-kilometers/.*

5. Burke, Stephanie. "Wi-Fi Alliance Introduces Wi-Fi CERTIFIED WPA3 Security." Wi-Fi Alliance, June 25, 2018. *https://www.wi-fi.org/news-events/newsroom/wi-fi-alliance-introduces-wi-fi-certified-wpa3-security/.*

Chapter 11

1. Schneider, Fred B., ed. *Trust in Cyberspace.* Washington, DC: National Academies Press, 1999.

2. Trend Micro home page. Accessed July 2, 2019. *https://www.trendmicro.com/vinfo/us/security/news/malware/.*

3. Sentryo. "Analysis of Triton Industrial Malware." March 27, 2018. *https://www.sentryo.net/analysis-of-triton-industrial-malware/.*

4. Barrantes, E.G., D.H. Ackley, T.S. Palmer, D.D. Zovi, S. Forrest, and D. Stefanovic, "Randomized Instruction Set Emulation to Disrupt Binary Code Injection Attacks." In *CCS '03: Proceedings of the 10th ACM Conference on Computer and Communications Security* (pp. 281–89). New York: Association for Computing Machinery, 2003.

Chapter 12

1. Oberhaus, Daniel. "What Is SS7 and Is China Using It to Spy on Trump's Cell Phone?" *Vice*, October 25, 2018. *https://vice.com/en_us/ article/598xyb/what-is-ss7-and-is-china-using-it-to-spy-on-trumps-cell-phone/.*

2. Browner, Ryan. "Hackers Are Using Blacklisted Bitcoin Apps to Steal Money and Personal Data, According to Research." *CNBC*, January 24, 2018. *https://www.cnbc.com/2018/01/24/hackers-targeting-apple-google-app -stores-with-malicious-crypto-apps.html.*

3. Miessler, Daniel. "An ICS/SCADA Primer." *Daniel Miessler* (blog), February 4, 2016. *https://danielmiessler.com/study/ics-scada/.*

4. Ivezic, Marin. "Stuxnet: The Father of Cyber-kinetic Weapons." *CSO*, January 22, 2018. *https://www.csoonline.com/article/3250248/cyberwarfare/ stuxnet-the-father-of-cyber-kinetic-weapons.html.*

5. Broad, William J., John Markoff, and David E. Sanger. "Israeli Test on Worm Called Crucial in Iran Nuclear Delay." *The New York Times*, January 15, 2011. *https://www.nytimes.com/2011/01/16/world/middleeast/ 16stuxnet.html.*

6. US Food & Drug Administration. "Cybersecurity Updates Affecting Medtronic Implantable Cardiac Device Programmers: FDA Safety Communication." October 11, 2018. *https://www.fda.gov/MedicalDevices/ Safety/AlertsandNotices/ucm623184.htm.*

7. Greenberg, Andy. "Hackers Remotely Kill a Jeep on the Highway— With Me in It." *Wired*, July 21, 2015. *https://www.wired.com/2015/07/ hackers-remotely-kill-jeep-highway/.*

8. McFarlane, Duncan. "The Origin of the Internet of Things." *RedBite* (blog), June 26, 2015. *https://www.redbite.com/the-origin-of-the-Internet -of-things/.*

9. Lynx Software Technologies. "HP Uses the LynxOS® Real-Time Operating System." Accessed July 2, 2019. *http://www.lynx.com/ hp-laserjet-printers/.*

10. HP Customer Support–Knowledge Base. "HP Printing Security Advisory—KRACK Attacks Potential Vulnerabilities." Hewlett-Packard, January 9, 2018, updated January 12, 2018. *https://support.hp.com/us-en/ document/c05872536.*

11. Tierney, Andrew. "Totally Pwning the Tapplock Smart Lock." Pen Test Partners, June 13, 2018. *https://www.pentestpartners.com/security-blog/ totally-pwning-the-tapplock-smart-lock/.*

12. Stykas, Vangelis. "Totally Pwning the Tapplock Smart Lock (the API Way)." *Medium*, June 15, 2018. *https://medium.com/@evstykas/ totally-pwning-the-tapplock-smart-lock-the-api-way-c8d89915f025/.*

13. Woolfe, Nicky. "DDoS Attack That Disrupted Internet Was Largest of Its Kind in History, Experts Say." *The Guardian*, October 26, 2016. *https:// www.theguardian.com/technology/2016/oct/26/ddos-attack-dyn-mirai-botnet/.*

Chapter 13

1. Target. "Target Confirms Unauthorized Access to Payment Card Data in U.S. Stores." Press release, December 19, 2013. *https://corporate.target .com/press/releases/2013/12/target-confirms-unauthorized-access-to-payment-car/.*

2. Target. "Target Provides Update on Data Breach and Financial Performance." Press release, January 10, 2014. *https://corporate.target.com/ press/releases/2014/01/target-provides-update-on-data-breach-and-financia/.*

3. Shu, Xiaokui, Ke Tian, Andrew Ciambrone, and Danfeng Yao. "Breaking the Target: An Analysis of Target Data Breach and Lessons Learned." arXiv, January 18, 2017, accessed July 2, 2019. *https://arxiv.org/ pdf/1701.04940.pdf.*

4. Schiela, Robert. "SEI CERT Coding Standards." Confluence: Carnegie Mellon University Software Engineering Institute, February 5, 2019. *https://wiki.sei.cmu.edu/confluence/display/seccode/SEI+CERT+Coding +Standards/.*

5. Gibson Research Corporation. "How Big is Your Haystack?". Accessed August 2, 2019. *https://www.grc.com/haystack.htm/.*

6. Litchfield, David, Chris Anley, John Heasman, and Bill Grindlay. *The Database Hacker's Handbook: Defending Database Servers.* Hoboken, NJ: Wiley, 2005.

7. Miller, Bart. "Computer Sciences Department, University of Wisconsin–Madison, CS 736, Fall 1998, Project List" (syllabus). Accessed July 2, 2019. *http://pages.cs.wisc.edu/~bart/fuzz/CS736-Projects-f1988.pdf.*

Chapter 14

1. Hartmans, Avery. "A Superstar Chinese Hacker Just Won $112,000 from Google, Its Largest Bug Bounty Ever." *Business Insider,* January 20, 2018. *https://www.businessinsider.com/guang-gong-qihoo-360-google-pixel-2-hacking -bug-bounty-2018-1.*

2. Security Onion homepage. Accessed July 2, 2019. *https://securityonion.net/.*

3. Ryznar, Barbara A. "Alert Fatigue: An Unintended Consequence." *Illuminating Informatics* (blog). *Journal of AHIMA,* July 3, 2018. *http:// journal.ahima.org/2018/07/03/alert-fatigue-an-unintended-consequence/.*

INDEX

bring-your-own-device (BYOD) policies, 161
browsers, 179
brute forcing, 68
buffer overflows, 151–152, 175
bug bounty programs, 200–201
Bugcrowd, 201
bugs, 130
Burp Suite, 187–188, 194
business competition, 103
business continuity planning (BCP), 122
Business Software Alliance (BSA), 56

C

Caesar cipher, 62
cameras, 168
Cameroon, 134
capabilities, 42–43
CAPTCHAs, 45
The Car Hacker's Handbook (Smith), 166
cars, 165–166
central management, 159–161
certificate authority, 73
certificates, 73–74
chain of custody, 55
Children's Internet Protection Act (CIPA) (2000), 86
Children's Online Privacy Protection Act (COPPA) (1988), 86
Chinese Wall model, 47–48
choke points, 134, 169, 193
Cisco, 25
class A and class B internal networks, 192
clean desk policies, 119
cleartext, 61
clickjacking, 42, 178–179
client-side attacks, 41, 178–179
cloud computing, 89–91, 194–195, 201
code, 183
collision, 72
compensating controls, 82
competitive intelligence and competitive counterintelligence, 103
Competitive Strategy: Techniques for Analyzing Industries and Competitors (Porter), 103
compliance. *See also* laws and regulations
    controls for achieving, 81–82
    frameworks for, 87–89
    maintaining, 82–83
    overview, 79–81
    technological changes and, 89–92

confidentiality, 5, 7
confidentiality, integrity, and availability (CIA) triad, 4–6, 8
configuration files, 180
confused deputy problem, 41
containers, 195
controller area network (CAN) bus, 165–166
controls, 14
corporate-owned business only (COBO) and corporate-owned personally enabled (COPE) mobile devices, 161
Cotton, Gerald, 92
countermeasures, 98
critical information assets, 96
cross-site request forgery (CSRF), 41–42, 178–179
cross-site scripting (XSS), 178
cryptocurrencies, 92, 163
cryptography
    algorithms, 61–66
    asymmetric key cryptography, 70–71
    attacks, 178
    elliptic curve cryptography (ECC), 71
    history of, 62–66
    keyless cryptography, 71–72
    overview, 61
    symmetric key cryptography, 68–69
    tools for, 67–74
    uses of, 74–77
cyber intelligence/digital network intelligence (CYBINT/DNINT), 114

D

data
    protection of, 127–129
    at rest and in motion, 9, 74–77
    storage of, 7, 128–129
databases, 181–184
Data-Life project, 169
deep packet inspection firewalls, 136
default accounts, 148–149
defense in depth strategy, 17–20
demilitarized zones (DMZs), 137
denial-of-service (DoS) attacks, 5
DES, 69–70
detective controls, 123–124
deterrence, 54

deterrent controls, 123
Diffie, Whitfield, 70
digital certificates, 73–74
digital network intelligence (DNINT), 114
digital signatures, 72–73
directory traversal attacks, 180
disaster recovery planning (DRP), 122
disclosure, alteration, and denial (DAD), 5. *See also* confidentiality, integrity, and availability (CIA) triad
discretionary access control (DAC) model, 43
distributed denial-of-service (DDoS) attacks, 170
DMZs (demilitarized zones), 137
dongles, 32
dynamic analysis, 199

E

Ecole de Guerre Economique (Economic Warfare School), 103
electronic intelligence (ELINT), 114
electronic protected health information (e-PHI), 85
elliptic curve cryptography (ECC), 71
embedded devices, 164–167, 169
encryption, 61, 70, 178
energy anomalies, 125
Enhanced Virus Protection, 152
Enigma machine, 64–65
enterprise mobility management, 161
environmental attributes, 45
equal error rates (EERs), 31
Equifax, 53
equipment, 129–132
EtherApe, 185
Ethereal, 142
ethical hacking, 195–200
evacuations, 126–127
executable space protection, 151–152
Execute Disable (XD) bit, 152
EXIF data, 111–112
exploit frameworks, 156

F

fabrication attacks, 10
Facebook, 109

factors, 26–27
false acceptance rates (FARs) and false rejection rates (FRRs), 31
falsified information, 25
Family Educational Rights and Privacy Act (FERPA) (1974), 86
Fazio Mechanical, 174
Federal Information Security Management Act (FISMA) (2002), 4, 84
Federal Risk and Authorization Management Program (FedRAMP), 85
Fighting Computer Crime (Parker), 6, 122
file metadata, 111
file system ACLs, 38–39
FIM (file integrity monitoring) tools, 203–204
financial intelligence (FININT), 114
fingerprints, 29–30. *See also* biometrics
firewalls, 135–137, 143–144, 152–153
flash media, 128
forensic investigations, 111
format string attacks, 176
frequency analysis, 67
FTP (File Transfer Protocol), 140
full disk encryption, 75
fuzzers, 188

G

General Data Protection Regulation (GDPR) (2018), 87
geospatial intelligence (GEOINT), 113
GitHub, 169
Global Positioning System (GPS) information, 112
Google, 110–111, 163, 200
Gramm–Leach–Bliley Act (GLBA) (1999), 86
gray-box testing, 198
Greenbone, 155
group permissions, 39

H

Haase, Kurt, 99
HackerOne, 201
hard-coded passwords, 177
hardware devices, 200
hardware tokens, 32–33
hash functions, 71–72

Health Insurance Portability and
    Accountability Act (HIPAA)
    (1996), 4, 52, 85
Hellman, Martin, 70
heuristics, 151
honeypots and honeynets, 143
hosts, 193
human intelligence (HUMINT), 108

I

IaaS (infrastructure as a service)
    environments, 89–91, 195
identification, 23–33
identity thieves, 25
impact, 11
impersonation attacks, 27–28
incident response process, 15–17
industrial control systems, 164–165
industrial espionage, 103
industry compliance, 80–81. *See also*
    compliance
information security policies, 81–82
infrastructure as a service (IaaS)
    environments, 89–91, 195
input validation attacks, 176, 180
integrity, 5, 7
Intel, 152
Interagency OPSEC Support Staff
    (IOSS), 104
interception attacks, 8
International Organization for
    Standardization (ISO), 88
Internet of Things (IoT) devices, 159,
    167–170
Internet Protocol (IP) addresses, 40
Internet Protocol Security (IPsec), 76
interruption attacks, 9
intrusion detection systems (IDSs)
    accountability and, 54–55
    implementation of, 138
    operating systems and, 152–153
intrusion prevention systems (IPSs),
    54–55
IOSS (Interagency OPSEC Support
    Staff), 104
IP addresses, 40

J

jailbreaking, 162–163
Java Virtual Machine (JVM), 37

Jefferson Disk, 62–64
job listings, 109
Joint Test Action Group (JTAG) debug
    ports, 200

K

Kali, 141
Kerckhoffs, Auguste, 66
key controls, 82
key exchange, 68
keyless cryptography, 71–72
keys, 61
keyword ciphers, 67
Kismet, 141, 143
KRACK vulnerability, 168

L

laws and regulations. *See also* compliance
    Children's Internet Protection Act
        (CIPA) (2000), 86
    Children's Online Privacy
        Protection Act (COPPA)
        (1988), 86
    familiarity with, 119
    Family Educational Rights and
        Privacy Act (FERPA)
        (1974), 86
    Federal Information Security
        Management Act (FISMA)
        (2002), 4
    General Data Protection Regulation
        (GDPR) (2018), 87
    Gramm–Leach–Bliley Act (GLBA)
        (1999), 86
    Health Insurance Portability and
        Accountability Act (HIPAA)
        (1996), 4, 52, 85
    international, 87
    overview, 4
    Sarbanes–Oxley Act (SOX) (2002),
        52, 55, 85
Linux operating systems, 141, 149, 185
logging, 56–57, 150
logical controls, 14

M

magnetic media, 127–129
malicious apps, 163
Maltego, 113

physical penetration testing, 199
physical security
    data, 75, 127–129
    devices, 168
    equipment, 129–132
    overview, 121–122
    people, 125–127
    threats, 122
plaintext, 61
platform as a service (PaaS)
            environments, 89–91, 195
Porter, Michael E., 103
ports, 40–41
port scanners, 141, 147–148, 153–155
possession, 7
Post Office Protocol (POP), 140
pretexting, 114
Pretty Good Privacy (PGP), 71
preventive controls, 124
principle of least privilege, 43–44, 149
printers, 167
Privacy Rights Clearinghouse, 100
privilege escalation attacks, 183–184
protected health information (PHI), 85
protocols
    FTP (File Transfer Protocol), 140
    Internet Protocol (IP) addresses, 40
    Internet Protocol Security
            (IPsec), 76
    Post Office Protocol (POP), 140
    Secure File Transfer Protocol
            (SFTP), 140
    Secure Sockets Layer (SSL)
            protocol, 71
    Signaling System No. 7 (SS7)
            protocol, 162
    vulnerabilities and, 182
proxy servers, 137
public key infrastructure (PKI), 74
public records, 109–110
public wireless networks, 139–141
Purple Dragon, 103
purple teams, 203

Q

Quadriga, 92
Qualys, 58, 191

R

race conditions, 175–176
RAID arrays, 128

reactive tools, 56–57
Reagan, Ronald, 104
real-time operating systems (RTOSs),
            164–165
red teams, 196
redundant arrays of inexpensive disks
            (RAID), 128
regulations. *See* laws and regulations
regulatory compliance, 80–81. *See also*
            compliance
remote code executions (RCEs), 53, 183
residual data, 129
resource attributes, 45
résumés, 109
risk-based approach, 84
risks. *See also* operations security
            (OPSEC)
    assessment of, 13, 98
    management processes, 11
    mitigation of, 14
    overview, 10
Rivest, Ron, 71
Rivest-Shamir-Adleman (RSA)
            algorithm, 71, 178
rogue access points, 139–140
role-based access control (RBAC)
            model, 44
ROT13 cipher, 62
rule-based access control, 44
rules of engagement, 196, 201

S

SaaS (software as a service)
            environments, 89–91
safety of people, 126
sandboxes, 37
Sarbanes–Oxley Act (SOX) (2002), 52,
            55, 85
SaverSpy, 100
scanners, 141, 153–155, 193–194. *See
            also* vulnerabilities
Scapy, 143
SCIP (Strategic and Competitive Intel-
            ligence Professionals), 103
scoping, 196
Secure File Transfer Protocol
            (SFTP), 140
secure protocols, 140
Secure Shell (SSH), 140
Secure Sockets Layer (SSL) protocol, 71
security through obscurity strategy, 65

V

Valasek, Chris, 166
validation, 176, 180
vehicles, 165–166
Vietnam War, 103
VPN (virtual private network)
　　　connections, 76, 118, 139
vulnerabilities. *See also* operations
　　　security (OPSEC)
　　　assessment of, 12–13, 58, 97,
　　　　　155–156, 191–195
　　　overview, 10
　　　protocols and, 182
　　　scanners, 141, 153–155, 193–194
　　　software development, 174–178

W

Washington, George, 102
web applications, 178–181
white-box testing, 197–198

Wi-Fi

Wi-Fi Protected Access (WPA, WPA2,
　　　and WPA3), 140
Wired Equivalent Privacy (WEP), 140
wireless networks, 139–140, 141
Wireshark, 142, 184–185

X

XD bit, 152
XSS (cross-site scripting), 178

Z

ZAP (Zed Attack Proxy), 186
zero-day attacks, 141

Foundations of Information Security is set in New Baskerville, Futura, and Dogma. The book was printed and bound by Sheridan Books, Inc. in Chelsea, Michigan. The paper is 60# Finch Offset, which is certified by the Forest Stewardship Council (FSC).

The book uses a layflat binding, in which the pages are bound together with a cold-set, flexible glue and the first and last pages of the resulting book block are attached to the cover. The cover is not actually glued to the book's spine, and when open, the book lies flat and the spine doesn't crack.